# Machine Vision - Applications and Systems

# Machine Vision - Applications and Systems

*Editor*

**Beata Akselsen**

scitus academics

**Machine Vision - Applications and Systems**

Edited by **Beata Akselsen**

ISBN: 978-1-68117-268-2
Library of Congress Control Number: 2016937436


www.scitusacademics.com
Box No. 4766, 616 Corporate Way,
Suite 2, Valley Cottage,
NY 10989



**Notice**

Reasonable efforts have been made to publish reliable data and views articulated in the chapters are those of the individual contributors, and not necessarily those of the editors or publishers. Editors or publishers are not responsible for the accuracy of the information in the published chapters or consequences of their use. The publisher believes no responsibility for any damage or grievance to the persons or property arising out of the use of any materials, instructions, methods or thoughts in the book. The editors and the publisher have attempted to trace the copyright holders of all material reproduced in this publication and apologize to copyright holders if permission has not been obtained. If any copyright holder has not been acknowledged, please write to us so we may rectify.

Printed in United States of America on Acid Free Paper

# Preface

Vision plays an important role for living beings, enabling them to cooperate with the environment effectively and competently. The main objective of Machine Vision is to provide artificial systems with sufficient capacity for dealing with non-predetermined situations. While computer vision is mainly focused on processing hardware images, machine vision usually requires additional hardware and computer networks to transmit information generated by other process components, such as a robot arm. Machine vision is a sub-category of machinery for IT, optics, mechanics and industrial automation. Product inspection, such as microprocessors, automobiles, food and pharmaceuticals, is one of the most common machine vision applications. Machine vision systems are increasingly used to solve problems with industrial inspection, automate the inspection process fully and improve its accuracy and efficiency. Like the inspection of products produced by people in the production line, digital cameras, intelligent cameras and image processing software are used for this purpose.

This book presents the possibility of applications for machine vision in the present. The book focuses on computer vision and image processing in engineering and technological aspects. Machine Vision is no longer limited to industrial environments where situations and tasks are reduced and very specific, but system solutions are now prevalent for routine life problems.

# Table of Contents

# Chapter 1

# A Novel Machine Vision System for the Inspection of Micro-Spray Nozzle

**Kuo-Yi Huang [1,*] and Yu-Ting Ye [2]**

[1]*Department of Bio-Industrial Mechatronics Engineering, National Chung Hsing University, Tai-Chung 402, Taiwan*

[2]*Department of Mechatronic Engineering, Huafan University, New Taipei City 223, Taiwan*

## ABSTRACT

In this study, we present an application of neural network and image processing techniques for detecting the defects of an internal micro-spray nozzle. The defect regions were segmented by Canny edge detection, a randomized algorithm for detecting circles and a circle inspection (CI) algorithm. The gray level co-occurrence matrix (GLCM) was further used to evaluate the texture features of the segmented region. These texture features (contrast, entropy, energy), color features (mean and variance of gray level) and geometric features (distance variance, mean diameter and diameter ratio) were used in the classification procedures. A back-propagation neural network classifier was employed to detect the defects of micro-spray nozzles. The methodology presented herein effectively works for detecting micro-spray nozzle defects to an accuracy of 90.71%.

**Keywords:** Micro-spray nozzle; Image processing; Neural network

# 1. INTRODUCTION

Nozzles are a common mechanical component and are widely used in agriculture, manufacturing and the service industry. A micro-spray nozzle is an important component in an agricultural sprayer, which is used to spray water, pesticides and nutrients. Real-time flow uniformity depends on the internal quality of the micro-spray nozzle. Unstable flow will be created because of internal defects. The price and quality of micro-spray nozzles are down due to such defects. The internal defects of micro-spray nozzles usually result during cutting procedures with a CNC (computer numerical control) machine. Chang and Yu [1] proposed a triangular-pitch shell-and-tube spray evaporator featuring an interior spray technique. The dry-out phenomenon is prevented, and the heat transfer performance is improved in their study. In addition, micro-spray nozzles have to be sorted manually, because the surface of the micro-spray nozzle is heterogeneous, which makes auto-detection very difficult.

Image processing techniques are a powerful method and are widely used to inspect industrial products. Chen*et al.* [2] designed an automatic damage detection system of an engineering ceramic surface with image processing techniques, pattern recognition and machine vision. Paniagua *et al.* [3] proposed a neuro-fuzzy classification system to inspect the quality of industrial cork samples by incorporating techniques based on Gabor filtering techniques and neuro-fuzzy computing with three wavelet-based texture quality features. A microscopic vision system [4] has been employed to measure the surface roughness of the micro-heterogeneous texture in a deep hole, by virtue of the frequency domain features of microscopic images and a back-propagation artificial neural network optimized by the genetic algorithm. Indeed, neural networks, geometric, color and texture features were often employed in the classification of plants and crops [5,6,7]. Shen *et al.* [8] used the Otsu method, HSI color system and Sobel operator to extract disease spot regions and calculate leaf areas. Park *et al.* [9] employed an unsupervised segmentation algorithm by Gaussian mixture models to segment color image regions.

However, to the best of the authors' knowledge, there is no literature on the inspection of the internal quality of micro-spray nozzles using image processing techniques. Some research [10,11,12] talked about the determination of drop sizes and shapes for spray nozzles. The drop size distribution of an irrigation spray nozzle was determined using image processing techniques, and the relationship between drop size distribution, operating pressure and nozzle size were discussed [10]. The droplet shape and size of a diesel spray had been detected using wavelet transform, a Gaussian filter and sub-pixel contour extraction [11]. The gray level gradient, boundary curvature detection, the Hough transform and the convex-hull method were employed to count and size particles in the field of sprays [12].

Currently, the internal damages of micro-spray nozzles are manually inspected (sorted) using stereomicroscopes. The procedures are laborious and ineffective. The labor cost was about 80% of the total cost for micro-spray nozzle products. The detection process has to be automated to reduce the total cost. Thus, this paper aims to develop a machine vision system to correctly and automatically inspect the micro-spray nozzle. The specific goals are: (1) to develop an algorithm to segment the defect region; (2) to extract the gray level and texture features; and (3) to classify different grades using the aforementioned features by a classifier.

In summary, we develop a machine vision system to correctly and automatically inspect and classify micro-spray nozzles. The system includes an extraction algorithm of defect regions, a feature estimation algorithm for defect regions and a classifier for the quality of micro-spray nozzles.

# 2. MATERIALS AND METHODS

## 2.1. Micro-Spray Nozzle Structure and Defects

Micro-spray nozzles (shown in Figure 1) are provided by Natural Fog Multi-Tech Precision Industry Corporation Ltd. (Tai-Chung, Taiwan). The structure profile of the micro-spray nozzle is shown in Figure 2. The outlet diameter of the micro-spray nozzle is 0.1 mm. There are two inclined annular-planes, A and B (as shown inFigure 2), on the inside surface of the micro-spray nozzle. Figure 3 depicts the circle textures in the inner image of micro-spray nozzles after CNC machine manufacturing. The defects of micro-spray nozzles were made by the CNC machine during the manufacturing procedures. The defects appear on the outlet and inclined planes A and B. Four possible defects, which include the outlet shape and deckle edge, pellet and stripe metal filings on inclined planes, are shown in Figure 3. The purpose of this study is to inspect the defects of micro-spray nozzles automatically using a machine vision system.

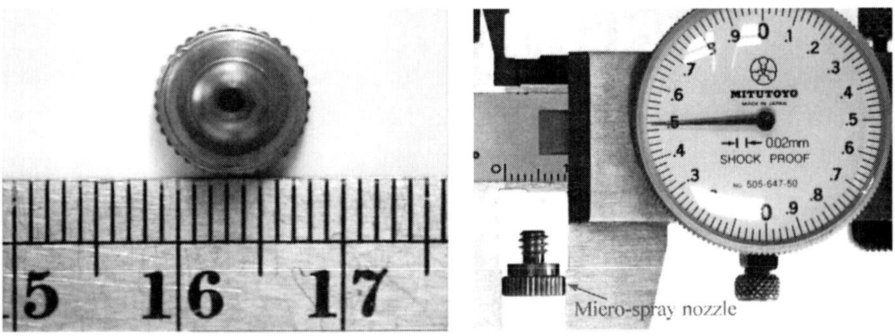


**Figure 1.** Micro-spray nozzle.

## 2.2. Hardware System

The machine vision system implemented to inspect the inner images of micro-spray nozzles is illustrated in Figure 4. This system includes an IEEE 1394 CCD color camera (DFK-31BF03, Imaging Source Inc., Bremen, Germany), a stereomicroscope (Stemi 2000-C, Zeiss Inc.,

Oberkochen, Germany), a front illuminating white light LED with a diffuse filter, a fixed table and a personal computer. Open Source Computer Vision Library (OpenCV1.0, Intel Corporation) and Visual C++ 6.0 programming are linked to the programs to grab images of 1024 × 768 pixels.

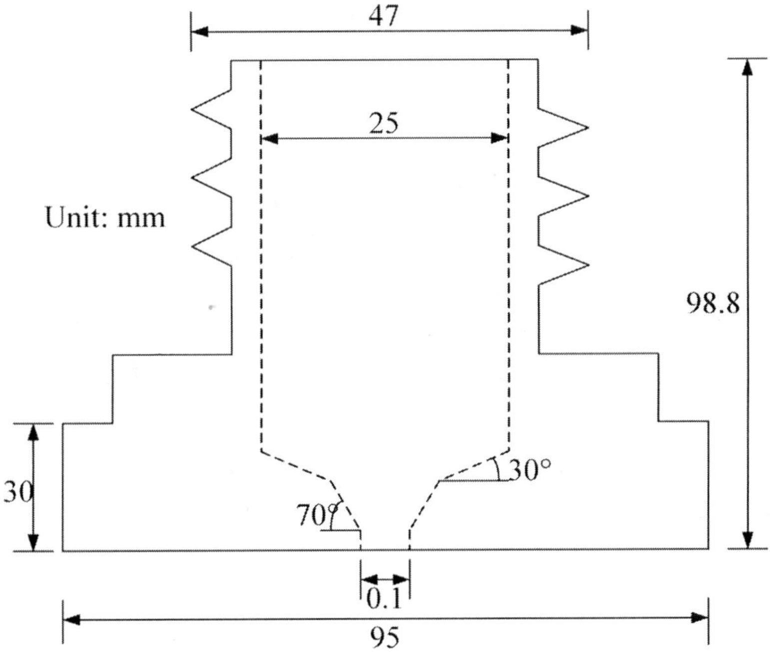


**Figure 2.** The profile of the micro-spray nozzle.

## 2.3. Region Segmentation and Features Extraction

Algorithms that include the estimation of the outlet's geometric feature and segmentation of the region of interest (ROI), a circle inspection (CI) algorithm and a classifier are proposed to detect micro-spray nozzle defects. Details of the proposed algorithms are described as follows.

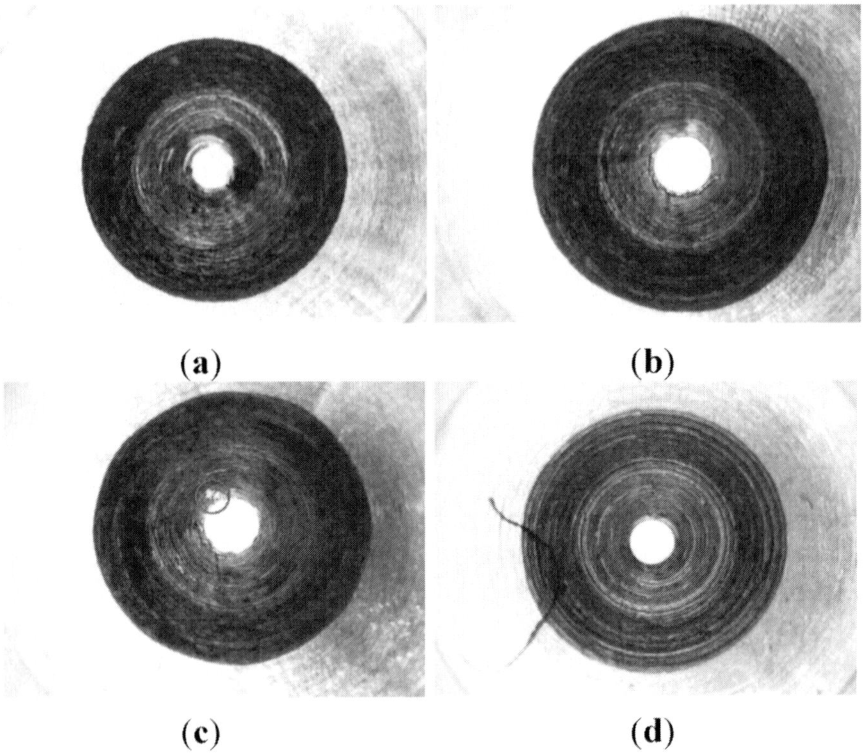


**Figure 3.** Four possible defects. (**a**) Small outlet; (**b**) Deckle edge of outlet; (**c**) Pellet metal fillings; (**d**) Strip metal fillings.

### 2.3.1. Outlet Extraction

Segmentation of the ROI image is an essential procedure once the features of the micro-spray nozzle have been extracted. Firstly, the outlet image (as shown in Figure 5) is segmented using Otsu's auto-thresholding method and hole-filling operations [13]. By assuming that the binary image of the outlet is $f(x_i, y_i)$ (where $i = 1, 2, \ldots, m$ and the total number of pixels is $m$), the centroid is obtained as $\overline{X} = \sum_{i=1}^{m} x_i / m$, $\overline{Y} = \sum_{i=1}^{m} y_i / m$. The covariance matrix is defined as $C = (\sum_{i=1}^{m} U_i U_i^T) / m - MM^T$ in which Ui is the *i*-th coordinate vector of the image and $M = (\sum_{i=1}^{m} U_i) / m$ is the mean vector. *T* indicates vector

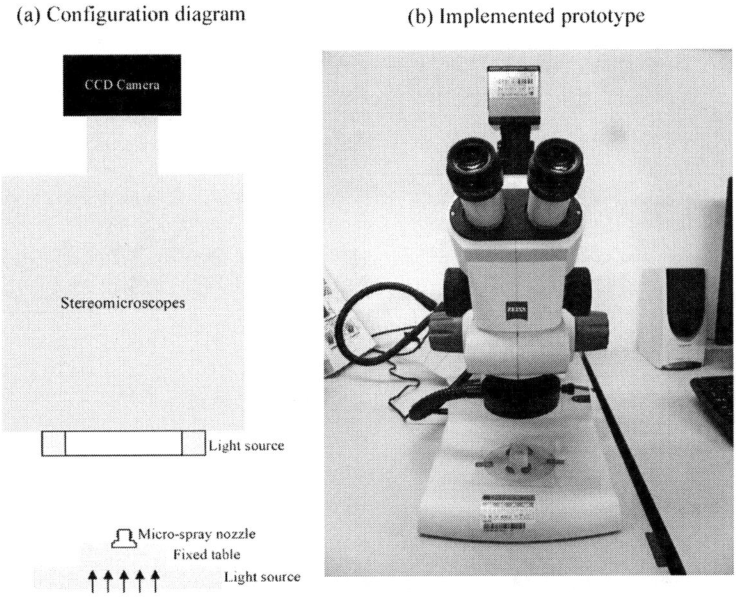


**Figure 4.** Illustration of the machine vision system for micro-spray nozzle defect inspection.

transposition. A pair of orthogonal eigenvectors of the covariance matrix is then calculated. The geometric features—principle axis length ($L_p$), secondary axis ($L_s$), centroid, area ($A$), perimeter ($P$), compactness ($P^2/4\pi A$), diameter ratio (min./max. diameter, $D_{mm}$) and mean diameter ($D_{mean}$) of the outlet—are computed using eigenvectors. Secondly, two geometric features—diameter ratio and mean diameter—are employed in the micro-spray nozzle classification process.

The ROI of inclined annular-planes is the internal image of the micro-spray nozzle, as shown in Figure 6. Segmenting the ROI effectively is an important procedure once the defects have been detected. Firstly, Canny edge detection [13], a randomized algorithm for detecting circles [14], hole-filling operation and the AND logic operator are used to segment the ROI of the inclined annular-planes.

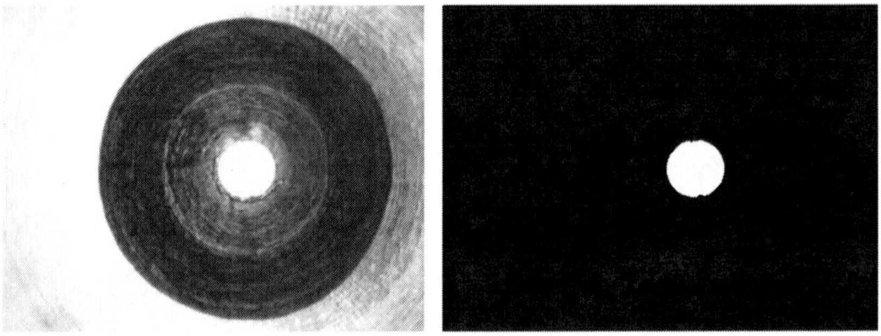

(a) (b)

**Figure 5.** Outlet image segmentation. (**a**) Orignal image; (**b**) Outlet image.

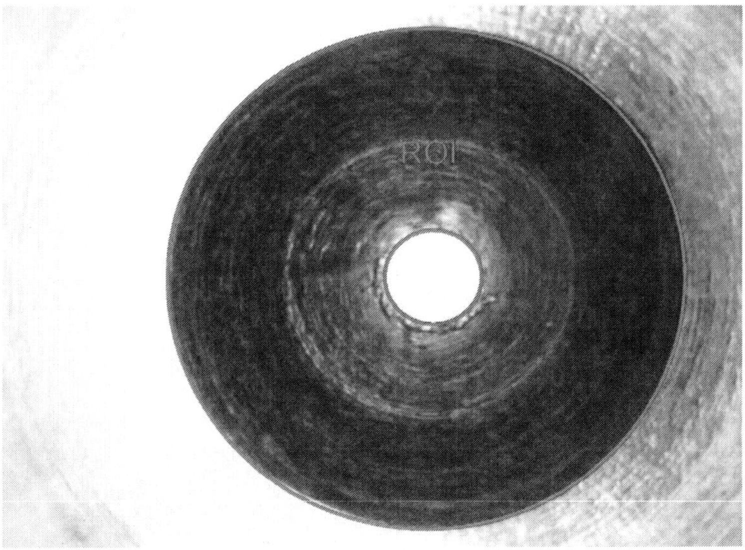


**Figure 6.** ROI diagram.

The procedures of extraction are as follows.

**Step 1.** Canny edge detection for the original image (Figure 7a), shown as Figure 7b.

**Step 2.** Randomized algorithm for detecting circles, shown as Figure 7c.

**Step 3.** The ring region is filled using a hole-filling operation, shown as Figure 7d.

**Step 4.** The ROI (shown as Figure 7e) is segmented using the AND logic operator for Figure 7a,d.

**Step 5.** Geometric features' computation.

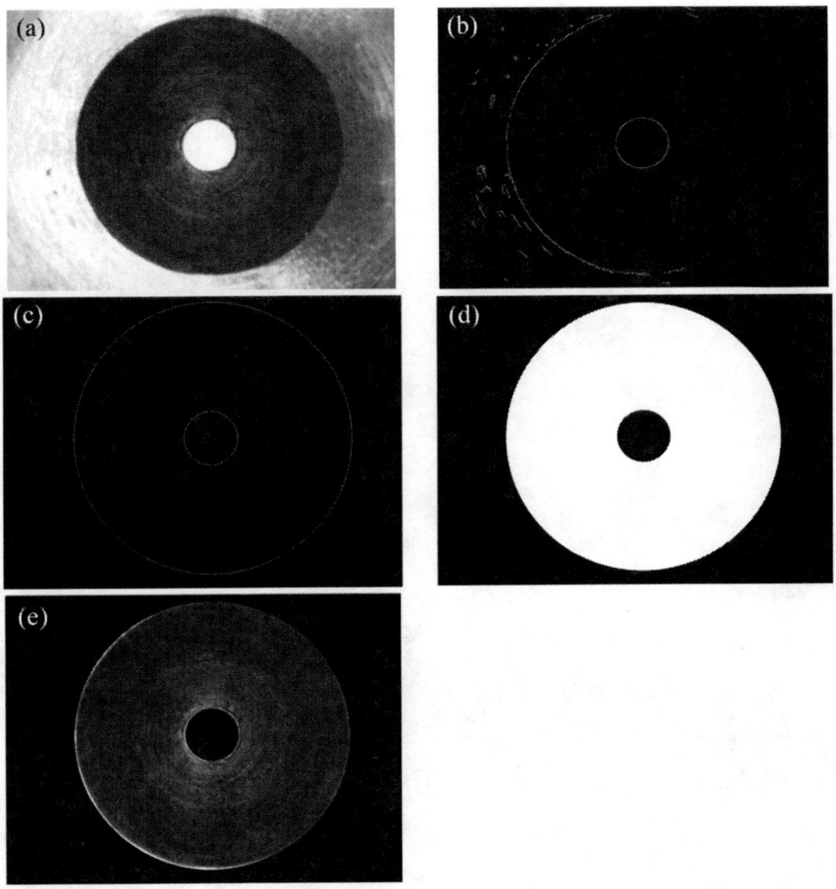


**Figure 7.** (**a**) Original image; (**b**) after Canny edge detection; (**c**) randomized algorithm for detecting circles; (**d**) the image after hole-filling operation; (**e**) ROI image with the AND logic operator for (a,d).

### 2.3.2. Possible Defect Segmentation

Segmenting defect regions is an important procedure before possible defects (including the deckle edge, pellet and stripe metal fillings) are detected and classified. A prior experiment proceeded as follows. Firstly, an inspection circle is used to find gray levels with scanning resolution in a pixel, as shown in Figure 8. There are different distribution forms of gray levels in different circles, as illustrated in Figure 9. However, the difference between defects and non-defects is difficult to distinguish using the thresholding method [13]. Therefore, a novel method, the circle inspection algorithm (CI algorithm), is proposed for defect region segmentation of micro-spray nozzles in this study.

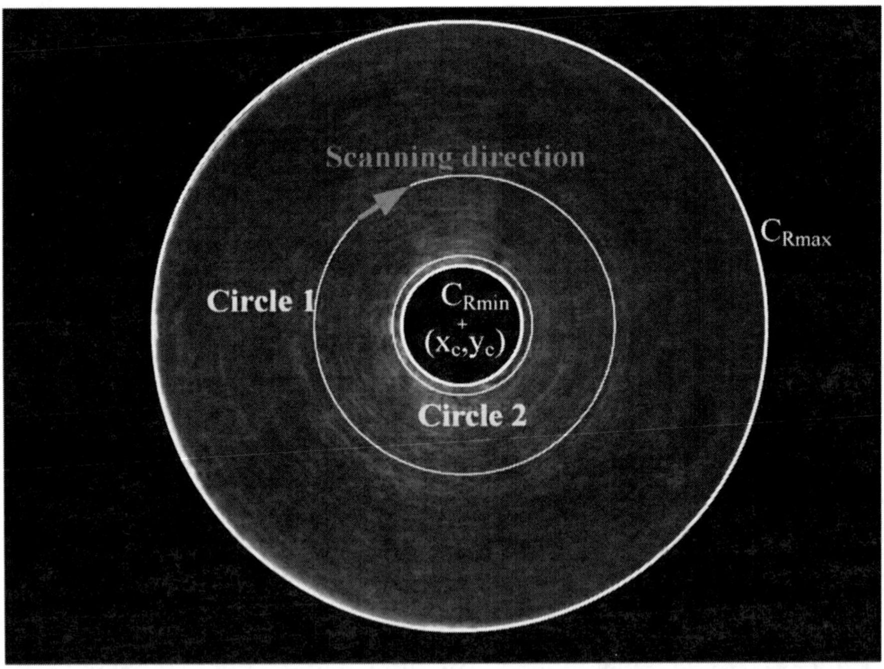


**Figure 8.** The scanning direction of the circle inspection for the ROI.

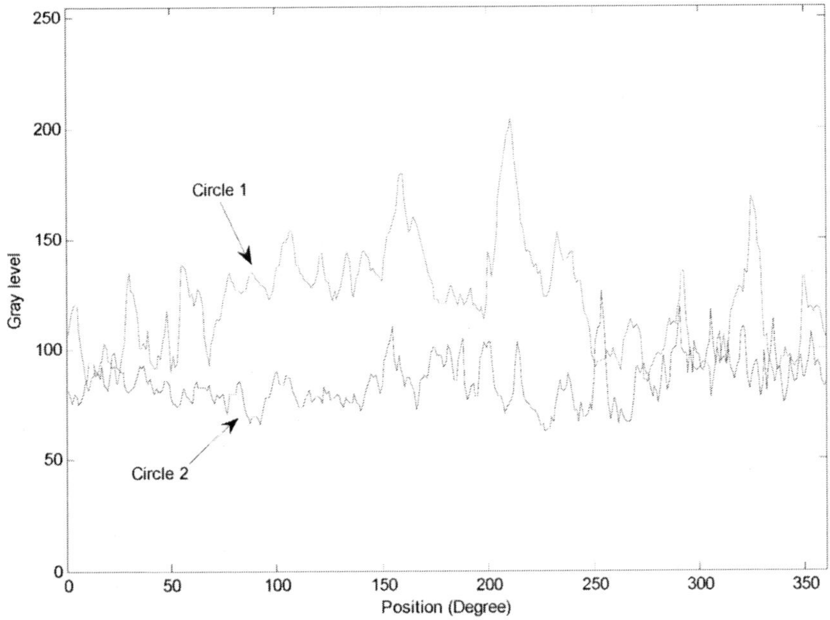


**Figure 9.** The distribution of gray levels of the circle inspection.

The CI algorithm is effectively executed to extract defect regions for internal images of micro-spray nozzles according to the differences of the gray level gradient. The CI algorithm is described as follows:

**Step 1.** The distribution of the gray level on the image is estimated along the circle $C_{Rj}$ (with scanning resolution in a pixel); $(x_c, y_c)$ is the center, and $R_{min} < R_j < R_{max}$.

**Step 2.** Compute the gray level gradient (Gi) of the circle, as demonstrated in Figure 10 on Circle 1.

$$G_i = \frac{1}{2}\left[\left(\frac{|g(i)-g(i-n)|}{n}\right)+\left(\frac{|g(i)-g(i+n)|}{n}\right)\right]$$
$$= \frac{1}{2n}|2g(i)-g(i-n)-g(i+n)| \quad (1)$$

where $g(i)$ is the gray level of the circle, $i$ is the position of the circle and $n$ is the distance.

**Step 3.** Segment the possible defect regions (*PDR*).

$$\begin{cases} If \quad G_i \geq T, \quad then \quad g(i) \in PDR \\ If \quad G_i < T, \quad then \quad g(i) \in Normal \end{cases} \tag{2}$$

where $T$ is a threshold value.

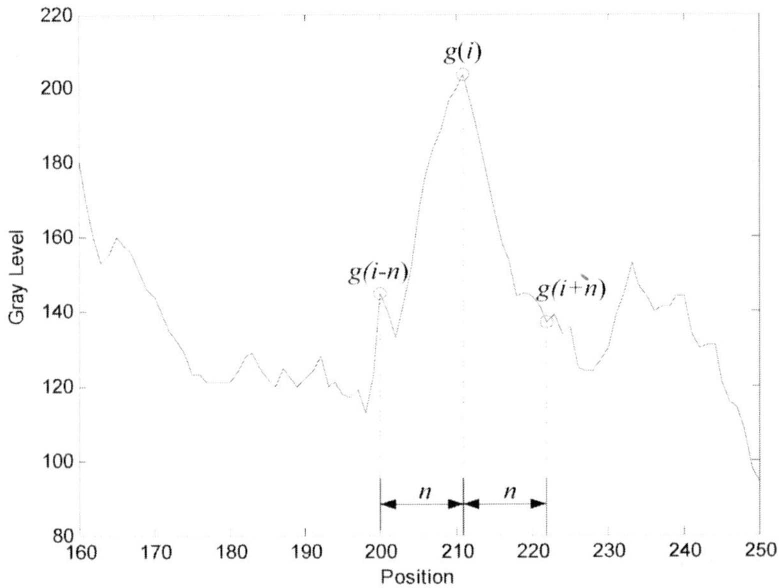


**Figure 10.** Parameters of gray level gradient computation.

## 2.4. Classification: Classifier

Geometric, texture and color features analysis have been widely employed in classification. With proper feature selections, the design of a classifier can be greatly simplified. This study adopts the geometric feature (mean diameter, diameter ratio, distance variance), the color features (mean gray level, variance of gray level) and texture features (contrast, energy and entropy from the gray level co-occurrence matrix (GLCMs) [15]) to classify defects and non-defects using a back propagation neural network [16] (BPNN, as shown in Figure 11). Mathematical formulations of these features are given in Table 1.

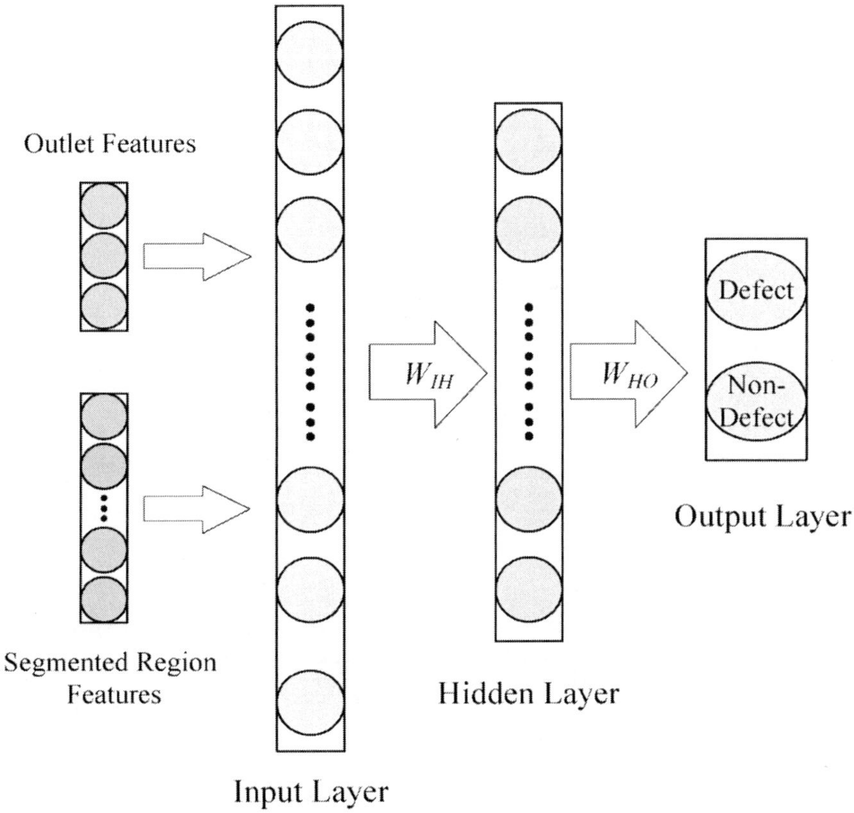


**Figure 11.** The structure of the back propagation neural network (BPNN) classifier.

In this study, the BPNN classifier consists of three layers: an input layer, a hidden layer and an output layer (as shown in Figure 11). The input layer has 17 nodes, which are related to 3 geometric features, 2 color features and 12 texture features, normalized between 0 and 1. The output layer is made of nodes, related to two categories: defect and non-defect. Initially, the number of nodes $n_H$ in the hidden layer is calculated using the following formula:

**Table 1.** Mathematical formulations of the features.

| | |
|---|---|
| Distance Variance | Variance of $\frac{1}{N}\sum_{i}^{N}(D(x_i,y_i)-\overline{D})$ |
| Mean gray level | $\overline{f}=\frac{1}{N}\sum_{i=1}^{N}f(x,y)$ |
| Gray level variance | $\frac{1}{N}\sum_{i}^{N}(f(x_i,y_i)-\overline{f})$ |
| Contrast (orientations 45°, 90°, 135° and 180°) | $\sum_{i}\sum_{j}(i-j)^2 p^2(i,j,d,\theta)$ |
| Entropy (orientations 45°, 90°, 135° and 180°) | $-\sum_{i}\sum_{j}p(i,j,d,\theta)\log(p(i,j,d,\theta))$ |
| Energy (orientations 45°, 90°, 135° and 180°) | $\sum_{i}\sum_{j}p^2(i,j,d,\theta)$ |

Note: $D(x_i, y_i)$ is the distance between location $(x_i, y_i)$ and the outlet center, $p(i, j, d, \theta)$ represents the relative frequency of a gray level co-occurrence matrix (GLCM) of an image $g(x_i, y_i)$, where $i$ is the gray level at location $(x, y)$ and $j$ represents the gray level of a neighboring pixel at a distance $d$ and an orientation from location $(x_i, y_i)$. The GLCM of distance 1 pixel and orientations 45°, 90°, 135° and 180° are used for the isolated image.

$$n_H = 0.5(n_I + n_O) + 2 \tag{3}$$

where $n_I$ is the number of input nodes and $n_o$ is the number of output nodes. The objective of the learning process is to find a relation in a pattern that was made by the features of each segmented region. The BPNN is trained, and the weights are changed until the error convergence criterion approaches 0.1. The error signal is given by:

$$E(t) = \sum_{k=1}^{2}(d_k(t) - y_k(t))^2 \tag{4}$$

where $d_k(t)$ is the desired response for neuron $k$ ($k$ = 1~2) and $y_k(t)$ is the output signal of neuron $k$ at iteration $t$.

### 2.5. Overall Descriptions

The overall steps involved in the defect region segmentation and classification are shown in Figure 12. The algorithm for the classification of defects included image processing techniques, the CI algorithm and the BPNN classifier, are fully described in the previous two sections.

The program employed for detecting and classifying the defects is written in Microsoft Visual C++ 6.0 and OpenCV 1.0.

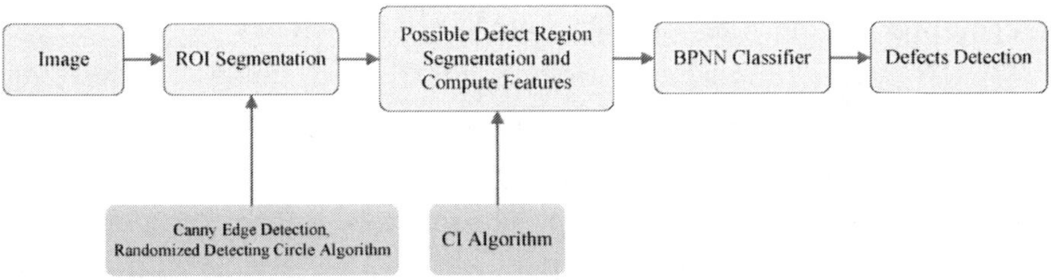


**Figure 12.** Segmentation and classification steps.

## 3. RESULTS AND DISCUSSION

In this paper, a defect detection (DD) software for a micro-spray nozzle is developed using image processing techniques and the CI algorithm (written in Visual C++ 6.0 with OpenCV 1.0), as outlined in the first few steps shown in Figure 12. The algorithm is summarized as follows:

**Step 1.** Two geometric features of the outlet are computed.

**Step 2.** The ROIs are segmented using Canny edge detection, a randomized algorithm for detecting circles, hole-filling and the AND logic operators.

**Step 3.** Possible defect regions are segmented by the CI algorithm.

**Step 4.** Estimate 15 features of the segmented regions.

**Step 5.** Establish and test the BPNN classifier to classify defects and non-defects.

The functions of DD include file operations (acquire, load and save images) and image analysis operations (binary operator, hole-filling, remove noises using closing, opening and Canny edge). The geometrics of the outlet, texture and color features of the segmented region are obtained, and defects can be detected by the DD computation accurately and rapidly.

The difference between defects and non-defect regions is not obvious in the original image of a micro-spray nozzle, as shown in Figure 13a. Possible defect regions, including defects and non-defects, are segmented using the CI algorithm (parameters $n = 6$, $T = 11$ are selected after some experimentations) and image processing techniques (such as hole-filling, erosion, dilation, opening, closing and Canny edge operators), as indicated in Figure 13b. Figure 13c results using the AND logic operator for Figure 13a,b. Hence, the defects of micro-spray nozzles (Figure 13d) are detected according to the BPNN classification.

In order to establish the BPNN classifier, 698 samples (with 565 non-defects and 133 defects) are randomly sampled. Eleven hidden nodes are obtained by Equation (3) according to 17 input features, and two output categories. The BPNN classifier is implemented using functions of MATLAB 8.0. For each configuration, the training sample set is randomly selected from all samples until the BPNN convergence is achieved. Over-fitting often occurs when the training set contains some incorrect samples in the BPNN. As the grades of micro-spray nozzles in training samples are already known before the training process, over-fitting is unlikely to occur. To ensure that the influence of over-fitting is trivial during the training process, the maximum number of iterations is set to 100,000. Further studies showed that the same inspection effect is obtained when the error rate convergence criterion is smaller than 0.1. Randomly-sampled images (1486 non-defects and 118 defects) are used to test the system. The accuracy of the classification is 90.71%. The accuracy of outlet shape and strip fillings is 100%. However, a few deckle edges and pellet fillings of the images can not be detected using the proposed algorithms, examples of classification failure and explanations are shown in Table 2.

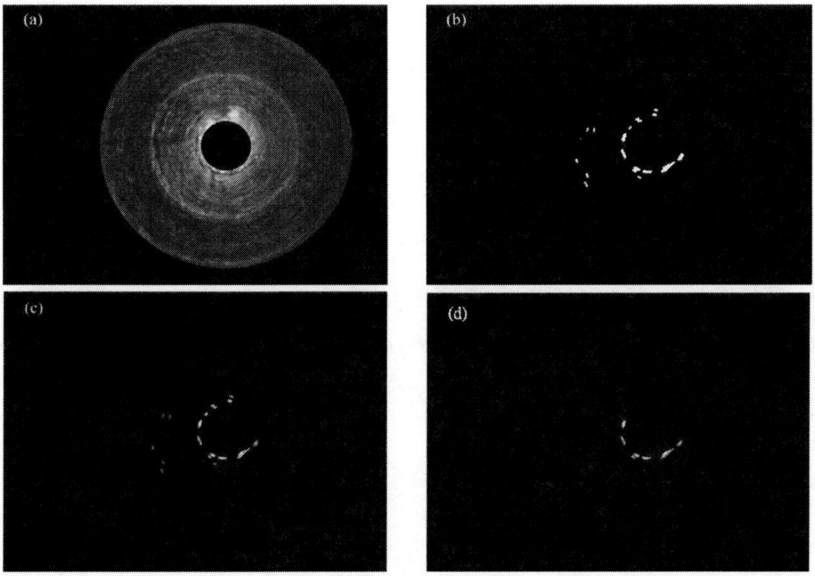


**Figure 13.** (**a**) Original image; (**b**) segmented binary image after the CI algorithm; (**c**) segmented image after the CI algorithm; (**d**) classification result.

**Table 2.** Examples of classification failure and explanations.

| | Original Image | ROI | Explanation |
|---|---|---|---|
| Case 1: Deckle edge | 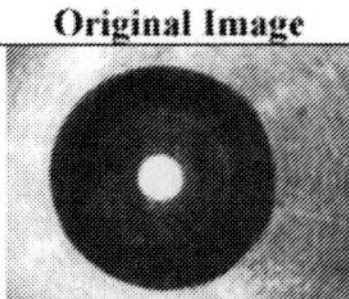 | 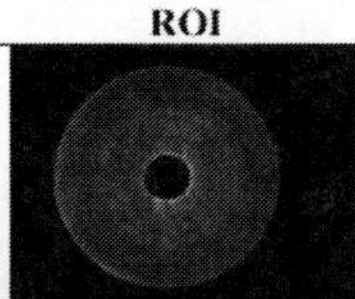 | Deckle edges are removed after ROI segmentation operator. |
| Case 2: Deckle edge | 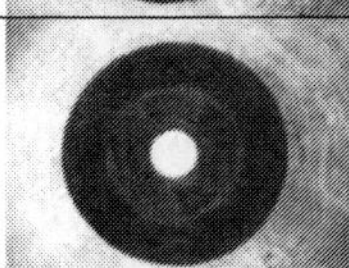 | 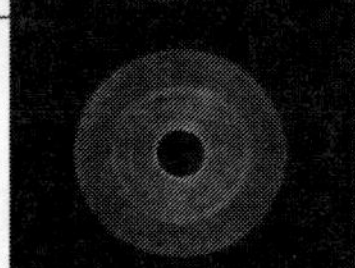 | Deckle edges cannot be segmented by the CI algorithm because they are not obvious. |
| Case 3: Pellet filings | 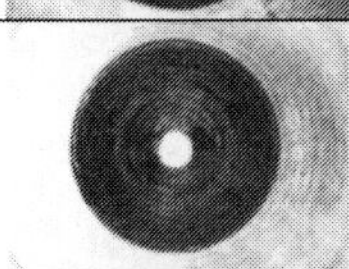 | 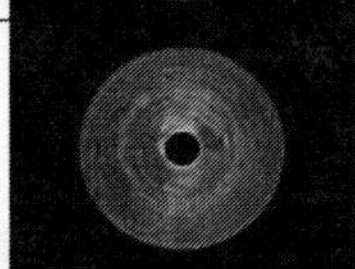 | Pellet fillings cannot be segmented by the CI algorithm because they are not obvious. |
| Case 4: Dark image | 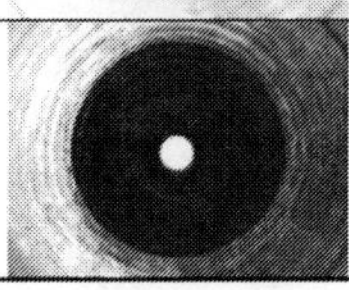 | 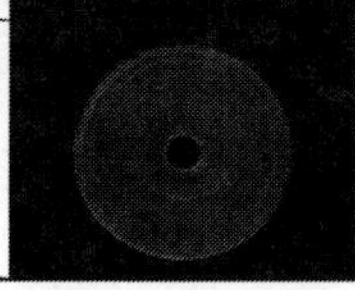 | The image is blurred and dark. |

In this study, the proposed system can detect and classify visible defects with a CCD camera accurately and efficiently. In the future, we hope that the detection and classification system can be applied to an auto-inspection system for micro-spray nozzles.

## 4. CONCLUSIONS

Real-time flow uniformity depends on the internal quality of the micro-spray nozzle, and unstable flow will result because of internal defects. A novel inspection system for internal defects of micro-spray nozzles is developed in this study. The image processing techniques, Canny edge detection, a randomized algorithm for detecting circles, the circle inspection algorithm and the BPNN classifier are used to establish the micro-spray nozzle detection system. Possible defects can be segmented efficiently using the CI algorithm and image processing techniques. Geometric, color and texture features of the defects are obtained to establish a BPNN classifier. Testing results show that the defects of the micro-spray nozzles can be detected efficiently using the proposed system. In a future study, we aim to refine the inspection algorithm in order to increase the inspection accuracy for the production line of micro-spay nozzles.

## AUTHOR CONTRIBUTIONS

All authors have made significant contributions to the paper. Huang K.Y. initiated the idea to develop the inspection system of micro-spray nozzles. Huang K.Y. and Ye Y.T. developed the inspection algorithms and the classifier together. Ye Y.T. wrote programs and performed the experiment. Huang, K.Y. contributed to the paper organization and technical writing to final version.

## REFERENCES

1. Chang, T.B.; Yu, L.Y. Optimal nozzle spray cone angle for triangular-pitch shell-and-tube interior spray evaporator. *Int. J. Heat Mass Transf.* **2015**, *85*, 463–472.

2. Chen, S.; Lin, B.; Han, X.; Liang, X. Automated inspection of engineering ceramic grinding surface damage based on image recognition. *Int. J. Adv. Manuf. Technol.* **2013**, *66*, 431–443.

3. Paniagua, B.; Vega-Rodríguez, M.A.; Gómez-Pulido, J.A.; Sánchez-Pérez, J.M. Automatic texture characterization using Gabor filters and neurofuzzy computing. *Int. J. Adv. Manuf. Technol.* **2011**, *52*, 15–32.

4. Liu, W.; Tu, X.; Jia, Z.; Wang, W.; Ma, X.; Bi, X. An improved surface roughness measurement method for micro-heterogeneous texture in deep hole based on gray-level co-occurrence matrix and support vector machine. *Int. J. Adv. Manuf. Technol.* **2013**, *69*, 583–593.

5. López-García, F.; Andreu-García, G.; Blasco, J.; Aleixos, N.; Valiente, J. Automatic detection of skin defects in citrus fruits using a multivariate image analysis approach. *Comput. Electron. Agric.* **2010**, *71*, 189–197.

6. Kavdir, I. Discrimination of sunflower, weed and soil by artificial neural networks. *Comput. Electron. Agric.* **2004**, *44*, 153–160.

7. Camargo, A.; Smith, J.S. An image-processing based algorithm to automatically identify plant disease visual symptoms. *Biosyst. Eng.* **2009**, *102*, 9–21.

8. Shen, W.; Wu, Y.; Chen, Z.; Wei, H. Grading method of leaf spot disease based on image processing. In Proceedings of the 2008 International Conference on Computer Science and Software Engineering, Wuhan, China, 12–14 December 2008; pp. 491–494.

9. Park, J.H.; Lee, G.S.; Park, S.Y. Color image segmentation using adaptive mean shift and statistical model-based methods. *Comput. Math. Appl.* **2009**, *57*, 970–980.

10. Sudheera, K.P.; Pandab, R.K. Digital image processing for determining drop sizes from irrigation spray nozzles. *Agric. Water Manag.* **2000**, *45*, 159–167.

11. Blaisot, J.B.; Yon, J. Droplet size and morphology characterization for dense sprays by image processing: Application to the diesel spray. *Exp. Fluids* **2005**, *39*, 997–994.

12. Lee, S.Y.; Kim, Y.D. Sizing of spray particles using image processing technique. *KSME Int. J.* **2004**, *18*, 879–894.

13. Gonzalez, R.C.; Woods, R.E. *Digital Image Processing*, 3rd ed.; Prentice Hall: Upper Saddle River, NJ, USA, 2002.

14. Chen, T.C.; Chung, K.L. An efficient randomized algorithm for detecting circles. *CVGIP Comput. Vis. Image Underst.* **2001**, *83*, 172–191.

15. Haralick, R.M.; Shanmugam, K.; Dinstein, I. Textual features for image classification. *IEEE Trans. Syst. Man Cybern.* **1973**, *3*, 610–621.

16. Fausett, L. *Fundamentals of Neural Networks: Architectures, Algorithms, and Applications*; Prentice-Hall: Upper Saddle River, NJ, USA, 1994.

# Chapter 2

# Robust 3D Object Model Reconstruction and Matching for Complex Automated Deburring Operations

**Alberto Tellaeche* and Ramón Arana**

*Smart and Autonomous Systems Unit, IK4-Tekniker, C/Iñaki Goenaga 5, Eibar 20600, Spain*

## ABSTRACT

The deburring processes of parts with complex geometries usually present many challenges to be automated. This paper outlines the machine vision techniques involved in the design and set up of an automated adaptive cognitive robotic system for laser deburring of metal casting complex 3D high quality parts. To carry out deburring process operations of the parts autonomously, 3D machine vision techniques have been used for different purposes, explained in this paper. These machine vision algorithms used along with industrial robots and a high tech laser head, make a fully automated deburring process possible. This setup could potentially be applied to medium sized parts of different light casting alloys (Mg, AlZn, etc.).

**Keywords:** 3D machine vision; Complex light casting parts; Automated deburring operation

# 1. INTRODUCTION

In die casting processes, ferrous and non-ferrous metallic alloys are taken to the liquid state, and products receive their final form by means of the injection and further solidification of these cast alloys in a mold. Casting of metals is one of the industrial activities with more tradition in Europe. The European industry is the second largest in the world for ferrous castings—far behind China—and the largest for forgings and non-ferrous castings. According to the European Foundry Association (CAEF), the most important market segments for castings in European Union are the automotive industry (50% of all castings), the engineering industry (30%), the construction industry (10%) and others, such as the aeronautics and electronics industry (10%). While the majority of volume falls upon the ferrous alloys family, the growing trend in the automotive sector towards lighter vehicles has resulted in an increased interest in light metals, particularly aluminum and magnesium. Regarding aluminum and its alloys, it has imposed itself as material of choice in key engine components such as cylinder heads, blocks, and pistons and even high-end car structures, due mainly to its excellent specific weight and corrosion resistance. Other sectors where aluminum has widespread use are aerospace, naval, railroad, furniture, and electric appliances.

On the other hand, the pressure from emerging economies has resulted in a general reduction in the market share at European level, especially in low/medium added value components. As a response to this phenomenon, and in order to maintain competitiveness, the sector has responded with an upgrade and optimization of its technologies, with the growing automation of the casting process one of its main consequences, taking machine vision as a fundamental technique for automated object recognition, grasping, and processing.

Among other operations, the deburring process is one of the most important finishing operations which are carried out during the manufacture of castings parts. The most common automated systems used for that purposes are based on cutting presses and robotized abrasive tools which are not flexible or adaptable to complex specific parts or to the production of short part series, which is a common problem for SMEs.

Cutting press machines are responsible for cutting the sharp edges or burrs generated on the component, or even thicker parts as sprues and runners, which are formed during the injection process.

Sometimes, given the complexity of the piece, the thickness, and type of material, the cutting is imprecise and generates unwanted geometric deviations on the parts. As a result, for certain types of pieces, it is necessary to add new operations, including inspection, review, and manual deburring and sanding with abrasive tools, which implies extra costs in the production process and a slower production. Other aspects that make the deburring stage more costly are the need to manufacture cutting dies and tools for each part geometry, as well as the wear that these cutting tools suffer after several production cycles, accelerated when burrs are thicker as a consequence of the progressive wear of the injection mold.

Nowadays, the cutting die cost is amortized when a high volume of parts is produced. However, a current trend in new markets is the production of short series. Therefore, new alternatives, capable of covering this deburring operation without cutting dies, open a new field of operation until now previously unfeasible.

Although deburring robots are well established in industry, most of them are based on mechanical tools and use fixed trajectories and force control, thus, the robot in these cases usually perform the same trajectory, applying mechanical abrasion with an identical force, always on the same points of the part, irrespective of the existence of burrs or not, eroding the part when no burrs are present. This existing approach implies a great disadvantage when processing high quality products, where finish quality is fundamental.

To overcome these limitations in the actual deburring techniques, and make this operation more flexible and adaptable to complex pars and small series, machine vision techniques can be applied as fundamental tools for the principal task of 3D part reconstruction and burr detection.

This paper is organized as follows: The following section reviews the state of the art in both deburring and machine vision applied to object recognition and inspection in robotics. Section 3 presents the problem of burr detection in complex parts carried out in this research, and finally, Section 4 and Section 5 present the results obtained and future work in this field.

## 2. STATE OF THE ART AND PREVIOUS RELATED WORKS

In many cases, deburring processes are not automated, depending on manual operation, however, the evolution in the manufacturing processes demands a sustancial improvement in these techniques [1].

The actual deburring techniques are not easily applicable to many new production lines, and a set of alternative methods are being applied, such as electrochemical or thermal deburring for high production volumes [2]. The limitations present in these processes have driven a new laser-based cutting approach for deburring, already tested in different materials: different types of steel [3,4,5,6,7,8], aluminum based alloys [9,10], titanium based alloys [11,12,13], copper [14,15], and even ceramics [16,17], glass [18,19], polymers [16,17], or composites [20,21]. These new approaches are generally applied in a fixed setup, requiring important changes in the deburring station to adapt the process to new geometries. The research presented in this paper presents a flexible setup based on machine vision to apply laser deburring to complex parts in a flexible way.

Machine vision is applied all over the process to solve two principal tasks: pose estimation and 3D reconstruction for burr detection.

Pose estimation problems appear continuously in many robotic environments. Research in robotics is focused on trying to solve problems with uncertainties, and one of these fundamental problems is manipulating objects in a 3D space. This problem, in its generic form, has been an active field of research in recent years [22]. In [23], they use color concurrence histograms and geometric modeling to identify objects for manipulation and grasping, using a classical learning framework for decision making.

Also, in many applications, such as the one proposed in this paper 3D reconstruction of point datasets is of vital importance. Good examples of these techniques applied to reconstruction can be found in [24,25]. In [26], they focus in the real time processing of the 3D point clouds acquired in real time. This is one of the fundamental problems to solve, because the processing of pure 3D point clouds is very computationally intensive.

Along with pose estimation, 3D matching of objects is another fundamental field of research in many applications, such as quality control, or part processing and manufactuning. In this research the very precise matching of the part with its CAD definition turns out to be fundamental for the correct detection of burrs and flaws in the part.

In some applications, CAD models are used to represent the knowledge of the world, giving information of the environment for object recognition and matching [27]. In this application, burr detection will be carried out by comparison of the 3D reconstruction with the STL model of the part.

Other approaches use different techniques for 3D object recognition and pose estimation, for example, in [28], 3D view-based eigen spaces are used, Features histograms are used in [29], and basic research has been carried out using single colored objects in [30] and keypoint features for robotic manipulation are used in [31]. Active appearance models are another approach used in [32].

During the last years, several new interesting research works have contributed to the development of new object matching approaches. In [33] a view-invariant object detection and pose estimation algorithm is proposed, using the object contours as input data. Another interesting work on recognizing objects in point clouds is described in [34]. In this case, a global model description based on oriented point pair features is used to match a model locally using a fast voting scheme.

Many approaches to the object matching and recognition problem are based on keypoints. A study is presented in [35] about the robustness and quality of keypoints to be used in matching problems.

Matching and recognition of objects are strictly related to what is called object retrieval, and studies carried out for this task are also applicable to the previous. In [36], object retrieval is done by using the 2D projections of the 3D object.

Finally, Tombari *et al.* [37] presents an interesting work, taking advantage of the current RGB-D sensors, with provide shape and texture information. This paper presents a novel descriptor that improves the accuracy obtained with other previous works based on descriptors.

## 3. PROBLEM DEFINITION

In the process of developing an automatic and robotized deburring station, complex automotive engine aluminum castings have been selected to demonstrate the technology. Initially, a flexible configuration has been considered, so that the deburring detection process is applicable to different parts, having the CAD model as an input.

Attending to this criteria, one complex part has been selected for machine vision algorithm testing, with a volume of 150 mm × 150 mm × 110 mm. Figure 1 presents the CAD representations of them.

Generally, in aluminium casting alloys, the areas where burrs are to be treated usually appear along the closure line of the mold. For reference, Figure 1, 10 different burr areas have been selected, and the thickness of each of them has been measured. The final roughness to be achieved in the parts has been obtained by evaluating the results using current finishing methods. The *Ra* parameter has been measured, according to standard ISO 4288, wherever possible, in a finished part. As an example, pictures with the burr zones defined by numbers are shown in Figure 2.

Table 1 summarizes the thickness in the sample part for each particular burr zone. The target surface roughness of 7.5 μm is the required finishing quality for the part, after eliminating the burr by the laser process. This second process is out of the scope of this paper.

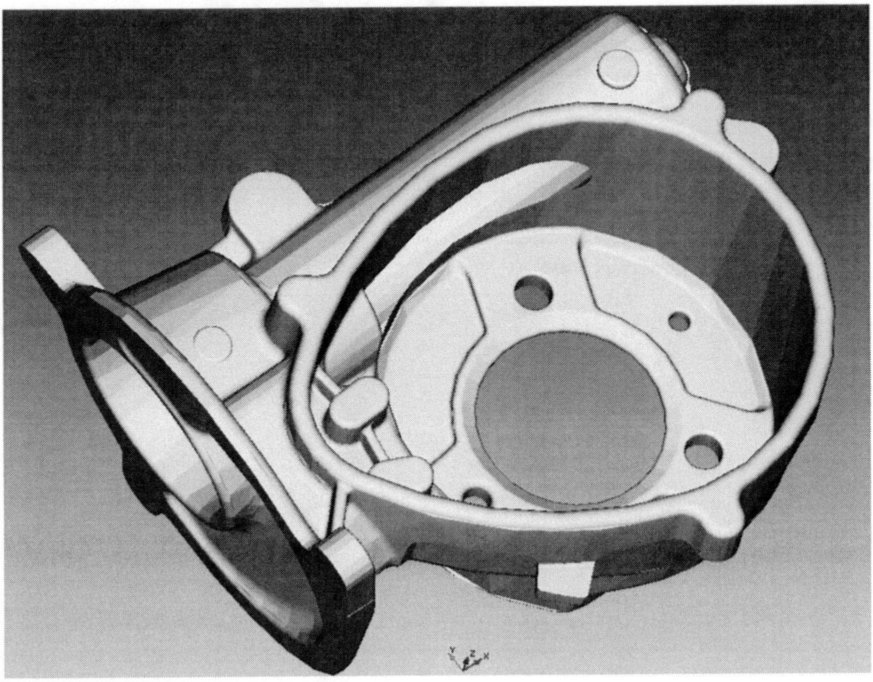

**Figure 1.** CAD representation of the part used for the research.

**Figure 2.** Burr examples in example part.

**Table 1.** Burr thickness for the different references.

| Zone in Sample Part | Burr Thickness (mm) |
|---|---|
| 1 | 3 |
| 2 | 3 |
| 3 | 1.5 |
| 4 | 1.4 |
| 5 | 1.7 |
| 6 | 0.25 |
| 7 | 1.6 |
| 8 | 1.6 |
| 9 | 1.2 |
| 10 | 0.9 |

For each part, the fundamental operations for the process must be carried out using 3D machine vision. These are, burr detection using 3D part reconstruction and matching with CAD model.

# 4. METHODS

The problem proposed, burr detection, consists of three principal steps:

1. 3D reconstruction of the part, using sheet of light techniques and registration methods to obtain a point cloud volume avoiding shadows and occlusions.
2. Point cloud filtering and clustering to obtain a robust model of the part under inspection.
3. Matching with the identified part CAD model, STL file in this case, to obtain volume differences corresponding to burrs.

The following subsections explain the different steps in both problems in more depth.

## 4.1. 3D Reconstruction and Partial View Registration

The sheet of light setup used for 3D reconstruction is a dual camera system, in a reversed ordinary setup configuration. According to [38], the reversed ordinary setup provides a good height resolution avoiding miss-register problems, provided the α angle is fixed between 15° and 65°. Smaller angles lead to bad sampling conditions, and larger angles lead to occlusions. The height resolution obtained with this setup can be expressed as follows, assuming that the pixels of the sensor are square:

$$\Delta z \approx \frac{\Delta x_{sensor}}{\sin(\alpha)} \tag{1}$$

where Δz is the resolution in Z axis in real world coordinates and Δxsensor is the increment of pixels in the *X*axis of the camera sensor.

The dual camera system is mounted in the sense of the relative movement of the part under inspection, so occlusions due to geometry are avoided. Figure 3 shows the real setup and the corresponding schematics. Additionally, for each of the two cameras, calibration has been performed so that the partial point clouds are obtained directly in real world coordinates, in this case, mm, which are the units in the part STL model.

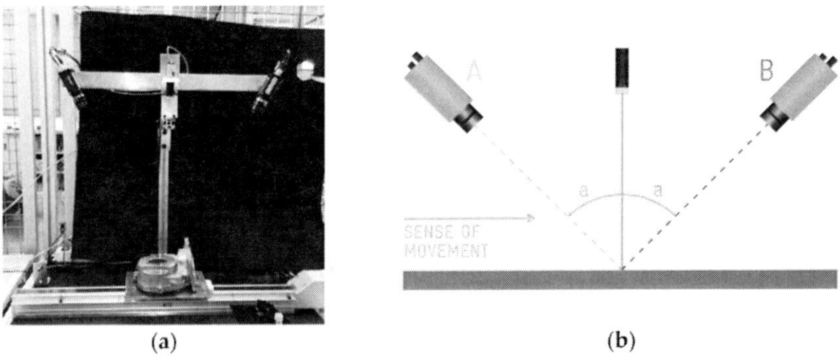


**Figure 3.** (**a**) Dual camera laser triangulation system, in reversed ordinary setup; (**b**) schematics of the setup.

The technical specifications of the system are summarized in the following points:

1. Two Dalsa Genie HM1400 matricial cameras, with a 1400 × 1280 pixel sensor, with a pixel size of 7.4 μm, and up to 75 fps. The image output format is GigE Vision.
2. High resolution optics, f 1.4, with a focal length of 16 mm.
3. Lasiris SLH-501L red laser line generator, with a 30° fan angle.
4. Working area of 200 mm in x axis. *Y* axis obtained by camera triggering.

5. System calibrated in X and Z using 100 × 100 mm squared calibration plate. Optimum height resolution has been found with a value of α = 30°.

6. The relative movement is carried out using a SMC LEFS32S3A linear axis with a 600 mm moving range and a resolution of 0.02 mm, commanded by a SMC LEC SA2-S3 servo motor.

For the registration of both partial reconstructions obtained from the part, key points have been extracted using the scale-invariant feature transform algorithm (SIFT) [39]. Having obtained the key points, the registration is performed in two steps, first using a FANN algorithm [40] for initial registration of clouds, and ICP [41] in a second step to minimize errors, obtaining as a result the affine transformation of the point cloud of the one camera with respect to the other, taking as coordinate reference the first camera in the sense of movement (A inFigure 3b):

$$H_{registration} = H_{icp}H_{fann} = \begin{bmatrix} R_{icp} \cdot R_{fann} & R_{icp} \cdot t_{fann} + t_{icp} \\ 0 \quad 0 \quad 0 & 1 \end{bmatrix} \tag{2}$$

Transforming the second partial point cloud by Equation (2) and adding the points to the first point cloud taken as reference, a first registration step is achieved. This initial step can be seen in Figure 4:

## 4.2. Point Cloud Preprocessing

After obtaining the registered point cloud, further processing is needed to obtain a suiTable 3D volume to be compared against the STL model of the ideal part. All needed configuration parameters in the different operations have been fixed empirically after performing some tests, and taking into account the characteristics of the initial point clouds in terms of number of points and spatial resolution of 0.25 mm/pix in *X* axis and 0.5 mm/pix in *Y* axis. Operations applied on the point cloud with brief description and parameters are listed below in order of application:

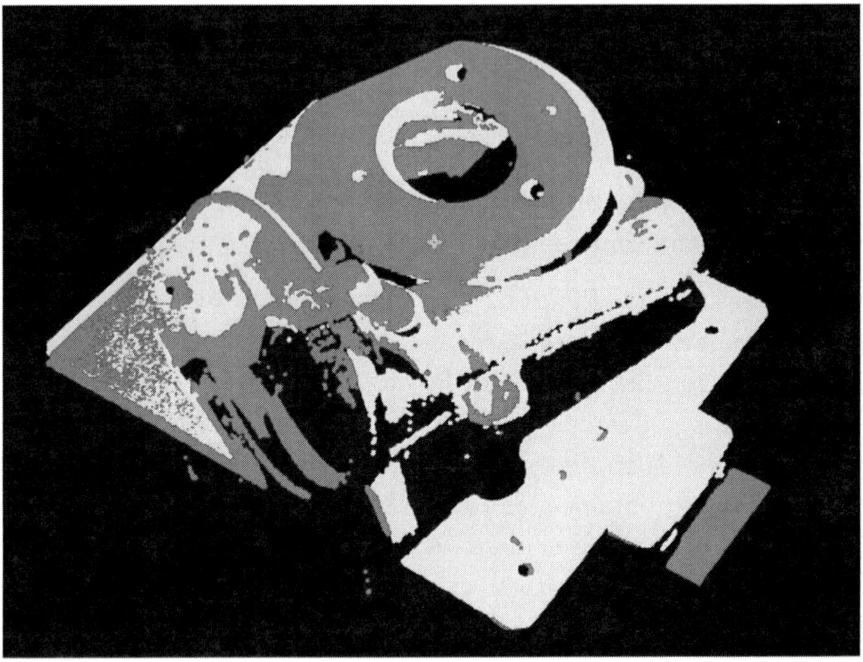

**Figure 4.** Registration of the two partial point clouds (red and green) obtained.

1. *Outlier removal*: Using the euclidean distance as measuring criterium, an outlier in the point cloud is defined as a point whose mean distance to the *k* nearest neighbours is bigger than *D* mm, with $k = 3$ and $D = 5$.

2. *Downsampling using a voxel grid filter:* All the points within voxel cubes of *d* mm of edge, are substituted by a new point, the cube centroid. Voxel cubes containing less than *n* points are removed from the point point cloud. $d = 0.5$ mm, $n = 5$ points.

3. *Smoothing of the downsampled pointcloud*: For point cloud smoothing the MLS algorithm is used, and fits a planar surface or a higher order polynomial surface to its *k* nearest points. The surface fitting is a standard weighted least squares parameter estimation of the plane or polynomial surface parameters, respectively. The closest neighbors of P have higher contribution

than the other points, which is controlled by the following weighting function with a parameter φ:

$$w(P^*) = e^{\left(-\frac{\|P^* - P\|^2}{\varphi^2}\right)} \tag{3}$$

The point being processed is then projected to the calculated local surface, with a relative φ = 1.0.

Applying these three steps to the initial registration process as explained in Section 4.1, a smoothed model with less noise is obtained, suitable to be used for detecting burrs in the part, by comparing it with the initial CAD model. Figure 5 shows the final model of the reconstructed part.

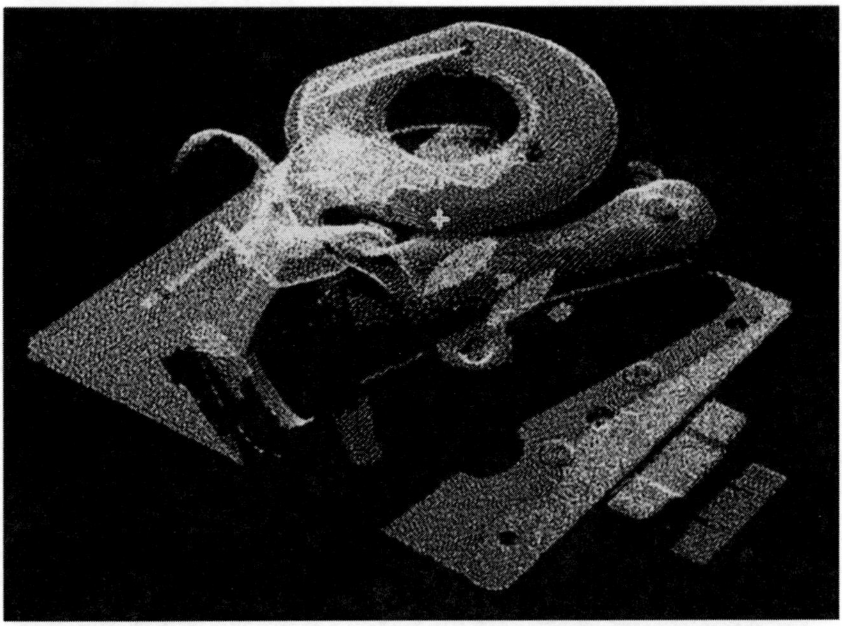

**Figure 5.** Final model after outlier removal, downsampling, and smoothing.

## 4.3. Matching with CAD Model and Burr Detection

For burr detection, the point cloud model generated in the previous section is used to carry out a registration with the STL model. The registration operation is based essentially on the same procedure explained in Section 4.1, taking as point clouds to register the generated 3D model from the scanned part, and the STL design model available. Once the complete registration is performed, distance from the scanned part to the nearest model surface is calculated, by establishing a threshold in distance of 0.1 mm. Points whose distances are above this threshold are marked as burr points.

The last step is a 3D clustering of these points, to obtain position and size of the burr that will be oblated by the laser, as illustrated in Figure 6.

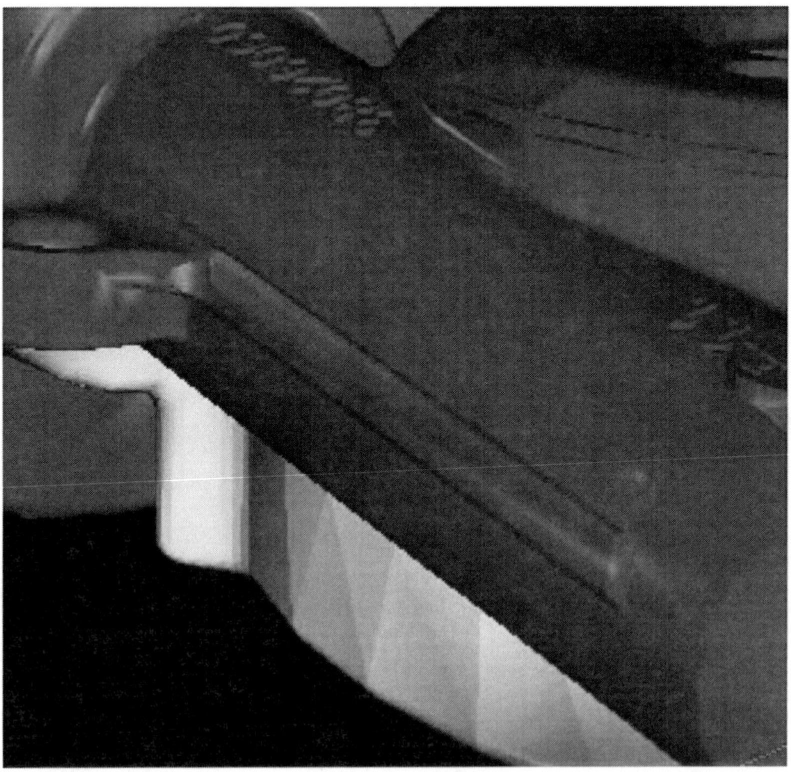

**Figure 6.** Detail of type 2 burr detection, in pink-red color.

**Table 2.** Burr detection. For each part and burr type, measured burr in mm.

| - | Burr Type | | | | | | | | | | | | | | | | | | | |
|---|---|---|---|---|---|---|---|---|---|---|---|---|---|---|---|---|---|---|---|---|
| Part N. | 1 | | 2 | | 3 | | 4 | | 5 | | 6 | | 7 | | 8 | | 9 | | 10 | |
| 1 | 2.9 | 3 | 2.7 | 2.8 | 1.8 | 1.8 | - | - | 2.1 | 2 | 0.5 | 0.5 | 1.5 | 1.6 | 1.5 | 1.5 | - | - | 0.9 | 1 |
| 2 | 2.9 | 2.8 | - | - | 1.4 | 1.5 | 1.3 | 1.4 | 2 | 2.1 | 0.7 | 0.7 | - | - | | | 1.1 | 1.3 | - | - |
| 3 | 3 | 2.9 | 2.9 | 2.7 | - | - | 1.8 | 1.7 | 2.1 | 2.2 | - | - | 1.7 | 1.7 | 1.7 | 1.8 | 1.7 | 1.7 | 1.2 | 1.2 |
| 4 | - | - | 3 | 3.1 | 1.6 | 1.7 | 2 | 1.9 | 2.2 | 2 | 0.3 | 0.4 | - | - | - | - | 1.5 | 1.6 | 1.3 | 1.3 |
| 5 | 2.8 | 3 | - | - | | | - | - | 2.3 | 2.3 | - | - | 1.6 | 1.7 | 1.6 | 1.7 | - | - | 1.1 | 1.2 |
| 6 | 3 | 3.1 | 3.2 | 3.2 | 1.6 | 1.4 | 1.6 | 1.6 | 2.2 | 2.2 | 0.7 | 0.5 | 1.5 | 1.5 | 1.4 | 1.4 | 1.6 | 1.5 | 1 | 0.9 |
| 7 | 2.9 | 2.8 | 2.6 | 2.7 | - | - | 1.5 | 1.5 | 2 | 2.1 | 0.5 | 0.3 | 1.8 | 1.8 | - | - | 1.8 | 1.7 | 1 | 1.1 |
| 8 | 2.9 | 2.7 | 2.6 | 2.6 | 2 | 1.9 | 1.7 | 1.8 | 2 | 2.1 | 0.5 | 0.5 | 1.4 | 1.4 | 1.7 | 1.6 | 1.8 | 1.6 | 0.9 | 1 |
| 9 | 3 | 3.1 | 3 | 3 | 1.7 | 2 | 1.7 | 1.7 | - | - | 0.7 | 0.6 | 1.6 | 1.7 | 1.8 | 1.9 | - | - | 1 | 0.8 |
| 10 | - | - | - | - | 1.9 | 1.8 | 1.4 | 1.3 | 2.3 | 2.4 | 0.3 | 0.4 | 1.6 | 1.6 | 1.6 | 1.5 | 1.5 | 1.5 | 1.3 | 1.3 |

# 5. RESULTS

Several experiments have been performed to assess the validation of the proposed process. In the first experiment, 10 parts have been taken directly from the production line are taken through the inspection procedure for burr detection. Not all the parts have all the classified types of burrs as described in Section 3. In these cases no data is provided. When a burr type is present, the left value indicates the thickness measured by the algorithm proposed, and the right value the real thickness of the burr measured manually. All the measurements are in mm. Table 2 shows the results for this test.

Several statistical measurements have been extracted after inspecting 100 different examples for each type of burr. The mean values of real thickness of the burr, mean values of the measured thickness, and the deviations between both values are presented in Table 3.

**Table 3.** Statistical error measurements.

| Burr Type | Mean Measured Thickness (mm) | Mean Real Thickness (mm) | Mean Error (mm) | Error Percentage over Real Measurement (%) |
|---|---|---|---|---|
| 1 | 2.9 | 3 | −0.1 | 3 |
| 2 | 3 | 3 | 0 | 0 |
| 3 | 1.5 | 1.6 | −0.1 | 6 |
| 4 | 1.6 | 1.7 | −0.1 | 6 |
| 5 | 2.0 | 2.2 | −0.2 | 9 |
| 6 | 0.6 | 0.8 | −0.2 | 25 |
| 7 | 1.5 | 1.5 | 0 | 0 |
| 8 | 1.6 | 1.7 | −0.1 | 5 |
| 9 | 1.3 | 1.4 | −0.1 | 7 |
| 10 | 1 | 1 | 0 | 0 |

# 6. CONCLUSIONS AND FUTURE WORK

Based on the results presented in the previous section, several important conclusions can be extracted about the performance and validity of the solution proposed. The main points to take into account are:

1. The thickness measured in the burrs is always smaller than the real thickness. This is important to avoid an excessive deburring of the part, compromising its mechanical properties.
2. The errors in measurements are proportionally much bigger when the burr size is smaller, however, never bigger than 0.2, an admissible tolerance for general deburring applications.
3. All the burr types defined in the reference part are correctly detected and with measurement errors smaller than 0.2, a tolerance that assesses the validation of this setup for industrial use in automatic deburring stations.

Taking into account the previous points, it can finally be concluded that this research can be directly applicable to industrial automated deburring setups, however several points could be developed further to obtain a more flexible and industrialized system from this initial research station. These developments could be:

1. Obtaining a more compact system, to be able to mount the complete set up as a robot tool.
2. Substitution of the linear axis by a small working area robot. With this new setup, any complex part could be scanned and reconstructed from different and variable angles, avoiding shadows and occlusions. In this case, precise calibration of the working area of the robot would be needed so that precise affine transformations could be done to the obtained partial point clouds, before proceeding to the global registration of them all to obtain the part surface model.

## ACKNOWLEDGMENTS

This research has been carried out within the scope of the experiment DEBUR—“Automated robotic system for laser deburring of complex 3D shape parts”. DEBUR experiment belongs to the ECHORD ++ (European Clearing House for Open Robotics Development Plus Plus) platform, an EU-funded project within the Seventh Framework Program, aiming to strengthen the cooperation between scientific research and industry in European robotics.

## AUTHOR CONTRIBUTIONS

Alberto Tellaeche and Ramón Arana designed the setup of the machine vision station for burr detection. Ramón Arana mounted the experiment setup, and programmed part of the code. Alberto Tellaeche finished the code and set final parameters, and also wrote the paper.

## REFERENCES


1. Lee, S.H. *Deburring Automation and Precision Laser Deburring*; University of California: Berkeley, CA, USA, 1996.
2. Lee, S.H.; Dornfeld, D.A. Precision laser deburring. *J. Manuf. Sci. Eng.* **2001**, *123*, 601–608.
3. Petring, D.; Abels, P.; Noldechen, E.; Presing, K.U. Laser beam cutting of highly alloyed thick section steels. In *Laser/Optoelectronics in Engineering*; Springer Verlag: Berlin, Germany, 1990; pp. 599–604.
4. Sato, S.; Takahashi, K.; Saito, S.; Fujioka, T.; Noda, O.; Kuribayashi, S.; Imatake, S.; Kondo, M. Five-kilowatt highly efficient electric discharge cw CO laser. In Proceedings of the Conference on Lasers and Electro-Optics, Baltimore, MD, USA, 24–28 April 1989.
5. Jones, M.; Chen, X. Thick section cutting with a high brightness solid state laser. In Proceedings of the 1999 Laser Materials Processing Conference (ICALEO '99), Orlando, FL, USA, 1999; pp. A158–A165.

6. Alfille, J.P.; Pilot, G.; Prunele, D. New pulsed YAG laser performances in cutting thick metallic materials for nuclear applications. In *High Power Lasers: Applications and Emerging Applications*; SPIE: Bellingham, WA, USA, 1996; pp. 134–144.

7. Kar, A.; Scott, J.E.; Latham, W.P. Theoretical and experimental studies of thick-section cutting with a chemical oxygen-iodine laser (COIL). *J. Laser Appl.* **1996**, *8*, 125–133.

8. Adams, M.J. Processes Introduction to Gas Jet Laser Cutting. *Met. Constr. Br. Weld. J.* **1970**, *2*, 1–8.

9. Carrol, D.L.; Kar, J.A.; Latham, W.L. Experimental analysis of the materials processing performance of Chemical Oxygen-Iodine Laser (COIL). In Proceedings of the Laser Materials Processing Conference (ICALEO '96), Orlando, FL, USA, 1996; pp. 19–27.

10. Juckenath, B.; Bergmann, H.W.; Geiger, M.; Kupfer, R. Cutting of aluminium and titanium alloys by $CO_2$lasers. In *Laser/Optoelectronics in Engineering*; Springer Verlag: Berlin, Germany, 1990; pp. 595–598.

11. Powell, J. *$CO_2$ Laser Cutting*; Springer: London, UK, 1998.

12. Bod, D.; Brasier, R.E.; Parks, J. A powerful $CO_2$ cutting tool. *Laser Focus* **1969**, *5*, 36–38.

13. Shigematsu, I.; Kozuka, T.; Kanayama, K.; Hirai, Y.; Nakamura, M. Cutting of TiAl intermetallic compound by $CO_2$ laser. *J. Mater. Sci. Lett.* **1993**, *12*, 1404–1407.

14. Daurelio, G. Copper sheets laser cutting: a new goal on laser material processing. In Proceedings of the 1987 Conference Laser Advanced Materials Processing (LAMP '87), Osaka, Japan, 21–23 May 1987; pp. 261–266.

15. Pocklington, D.N. Application of lasers to cutting copper and copper alloys. *Mater. Sci. Technol.* **1989**, *5*, 77–86.

16. Powell, J.; King, T.G.; Menzies, I.A.; Frass, K. Optimization of pulsed laser cutting of mild steels. In Proceedings of the 3th International Congress on Lasers in Manufacturing; Springer Verlag: Paris, France, 1986; pp. 67–75.

17. Lunau, F.W.; Paine, E.W. $CO_2$ laser cutting. *Weld. Met. Fabr.* **1969**, *27*, 3–8.

18. Chui, G.K. Laser cutting of hot glass. *Am. Ceram. Soc. Bull.* **1975**, *54*, 515–518.

19. Dobbs, R.; Bishop, P.; Minardi, A. Laser Cutting of Fibrous Quartz Insulation Materials. *J. Eng. Mater. Technol.* **1994**, *116*, 539–544.

20. Kawaga, Y.; Utsunomiya, S.; Kogo, Y. Laser cutting of CVD-SiC fibre/A6061 composite. *J. Mater. Sci. Lett.* **1989**, *8*, 681–683.

21. Rieck, K. Laser cutting of fiber reinforced materials. In Proceedings of the 3rd European Conference Laser Treatment of Materials (ECLAT '90), Coburg, Germany, 17–19 September 1990; pp. 777–788.

22. Andreopoulos, A.; Tsotsos, J.K. 50 Years of object recognition: Directions forward. *Comput. Vis. Image Underst.* **2013**, *117*, 827–891.

23. Ekvall, S.; Kragic, D.; Hoffmann, F. Object recognition and pose estimation using color cooccurrence histograms and geometric modeling. *Image Vis. Comput.* **2005**, *23*, 943–955.

24. Eggert, D.W.; Fitzgibbon, A.W.; Fisher, R.B. Simultaneous registration of multiple range views for use in reverse engineering of CAD models. *Comput. Vis. Image Underst.* **1998**, *69*, 253–272.

25. Fitzgibbon, A.W. Robust registration of 2D and 3D point sets. *Image Vis. Comput.* **2003**, *21*, 1145–1153.

26. Beserra, R.; Marques, B.; Karin de Medeiros, L.; Vidal, R.; Pacheco, L.C.; Garcia, L.M. Efficient 3D object recognition using foveated point clouds. *Comput. Graph.* **2013**, *37*, 496–508.

27. Aldoma, A.; Vincze, M.; Blodow, N.; Gossow, D.; Gedikli, S.; Rusu, R.B.; Bradski, G. CAD-model recognition and 6DOF pose estimation using 3D cues. In Proceedings of the 2011 IEEE International Conference on Computer Vision Workshops (ICCV Workshops), Barcelona, Spain, 6–13 November 2011; pp. 585–592.

28. Morency, L.; Sundberg, P.; Darrell, T. Pose estimation using 3D view-based eigenspaces. In Proceedings of the 2003 IEEE International Workshop on Analysisn and Modeling of Faces and Gestures, Nice, France, 17 October 2003; pp. 45–52.

29. Rusu, R.B.; Bradski, G.; Thibaux, R.; Hsu, J. Fast 3D recognition and pose using the Viewpoint Feature Histogram. In Proceedings of the 2010 IEEE International Conference on Intelligent Robots and systems (IROS), Taipei, Taiwan, 10–12 October 2010; pp. 2155–2162.

30. Azad, P.; Asfour, T.; Dillmann, R. Accurate shape-based 6-DoF pose estimation of single-colored objects. In Proceedings of the 2009 IEEE International Conference on Intelligent Robots and Systems (IROS), St. Louis, MO, USA, 10–15 October 2009; pp. 2690–2695.

31. Changhyun, C.; Christensen, H.I. Real-time 3D model-based tracking using edge and keypoint features for robotic manipulation. In Proceedings of the 2010 IEEE International Conference on Robotics and Automation (ICRA), New Orleans, LA, USA, 26 April–1 May 2010; pp. 4048–4055.

32. Mittrapiyanumic, P.; DeSouza, G.N.; Kak, A.C. Calculating the 3D-pose of rigid-objects using active appearance models. In Proceedings of the 2004 IEEE International Conference on Robotics and Automation (ICRA), 2004; pp. 5147–5152.

33. Payet, N.; Todorovic, S. From contours to 3D object detection and pose estimation. In Proceedings of the 2011 IEEE International Conference on Computer Vision (ICCV), Barcelona, Spain, 6–13 November 2011; pp. 983–990.

34. Drost, B.; Ulrich, M.; Navab, N.; Ilic, S. Model globally, match locally: Efficient and robust 3D object recognition. In Proceedings of the 2010 IEEE Conference on Computer Vision and Pattern Recognition (CVPR), San Francisco, CA, USA, 13–18 June 2010; pp. 998–1005.

35. Mian, A.; Bennamoun, M.; Owens, R. On the Repeatability and Quality of Keypoints for Local Feature-based 3D Object Retrieval from Cluttered Scenes. *Int. J. Comput. Vis.* **2010**, *89*, 348–361.

36. Gao, Y.; Wang, M.; Zha, Z.J.; Tian, Q.; Dai, Q.; Zhang, N. Less is More: Efficient 3-D Object Retrieval With Query View Selection. *IEEE Trans. Multimed.* **2011**, *13*, 1007–1018.

37. Tombari, F.; Salti, S.; Di Stefano, L. A combined texture-shape descriptor fon enhanced 3D feature matching. In Proceedings of the 18th International Conference on Image Processing, Brussels, Belgium, 11–14 September 2011; pp. 809–812.

38. Boehnke, K.E. Hierarchical Object Localization for Robotic Bin Picking. Ph.D. Thesis, Faculty of Electronics and Telecommunications, Politehnica University of Timisoara, Timisoara, Romania, September 2008.

39. Lowe, D.G. Object recognition from local scale-invariant features. In Proceedings of the Seventh IEEE International Conference on Computer Vision, Kerkyra, Greece, 20–27 September 1999; pp. 1150–1157.

40. Muja, M.; Lowe, D.G. Fast Approximate Nearest Neighbors with Automatic Algorithm Configuration. In Proceedings of the 2009 International Conference on Computer Vision Theory and Applications (VISAPP'09), Lisboa, Portugal, 5–8 February 2009.

41. Besl, P.J.; McKay, N.D. A Method for Registration of 3-D Shapes. *IEEE Trans. Pattern Anal. Mach. Intell.* **1992**, *14*, 239–256.

# Chapter 3

# Towards Realizing High-Throughput, Roll-to-Roll Manufacturing of Flexible Electronic Systems

**Xiaohui Lin [1], Harish Subbaraman [2,*], Zeyu Pan [1], Amir Hosseini [2], Chris Longe [1], Klay Kubena [1], Paul Schleicher [1], Phillip Foster [1], Sean Brickey [1] and Ray T. Chen [1]**

[1]*Department of Electrical and Computer Engineering, the University of Texas at Austin, Austin, TX 78758, USA*

[2]*Omega Optics, Inc., 8500 Shoal Creek Blvd, Building 4, Suite 200, Austin, TX 78757, USA*

## ABSTRACT

High-rate roll-to-roll (R2R) tracker systems are utilized for large volume flexible electronic device manufacturing, and the current alignment mechanism between layers is mainly achieved by relying on passive techniques. In this paper, we present a machine vision based alignment strategy that is used to achieve precise registration for stacking multilayers. Based on this strategy, we demonstrate two-layer printing with alignment accuracy better than 100 μm in web moving direction and 200 μm in lateral direction at a web rate of 5 m/min.

**Keywords:** Roll-to-roll; Ink-jet printing; Flexible electronics; Alignment

# 1. INTRODUCTION

Over the last decade, the printed electronics industry has been undergoing a significant growth in the market. Printed electronics refers to a set of printing methods, such as screen printing, flexography, gravure, offset lithography, inkjet printing, *etc.*, used to create electronic devices on various substrates. Among these methods, inkjet printing is an ideal solution for low cost, high speed printed electronics, due to the low material consumption, low equipment costs, and possibility for mass customization [1]. Some important application areas include RFID [2,3], solar cells [4,5], and displays [6,7], where device structures are mainly formed by stacking patterned layers, and where the critical dimension is in the tens of microns to millimeter range. The registration accuracy between layers is of great importance in determining the quality of the devices. For a tabletop printer, such as the ones printing on small area substrates, layer to layer registration is achieved via a microscopic system. The system determines the printing origin, and both the *X* and the *Y* direction offset values, with respect to previous layers. Therefore, one can precisely align two patterns with a maximum offset of the mechanical moving part accuracy, or to be more specific, the step motor accuracy.

However, the alignment strategy for a table-top printer is not applicable for a high-rate roll-to-roll system, where the registration needs to be performed while the substrate is moving at a high speed. There are several technologies that are used to realize roll-to-roll registration. For example, Krebs *et al.* punch a series of registration holes along the edge of the web so that the position of the web is kept relatively constant with respect to the printer head [8]. Jung *et al.* utilize no external setup for registration, but the mechanical system is capable of providing overlay printing registration accuracy of ±20 μm [2]. It is a practical way to make use of the precise tracking mechanism and the edge sensor to ensure minimum sideways wander of the web. However, such "passive" alignment strategies may encounter some off-registration problems if the original web has poor edge condition (e.g., edge flatness) that affects the width of the substrate. Due to the above-mentioned problems, in the actual industry environment, most ink-jet based roll-to-roll systems are only used to deposit the first layer, which does not require accurate alignment. For stacking of subsequent layers, screen printing is employed where the registration is performed when the web is stationery. This limits the final throughput of the manufacturing process.

In this research, we introduce an “active” alignment strategy using machine vision and demonstrate the entire system setup, including the software and hardware in order to realize multi-layer alignment. A feature of our method is that the active alignment is tolerant to the imperfections in the substrate condition, and does not pose demanding requirements on the web tracking system.

To better illustrate the system details, in Section 2, we first introduce the basic idea for realizing roll-to-roll registration. Based on this idea, the main system modules are determined. Next, based on the detailed system requirements, we specify the components in every module. A customized software implementation is described for synchronizing all the components for proper functioning in Section 3 Finally, multi-layer printing test is performed and the results are analyzed in Section 4.

## 2. SYSTEM COMPONENTS

### 2.1. Basic Idea

The Roll-to-Roll ink-jet printing system with alignment capability is a complex electro-mechanical system. In order to realize a high-speed, multi-layer printing system with good registration, an active alignment method should be considered. It should be noted that, in designing the system, the anisotropic mechanical properties of the flexible substrate also needs to be considered, since it plays an important role in achieving good alignment accuracy in a roll-to-roll process. In order to demonstrate the feasibility of our approach, and simplify the hardware, Kapton polyimide substrate is considered in our work due to its superior mechanical properties.

Alignment marks are utilized to determine the reference position, and all subsequent layer patterns are placed with respect to this reference position. Different from the table top printer used in our previous work [9,10,11], the printhead in the high-rate roll-to-roll system is stationary, which means that the alignment marks printed on first layer are not always exposed continuously to the same range of nozzles for the second layer printing due to sideways wander of the web.

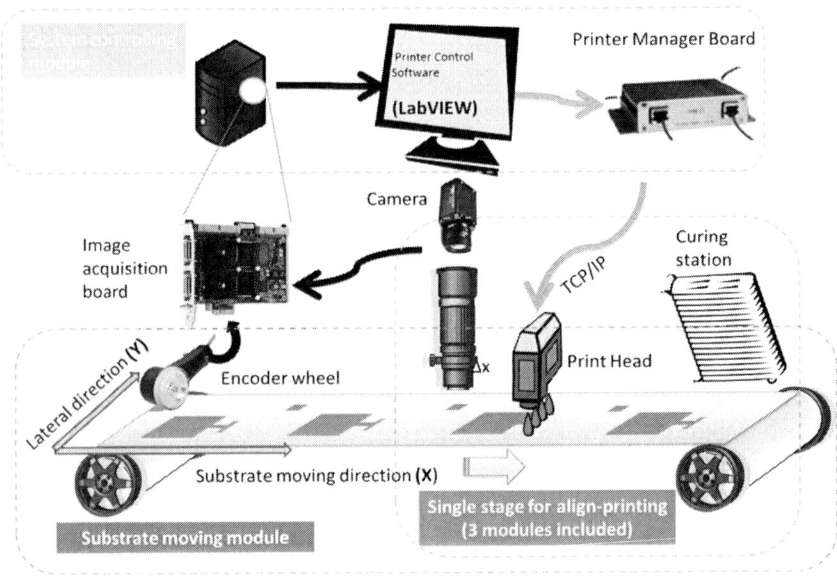


**Figure 1.** Schematic drawing of the main components in the roll-to-roll printing system with active alignment function. The main modules are (1) substrate moving module; (2) pattern detection module; (3) material ink-jet printing module; 4) fast curing module and (5) system control module. Modules (2) (3) and (4) form a standalone single stage system for aligned-printing, and can be configured in series to realize multi-stage continuous printing.

A viable solution to this problem is to utilize a high speed imaging system to get the real-time alignment mark position, and adjust the printer nozzle actuation accordingly for each copy of the pattern. Additionally, the system should also be configured to provide correct timing to start the second layer printing by using a Print/Go device.

## 2.2. Main System Modules

Based on the above discussions, we determined the main modules for a single stage printer: pattern detection module, ink-jet printing module and fast curing module. To complete the web transfer and printing function, some other modules including substrate moving module (web tracker, encoder), system control module (desktop with the controlling software) are also needed. A cartoon briefly depicting all the components in a single stage system is shown in Figure 1.

The main functions of these modules are listed below:

- The substrate moving module delivers the web at a controlled speed.
- The pattern detection module captures the positions of the alignment and the Print/Go marks.
- The ink-jet printing module retrieves and prints patterns with the desired material.
- The curing system provides in-line fast curing of the ink.
- The system control module processes images from the image acquisition module, and controls the ink-jet printing module.

## 2.3. Web Tracking Module

The tracking system contains an edge detection sensor. The sensor detects the substrate edge and controls the tilting angle of a suspending shaft so that the web edge is aligned in real time to minimize the lateral direction (*Y*) offset and the sideways wander of the web. Although the edge detection sensor and the actuator system can ensure rough alignment of the web edge, the sideways wander is still inevitable. Moreover, since the width variations in the web can be large (which is common for commercial substrate material rolls), edge detection by itself is not sufficient to give satisfying registration results. In the current situation, the sideways wander is observed to be around 2 mm in each direction (4 mm total).

The maximum sideway wander determines the minimum required camera field of view (FOV). Generally speaking, reducing the FOV increases the physical resolution of the captured images. However, this requires the tracker to have less sideways wander, so that all the alignment marks can be captured. Another component in the web tracking module is the TR1 wheel encoder which provides a resolution of 15 μm per pulse. The purpose of this encoder is to feedback the real time web running speed for the ink-jet printing module to make sure the printed patterns have the correct aspect ratio.

## 2.4. Pattern Detection Module

The purpose of the pattern detection module is to capture the alignment and the Print/Go marks on the running web. We choose a line-scan camera and an optical system with coaxial illumination to build our image acquisition setup. With a single line of pixels, line-scan sensors build continuous images not limited in their vertical resolution. Vertical resolution is dependent on the web speed.

The line-scan camera has $n = 2048$ pixels, and the optical zoom lens is adjusted to set the FOV to 6 mm, which yields a camera system resolution of 3 μm/pixel. The image resolution can be increased further by reducing the FOV and/or increasing the line-scan camera pixels.

The Print/Go signal is generated by a photoelectric sensor. The signal is used to trigger the actuation of the printhead. When a Print/Go mark is detected, the sensor output produces a falling edge of a TTL signal, which in turn triggers the printing. As shown in Figure 2, the alignment mark first enters the FOV for determining the *Y*offset.

Then, the photoelectric sensor sees the Print/Go mark in order to actuate the printing.

## 2.5. Material Ink-Jet Printing Module

The ink-jet printhead used in the current program is a high-speed head consisting of 1024 nozzles. The actuation of the cartridge is controlled by a "Print Manager Board" (PMB), which acts as the interface between the computer and the printhead. A "Print Server" software controls the PMB. It accepts external synchronizing signals from the encoder and routes the TCP/IP commands to the printhead. It also provides options for changing the waveform settings so that the jetting speed, jetting volume, and the transfer mechanism can be specified. In our system, the jetting speed is set at 5 m/s, providing a jetting volume of 14 pL per drop.

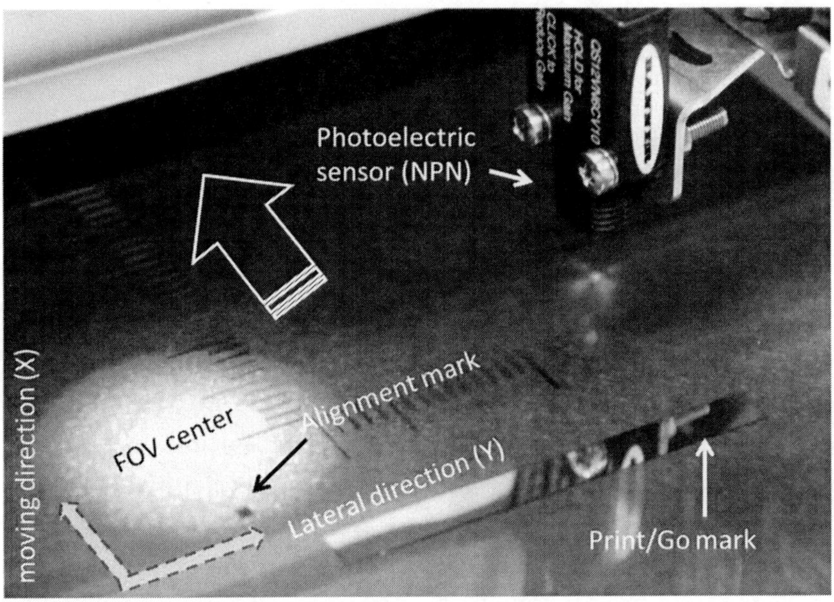


**Figure 2.** Alignment mark detection using line-scan camera, and Print/Go mark detection using photoelectric sensor.

## 2.6. Photonic Curing System

For the current roll-to-roll printing system, it is crucial to cure the printed ink quickly before it enters the next module. For inks and coatings containing nanoparticles, this process is called sintering. A conventional sintering process requires heating above 150 °C. However, it limits the applicable substrate, especially when the metal has a higher melting point than the flexible substrate, making it impossible to achieve sintering without causing subsequent damage to the substrate. Additionally, the curing speed of conventional systems is also relatively low for heating the ink above its melting points. To overcome these problems, a photonic curing/sintering method using high energy light pulse has been implemented.

Our photonic curing tool contains a 4.2" diameter spiral lamp (240 nm spectral cutoff). In our system, a 1.5 s exposure to 3 pulses, with a pulse energy 1500 Joules/pulse, completely sinters a printed silver nanoparticle film.

## 2.7. System Control Module

The system control module mainly refers to a PC equipped with the required hardware and software to perform the printing task, including acquiring images from the camera, processing the images, and sending the commands to the printhead.

The printer control is realized by TCP/IP commands. The client application initializes a command which is received by the server. The server processes the client command and starts the print engine operation. Once the operation is completed, the engine components respond to the server and the server feedbacks the client with related information. We set the printer to work in the queue print mode, thus enabling continuous addition of pre-offset images to the print queue.

# 3. SYSTEM INTEGRATION

With the basic functions realized by each individual module, system integration is realized by applying certain algorithm for aligning multi-layers. The detailed alignment strategy is discussed in the following sub-sections, along with software implementation using National Instruments NI 2011 LabVIEW software.

## 3.1. Alignment Strategy in the Y Direction (Lateral Direction)

The *Y* direction alignment is realized by the camera image processing. There are two steps involved: (a) determining the alignment mark offset; and (b) choosing the corresponding pre-offset second layer pattern to print.

By setting the correct FOV, one can make sure that whenever an alignment mark begins to pass under the camera, it appears in the FOV. The next step is to recognize the alignment mark and output its position. The alignment mark can be detected by utilizing pattern matching, which compares the captured image with a standard alignment mark template stored on the hard drive, and outputs the position error if they match to a certain degree. Alternatively, one can utilize an edge detection method as described below, which is preferred due to its lower processing time.

Edge detection is a set of mathematical methods which aims at identifying points in a digital image at which the image brightness changes sharply. It results in a highly reliable technique for detecting the alignment mark. The cartoon shown in Figure 3 presents the basic idea of detecting an alignment mark.

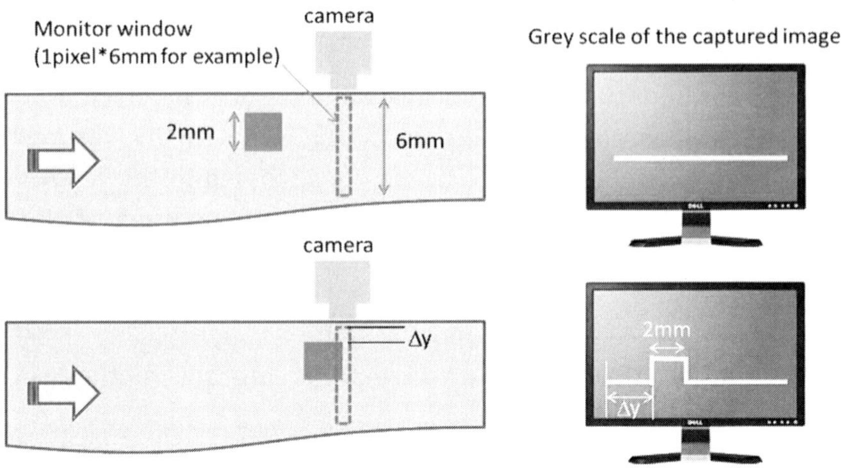


**Figure 3.** Edge detection scheme for *Y* direction alignment.

When an alignment mark passes under the camera, the abrupt greyscale image change is captured by the camera, and the first and last edge positions will be recorded. It should be noted, as mentioned above, that the line-scan camera has 2048 pixels, thus the direct output from the edge detection program is a value in pixel (0–2047). Here, in our application, we make use of the first edge to represent the position of the alignment mark. The last edge value is also recorded and used for checking the validity of the alignment mark.

The image processing speed should be able to match the image acquisition speed. All image processing applications are based on individual acquired images. When it comes to the case of line-scan camera, each image is formed by combining several line readout results together. For example, an image size of 2048 × 500 is formed by combining the results of 500 line readouts, with each line readout containing 2048 points. The line rate (number of line readouts per second) should be large enough in order to enable the capture of all the alignment marks. Therefore, the number of images, $N$ that the system can acquire is determined using $N$ = line rate/image height. A typical line rate is 20,000 Hz, and if we set the image height to be 200 pixels, it will generate $N$ = 100 images per second for processing.

The image processing step should be efficient enough so that each acquired image can be processed. In our system, the line edge detection method takes around 0.2 ms, while the pattern matching method takes around 2.5 ms, which is about 10 times longer. During this processing time, the web is still being transferred, causing an uncontrollable registration error in the *X* direction. Thus, the image processing time should be as short as possible. This makes edge detection a natural choice for achieving aligned printing at high-rates.

After receiving the offset value, there are three methods to print the offset images. The first method involves physically moving the printhead, which requires a high cost, fast, and precise moving mechanism. For high-rate printing, the mechanical motion may not catch up with the web speed, thereby limiting the throughput. The second method involves offsetting the nozzles using a program. However, our current system does not provide this function. The third method involves loading the images with pre-offset patterns, and it turns out to be the most practical one. In this method, we build an array of bitmap (*.bmp) images with different pre-offset values and name them sequentially when storing in the hard disk. The images are formed by moving all "black pixels" down by 1 pixel (70.5 μm in physical offset) while maintaining the entire image size. We have developed a MATLAB code that offsets the input image by 1 pixel each time, and then stores the images in the hard drive. By mapping the offset value from edge detection to the image ID, the image with correct offset value can be selected and sent to print server for printing.

## 3.2. Alignment Strategy in the X Direction (Web Moving Direction)

After choosing the proper pre-offset image to print, we also need to determine the correct time to start printing. Therefore, we also need the *X* direction alignment, which is aimed at setting the right timing for the printhead to start printing the patterns. We use a photoelectric sensor with Print/Go mark to determine the printhead actuation moment. For example, as illustrated in Figure 4, we need to print a second layer pattern (UT AUSTIN filled in RED) on top of the first layer image. The alignment marks and Print/Go marks are placed at the ending positions of each copy of the first layer pattern (unfilled UT AUSTIN). The camera will first detect the alignment mark, and initiate the TCP/IP protocol. This triggers a chain of events, leading up to the availability of an error corrected print pattern ready for printing. When the Print/Go signal is detected by the photoelectric sensor, the print ready pattern is printed. The time delay between the detection of the alignment mark and the detection of the Print/Go signal on the same copy is called buffer time, and it should be set long enough to finish the processing, image loading and transfer tasks. In the actual setup, the buffer time can be adjusted by changing the value of B and D, which represent the distances between the photoelectric sensor and the camera to the Print/Go mark, respectively, as illustrated in Figure 4.

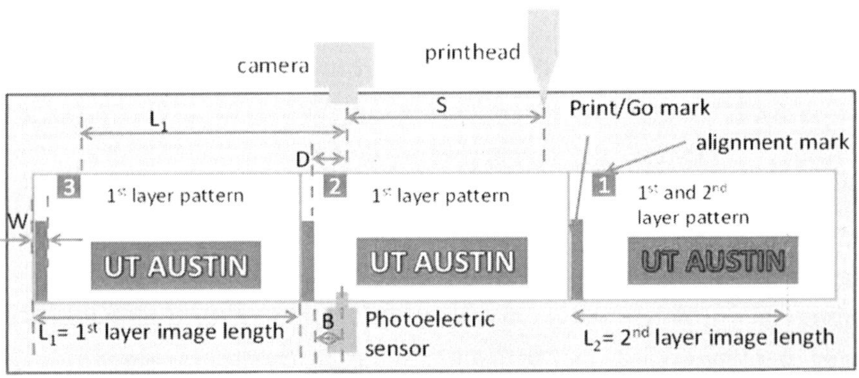


**Figure 4.** Alignment strategy in the *X* direction showing the relative positions of the printhead, camera, alignment mark, Print/Go mark and the photoelectric sensor.

### 3.3. Software Development Using NI LabVIEW

We use LabVIEW from National Instruments (NI) to integrate all the functional modules needed. Our software performs three major roles: image acquisition, image processing and printer control.

# 4. MODULE TESTING

## 4.1. Alignment Mark Detection

Whenever an alignment mark enters the field of view, it will be captured. The processed result is then used to select the corresponding pre-offset image, and the print command is sent out immediately. Figure 5 shows an offset testing result with 20 consecutive alignment marks captured by the camera. A non-flat behavior is typically expected due to sideways wander of the web. From the graph, the maximum sideways wander range of the web is calculated to be about 4 mm.

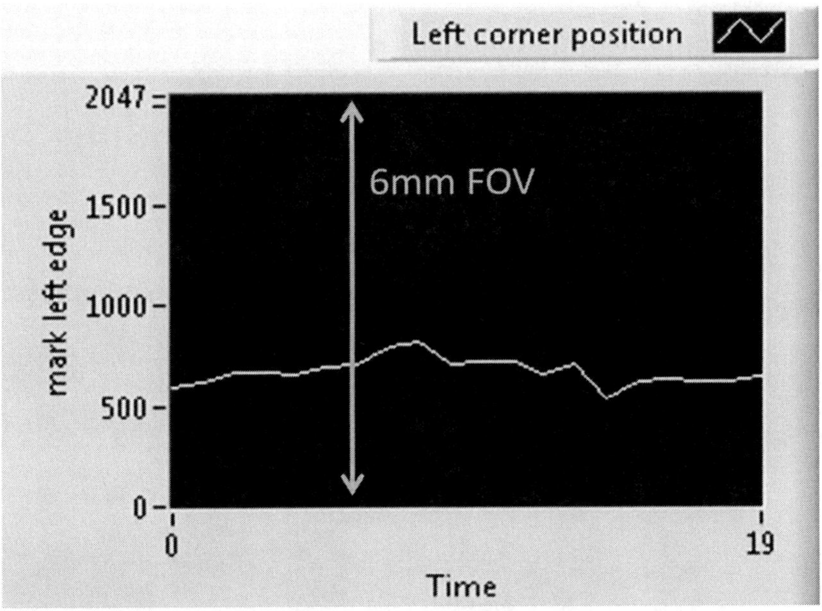


**Figure 5.** Detected positions of 20 consecutive alignment marks, indicating the web sideway wander of around 1.5–2 mm each way for this pass.

## 4.2. Registration for Multi-Layer Printing

We perform real-time aligned printing using a test pattern, as shown in Figure 6A. The first layer pattern contains a 2 mm × 2 mm square alignment mark, Print/Go mark and reference scales in $X$ and $Y$ directions. The second layer is a cross hair mark that is centered at $X$ = 40 mm, $Y$ = 10 mm location. In the experiment, we printed the first and the second layers using silver nanoparticle ink at a web rate of 5 m/min. The result is shown inFigure 6B, where the cross is printed at the desired location. We also perform continuous printing of 20 second-layer patterns to test its repeatability. The misalignment distribution with respect to the designed location results is shown in Figure 7, with inset pictures showing typical printed results on the web. As can be seen, for all copies, the off-registration errors are <100 μm in $X$ and <200 μm in $Y$ directions, which indicates the feasibility of our alignment strategy.

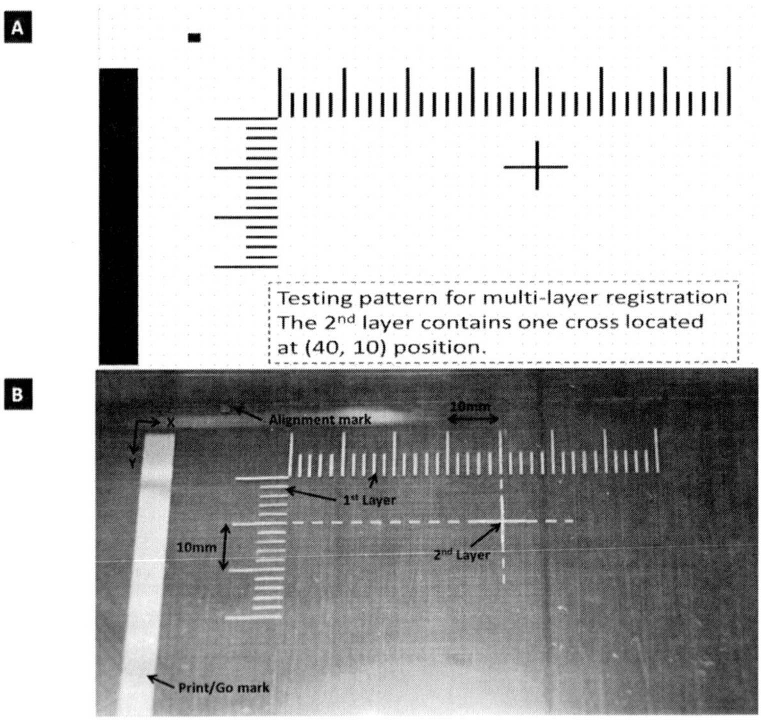


**Figure 6.** (**A**) Test pattern for aligned printing; (**B**) printed results showing registration of two layers with off-alignment less than 100 μm in both $X$ and $Y$ directions.

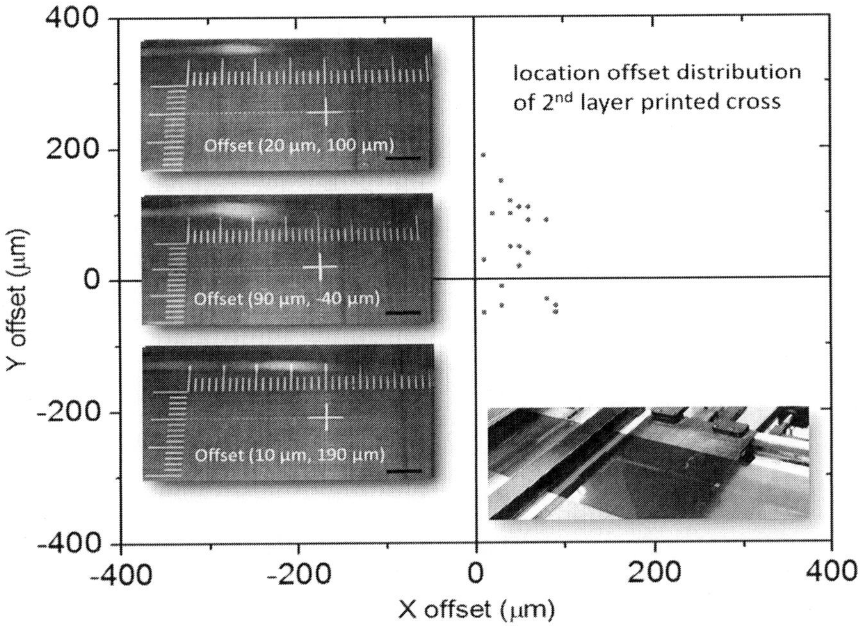


**Figure 7.** Registration offsets distribution showing continuous printing of 20 second-layer patterns with $\Delta X < 100$ µm and $\Delta Y < 200$ µm for all copies. The inset pictures have scale bars of 10 mm.

## 5. PERFORMANCE OVERVIEW

Although precise and effective algorithms are applied to ensure best registration accuracy, there are still several factors that need to be considered to minimize their effects to the system performance and auto registration accuracy. Factors that need further attention are:

- The resolution of the printhead.
- The time required to initialize the Print Server software.
- The time between the print command being sent and the Print Server being ready to start printing.
- Image acquisition and processing delays.
- The number of PMBs or printheads which can be connected to a single PC.

It is challenging to precisely predict or guarantee the performance of the software, as there are a number of different factors which contribute to it. These factors include:

- The operating system setup.
- The PC hardware.
- The other software or operations running on the PC.
- The Print Server configuration.

**Table 1.** Limiting factors for registration error.

| *X* Direction (absolute value) | |
|---|---|
| Limiting factors | Offset introduced |
| Encoder error due to slip when start/stop | 100–200 μm |
| Printer delay (4 ms delay, web running is 5m/min) | 333 μm during 4 ms |
| Image file transfer delay (uncertain) | Estimate ≈ 500 μm (500 KB file size) (*) |
| LabVIEW program image processing time (1 ms) | 80 μm |
| Actual tested offset | <100 μm |
| ***Y* Direction (absolute vale)** | |
| Limiting factors | Offset introduced |
| Printer nozzle offset | 70.5 μm |
| Sideway wander offset while transferring from FOV to printhead | Up to 2000 μm |
| Camera resolution | 3 μm |
| Actual tested offset | <200 μm |

(*) Including PMB-PC via USB (250 MB/s), thus 500 KB needs 2 ms Hard disk readout time: for 5400 rpm hard drive, 100 MB/s thus 500 KB needs 5 ms Total 7 ms delay (≈500 μm).

To be specific for our system, some limiting factors affecting the overall system registration resolution are shown in Table 1. In the *X* direction, the introduction of Print/Go marks gives the system extra buffering time for file loading/transferring and provides the exact timing to start printing. In the print runs, the buffer length (B) is set at around 10 mm (adjustable) which gives about 120 ms buffering time when the web is running at 5 m/min. Thus, many issues related to PC performance are eliminated, and the alignment errors are controlled well within 100 μm. This error is mainly due to the slip of the encoder. In the *Y* direction, the main limiting factors come from the printer nozzle offset and the web sideways wander. The printer nozzles have a pitch of 70.5 μm, which is larger than the camera resolution. Thus, the offset values will be rounded and mapped to the nearest integer when choosing the pre-offset images, as shown in Table 1. Besides, after a correct second layer image is selected, and until the moment printing starts, the web would have moved sideways due to web wander, which is beyond our current control. From the design point of view, reducing the camera/printhead separation and the second layer pattern width would be helpful in minimizing the effect of this uncertainty. In order to further improve the alignment accuracy, dynamic position control of printhead location can be utilized. Currently, the position of the printheads is fixed relative to the substrate. Mounting the printheads on precision motors will provide an additional degree of freedom for future systems in order to achieve sub 10 μm alignment accuracy, however, with a small throughput penalty. To ensure high yield, enough tolerance should be given for off-registration when designing the device pattern. In the future, we will also consider the effects of substrate shrinkage and buckling on the alignment accuracy.

## 6. CONCLUSIONS

In this paper, we demonstrated a customized, machine vision aided roll-to-roll ink-jet printing system for high rate, high yield device fabrication. Based on an active alignment technique, we built up all the necessary modules and developed the software to realize auto-registration for multi-layer stacking. The *X* direction registration was realized by in-line capturing the alignment mark and determining the onset moment of printing. The *Y* direction registration was achieved by real time image processing to get the alignment mark offset, and selecting the pre-offset images to compensate for the deviation. Several limiting factors, including the resolution of the printhead, the time required to initialize the Print Server software, the time between the print command being sent and the Print Server being ready to start printing, Image acquisition and processing delays, and the number of PMBs or printheads which can be connected to a single PC, affect the overall system performance. Specifically for registration, the printer nozzle offset, camera resolution, encoder error, print delay, image processing delay, leads to a current registration error of about 100 μm and 200 μm for the *X* and the *Y* directions, respectively.

## ACKNOWLEDGMENTS

This work was supported by the Office of Naval Research (ONR) Small Business Technology Transfer (STTR) contract N00014-11-C-0704 monitored by Khershed Cooper. We would also like to acknowledge Ed Garcia from Industrial Inkjet Ltd and Kaj Larsen from KAJ's Technical services for their valuable suggestion in setting up the system.

## AUTHOR CONTRIBUTIONS

Xiaohui Lin, Harish Subbaraman contributed to the system design, component selection, system setup, data analysis, and manuscript preparation. Zeyu Pan and Amir Hosseini contributed to data analysis and manuscript preparation. Chris Longe, Klay Kubena, Paul Schleicher, Phillip Foster, and Sean Brickey contributed to the alignment software development. Ray T. Chen contributed to overall system design, data analysis, and manuscript preparation.

## REFERENCES

1. Parashkov, R.; Becker, E.; Riedl, T.; Johannes, H.; Kowalsky, W. Large area electronics using printing methods. *Proc. IEEE* **2005**, *93*, 1321–1329.
2. Jung, M.; Kim, J.; Noh, J.; Lim, N.; Lim, C.; Lee, G.; Kim, J.; Kang, H.; Jung, K.; Leonard, A.D.; *et al*. All-Printed and Roll-to-Roll-Printable 13.56-MHz-Operated 1-bit RF Tag on Plastic Foils. *IEEE Trans. Electron Devices.* **2010**, *57*, 571–580.

3. Noh, J.; Dongsun, Y.; Lim, C.; Cha, H.; Han, J.; Kim, J.; Park, Y.; Subramanian, V.; Cho, G. Scalability of Roll-to-Roll Gravure-Printed Electrodes on Plastic Foils. *IEEE Trans. Electron. Packag. Manuf.* **2010**, *33*, 275–283.

4. Bundgaard, E.; Krebs, F.C. Low band gap polymers for organic photovoltaics. *Sol. Energy Mater. Sol. Cells.* **2007**, *91*, 954–985.

5. Jørgensen, M.; Norrman, K.; Krebs, F.C. Stability/degradation of polymer solar cells. *Sol. Energy Mater. Sol. Cells.* **2008**, *92*, 686–714.

6. Jacobson, J.; Comiskey, B.; Albert, J. Microencapsulated electrophoretic display. U.S. Patents US5961804 A, 5 October 1999.

7. Kim, C.A.; Myoung, H.J.; Kang, S.-Y.; Chung, H.-S.; Kim, G.H.; Ahn, S.D.; You, I.-K.; Oh, J.; Baek, K.H.; Soo, K. Towards a Colored Electronic Paper through a Fabrication of Color Microencapsulated Electrophoretic Display Panel. In Proceedings of Imid/Idmc 2006: The 6th International Meeting on Information Display/the 5th International Display Manufacturing Conference, Digest of Technical Papers, Daegu, Korea, 22–25 August 2006; pp. 1415–1418.

8. Krebs, F.C.; Tromholt, T.; Jørgensen, M. Upscaling of polymer solar cell fabrication using full roll-to-roll processing. *Nanoscale* **2010**, *2*, 873–886.

9. Lin, X.; Ling, T.; Subbaraman, H.; Zhang, X.; Byun, K.; Guo, L.J.; Chen, R.T. Ultraviolet imprinting and aligned ink-jet printing for multilayer patterning of electro-optic polymer modulators. *Opt. Lett.* **2013**, *38*, 1597–1599.

10. Lin, X.; Ling, T.; Subbaraman, H.; Guo, L.J.; Chen, R.T. Printable thermo-optic polymer switches utilizing imprinting and ink-jet printing. *Opt. Express* **2013**, *21*, 2110–2117.

11. Subbaraman, H.; Pham, D.T.; Xu, X.; Chen, M.Y.; Hosseini, A.; Lu, X.; Chen, R.T. Ink-Jet Printed Two Dimensional Phased-Array Antenna on a Flexible Substrate. *IEEE Antennas Wirel. Propag. Lett.* **2013**, *2*, 170–173.

# Chapter 4

## Hardware implementation of machine vision systems: image and video processing

**Guillermo Botella, Carlos García and Uwe Meyer-Bäse**

*Department of Computer Architecture and Automation, Complutense University*

## ABSTRACT

This contribution focuses on different topics covered by the special issue titled 'Hardware Implementation of Machine vision Systems' including FPGAs, GPUS, embedded systems, multicore implementations for image analysis such as edge detection, segmentation, pattern recognition and object recognition/ interpretation, image enhancement/restoration, image/video compression, image similarity and retrieval, satellite image processing, medical image processing, motion estimation, neuromorphic and bioinspired vision systems, video processing, image formation and physics based vision, 3D processing/coding, scene understanding, and multimedia.

**Keywords:** Computer vision Hardware implementation Image processing Video processing

# INTRODUCTION

Machine Vision systems represent an extensive area belonging to the digital signal processing with vast applications nowadays for industrial environment, robotics, vehicular/avionics/space technology, multimedia, entertainment, security, medicine, scientific, and so on. Nevertheless, mostly these techniques cannot be achieved "off-line" due to the physical constraints of the complex environment and the context where they are applied. Additionally, as these systems are becoming complex, huge computational resources are demanding, mostly if hard real-time constraint is required.

The hardware implementation and the acceleration of these systems are gaining importance nowadays in order to accomplish with the requirements of the systems being usually needed to keep a scrupulous trade-off between accuracy, efficiency, and power consumption. The use of GPGPUs, cells, FPGAs, and DSPs as accelerators, thus, achieves speedups of orders of magnitude vs. any optimized CPU implementation. Each appropriate implementation solution is carried out depending on many final demands as power consumption, performance, accuracy, reliability, rapid prototyping, final cost, capability, and reconfigurability among others [1–6].

The objective of this special issue has been to bring together high-quality state-of-the-art research contributions as well as review articles that address recent developments in the hardware implementation of machine vision systems.

## Specific contributions

In this special issue, we have detailed fundamental aspects related to hardware acceleration of image and video processing through different heterogeneous systems as commented previously. The applications described in this issue covers from multimedia coding to many machine vision topics.

Regarding this last aspect [7, 8], we can remark that low-level vision gets useful measurements such as color, spatial frequency, binocular disparity, motion processing, etc., from several channels. Some of the aforementioned channels or space-temporal filters can be identified with receptive fields that deliver information to the retina. Others, such as binocular disparity or motion processing, are combinations of the previously mentioned ones. Mid-level vision integrates primitives processes at a previous level. Information delivered at this stage corresponds to real-world inferences such as egomotion and independent moving objects (IMOs). They are called causal actions or object candidates in connection with any multimodal characterization. Examples of these are the combination of luminance measurements to infer lightness, shape from shading, perceptual grouping, figure organization, etc. Finally, high-level vision interprets the scene through specific tasks such as relational reasoning, knowledge building, object recognition, etc.

As resumed, in the initial classification, two principal topics are covered in 12 top quality research articles:

1. New advances in hardware acceleration techniques for multimedia content representation/coding and transmission
2. Hardware acceleration techniques for machine vision systems belonging to low-, mid- and high-level vision (according to the aforementioned taxonomy)

The first topic is covered by the five following contributions:

- In the article entitled 'MPCM: a hardware coder for super slow motion video sequences' [9] by Estefania Alcocer et al., the authors develop a fast FPGA implementation of a simple codec called modulo-pulse code modulation (MPCM) which is able to reduce the bandwidth requirements up to 1.7 times at the same image quality when compared with PCM coding. This allows current high-speed cameras to capture in a continuous manner through a 40-Gbit Ethernet point-to-point access.

- In the article entitled 'Enhancing LTW image encoder with perceptual coding and GPU-optimized 2D-DWT transform' [10] by Miguel Martínez-Rach et al., the authors propose an optimization of the wavelet image coder (specifically E_LTW encoder) with the aim to increase its rate/distortion (R/D) performance through perceptual encoding techniques and reduce the encoding time by means of a graphics processing unit-optimized version of the two-dimensional discrete wavelet transform. The results show that in both performance dimensions, our enhanced encoder achieves good results compared with Kakadu and SPIHT encoders (optimized versions of JPEG2000), achieving speedups of six times.

- In the article entitled 'GPU-based 3D lower tree wavelet video encoder' [11] by Vicente Galiano et al., the authors introduce a fast GPU-based encoder which uses 3D-discrete wavelet transform and lower trees, presenting also an exhaustive analysis of the use of GPU memory. This approach demonstrates a good trade-off between R/D, coding delay (as fast as MPEG-2 for high definition) and memory requirements (up to six times less memory than ×264 encoder).

- In the article entitled 'Adapting hierarchical bidirectional inter prediction on a GPU-based platform for 2D and 3D H.264 video coding' [12] by Rafael Rodríguez-Sánchez et al., the authors present an algorithm that concurrently performs the inter prediction carried out over *P*- and *B*-frames. The approach implements the hierarchical B frame prediction implemented in the H.264/AVC JM 17.2 reference software encoder, and it is tested using the main and the stereo high profile. Thus, a GPU-based implementation of an H.264/AVC and H.264/MVC inter prediction algorithm on a graphics processing unit is developed. The results show a negligible rate distortion drop with a time reduction of up to 98% for the complete H.264/AVC encoder.

- The last article regarding this first topic is entitled 'Modeling of a method of parallel hierarchical transformation for fast recognition of dynamic images' [13] by Leonid Timchenko et al.; the authors present principles necessary to develop a method, and computational facilities for the parallel hierarchical transformation based on high-performance GPUs are discussed in the paper. Mathematical models of the parallel hierarchical (PH) network training for the transformation and a PH network training method for recognition of dynamic images are developed.

- The second topic is discussed by the seven following contributions:
- Filter design optimization is a low-level vision task that has been covered in the paper entitled 'FIR Filter optimization for video processing on FPGAs' [14] by Michael Kumm et al.; the authors develop two proposed optimization techniques for high-speed implementations of the required multiplications in FIR filters with the least possible number of FPGA components. Both methods use integer linear programming formulations which can be optimally solved by standard solvers. In the first method, a formulation for the pipelined multiple constant multiplication problem is presented. In the second method, multiplication structures based on look-up tables are also taken into account. Due to the low coefficient word size in video processing, filters of typically 8 to 12 bits of an optimal solution is found for most of the filters in the benchmark used. A complexity reduction of 8.5% is achieved compared to the state-of-the-art heuristics.
- Super-resolution is also a low-level vision task that has been detailed in the paper entitled 'Exploring super-resolution implementations across multiple platforms' [15] by Bryan Leung et al. The authors implement and analyze a super-resolution algorithm across multiple platforms ranging from purely hardware to purely software and even a mix of both hardware and software. More specifically, they examine the performance for a FPGA implementation on two different FPGAs, a software/hardware solution on a FPGA with a soft core processor (embedded system), a GPGPU implementation, and a MATLAB implementation. Overall, they are very interesting in terms of architecture and performance over different platforms.

- Regarding low-level vision, the optimization of hyperspectral imaging is a relevant topic nowadays belonging to remote sensing, that has been addressed in the paper entitled 'Performance versus energy consumption of hyperspectral unmixing algorithms on multi-core platforms' [16] by Alfredo Remón et al. The authors provide a detailed assessment of the performance versus energy consumption of different hardware architectures which have not been conducted as of yet in the field of hyperspectral imaging, particularly relevant to achieve processing results in real-time. They focus a thoughtful perspective on this relevant issue and analyze the performance versus energy consumption ratio of different processing chains for spectral unmixing when implemented on multi-core platforms.
- At this point, it is worthy to pay attention to an important aspect regarding low-level vision - the motion estimation - existing nowadays. It has many important applications and is crucial to the hardware acceleration of these algorithms. Two papers representing different family methods: "gradient-family" and "matching-family" are presented in this special issue.

A gradient family-based method is presented in the contribution 'Robust motion estimation on a low-power multi-core DSP' [17] authored by Francisco D. Igual et al., which addresses the efficient implementation of a robust gradient-based optical flow model in a low-power platform based on a multi-core digital signal processor (DSP C6678 DSP from Texas Instruments, Dallas, TX, USA). The aim of this work was to carry out a feasibility study on the use of these devices in autonomous systems such as robot navigation, biomedical assistance, or tracking with not only power restrictions but also real-time requirements. The interest of this research is particularly relevant in optical flow scope because this system can be considered as an alternative solution for mid-range video resolutions when a combination of in-processor parallelism with optimizations such as efficient memory-hierarchy exploitation and multi-processor parallelization are applied.

A matching family-based method is presented in the contribution 'Acceleration of block-matching algorithms using a custom instruction-based paradigm on a Nios II microprocessor' [18] authored by Diego González et al.; this paper focuses on the optimization of matching algorithms widely used for video coding standards using an Altera custom instruction-based paradigm and a combination of synchronous dynamic random access memory (SDRAM) with on-chip memory in Nios II processors. A complete profile of the algorithms is achieved before the optimization, which locates code leaks and, afterward, creates a custom instruction set, which is then added to the specific design, enhancing the original system. As well, every possible memory combination between on-chip memory and SDRAM has been tested to achieve the best performance. The final throughput of the complete designs are shown. This manuscript outlines a low-cost system, mapped using very large scale integration technology, which accelerates software algorithms by converting them into custom hardware logic blocks and showing the best combination between on-chip memory and SDRAM for the Nios II processor.

- Keeping it going at a low-level vision layer, the next contribution focuses on augmented vision for impaired people; this paper is entitled 'A reconfigurable real-time morphological system for augmented vision' [19] authored by Ryan B. Gibson et al. Augmented visual aid devices require highly user-customizable algorithm designs for subjective configuration per task, where current digital image processing visual aids offer very little user-configurable option. The high spatial frequencies of an image can be extracted by edge detection techniques and overlaid on top of the original image to improve visual perception among the visually impaired. This paper presents a highly user-reconfigurable morphological edge enhancement system on FPGA, where the morphological, internal and external edge gradients can be selected from the presented architecture with specified edge thickness and magnitude. In addition, the morphology architecture supports reconfigurable shape structuring elements and configurable morphological operations. The proposed morphology-based visual enhancement system introduces a high degree of user flexibility in addition to meeting real-time constraints capable of obtaining 93 fps for high-definition image resolution.

- Finally, the last paper contributed in this special issue is entitled 'Parallel embedded processor architecture for FPGA based image processing using parallel software skeletons' [20] authored by Hanen Chenini et al. This application belongs to the mid-level vision, the authors provide a rapid prototyping tool as a graphic programming environment (CubeGen). Further, it offers a set of parallel software skeletons as a communication library, providing a software abstraction to enable quick implementation of complex image processing applications on the FPGA platform. The design of homogeneous network of communicating processor is presented from the hardware and software specification down to synthesizable hardware description. Additionally, the present approach is extended to support more complex applications by implementing a soft multiprocessor and show the impact of various configuration choices to match the specific application needs. Using images of a real road scene, the performance results of the road recognition algorithm on a Xilinx Virtex-6 FPGA platform not only achieve the desired latency but further improve the tracking performance which depends mainly on the number of hypotheses.

## CONCLUSIONS

This editorial paper has covered the accepted contributions as well as the topics covered for the special issue 'Hardware Implementation of Machine Vision Systems: Image and Video Processing' in the Journal on Advances Signal Processing (JASP), 2013.

# DECLARATIONS

## Acknowledgements

The guest editors would like to thank the authors for their cooperation, interest, and their top-quality contributions presented in this special issue. Also, the guest editor wants to thank our Editor-in-Chief Professor Geert Leus (as well as Professor Phillip Regalia, the former Editor-in-Chief when this special issue was launched). Finally, we thank the entire Editorial Office Staff for their dedication and effort devoted to this special issue. Also, we want to acknowledge the Spanish Project TIN 2012/32180.

# REFERENCES

1. Ayuso F, Botella G, García C, Prieto M, Tirado F: GPU-based acceleration of bioinspired motion estimation model. In *Concurrency and Computation: Practice and Experience*. New York: Wiley; 2013:1037-1056. 25

2. Botella G, García A, Rodriguez-Alvarez M, Ros E, Meyer-Bäse U, Molina MC: Robust bioinspired architecture for optical-flow computation. *IEEE Trans. VLSI Syst.* 2010, 18(4):616-629.

3. García C, Botella G, Ayuso F, Prieto M, Tirado M: Multi-GPU based on multicriteria optimization for motion estimation system. *EURASIP J. Adv. Signal Processing* 2013, 2013: 23.

4. Botella G, Meyer-Bäse U, García A: Bio-inspired robust optical flow processor system for VLSI implementation.*Electronics Letters* 2009, 45(25):1304-1305.

5. Botella G, Ros E, Rodriguez M, García A, Romero S: Pre-processor for bioinspired optical flow models: a customizable hardware implementation. In *Proceedings of the 13th IEEE Mediterranean Electrotechnical Conference, MELECON 2006, Benalmádena, 16-18 May*. Benalmádena; 2006:93-96.

6. González D, Botella G, Meyer-Baese U, García C, Sanz C, Prieto-Matías M, Tirado F: A Low cost matching motion estimation sensor based on the NIOS II microprocessor. *Sensors* 2012, 12: 13126-13149.

7. Szelinsky R: *Computer Vision Algorithms and Applications*. Berlin, Germany: Springer; 2011.

8. Dudek P, Lopich A, Gruev V: A pixel-parallel cellular processor array in a stacked three-layer 3D silicon-on-insulator technology. In *European Conference on Circuit Theory and Design, 2009*. Antalya: ECCTD 2009; Aug 2009:23-27.

9. Alcocer E, López-Granado O, Gutierrez R, Malumbres MP: MPCM: a hardware coder for super slow motion video sequences. *EURASIP J. Adv Signal Processing* 2013, 2013: 142.

10. Martínez-Rach , Miguel O, López-Granado O, Galiano V, Migallón H, Llor J, Malumbres MP: Enhancing LTW image encoder with perceptual coding and GPU-optimized 2D-DWT transform. *EURASIP J. Adv Signal Processing* 2013, 141: 2013.

11. Galiano V, López-Granado O, Drummond LA, Malumbres MP, Migallón H: GPU-based 3D lower tree wavelet video encoder. *EURASIP J. Adv Signal Processing* 2013, 2013: 141.

12. Rodríguez-Sánchez R, Martínez J, Cock J, Fernández-Escribano G, Pieters B, Sánchez JL, Claver JM, De Walle R: Adapting hierarchical bidirectional inter prediction on a GPU-based platform for 2D and 3D H.264 video coding. *EURASIP J. Adv Signal Processing* 2013., 67:

13. Timchenko LI, Kokryatskaya NI, Shpakovych VV: Modeling of a method of parallel hierarchical transformation for fast recognition of dynamics images. *EURASIP J. Adv Signal Processing* 2013, 2013: 87.

14. Kumm M, Fanghänel D, Möller K, Zipf P, Meyer-Baese U: FIR Filter optimization for video processing on FPGAs. *EURASIP J. Adv Signal Processing* 2013, 2013: 111.

15. Leung B, Memik S: Exploring super-resolution implementations across multiple platforms. *EURASIP J. Adv Signal Processing* 2013, 2013: 116.

16. Remón A, Sánchez S, Bernabé S, Quintana-Ortí ES, Plaza A: Performance versus energy consumption of hyperspectral unmixing algorithms on multi-core platforms. *EURASIP J. Adv Signal Processing* 2013, 2013: 68.

17. Igual FD, Botella G, García C, Prieto M, Tirado F: Robust motion estimation on a low-power multi-core DSP.*EURASIP J. Adv Signal Processing* 2013., 99:

18. González D, Botella G, García C, Prieto M, Tirado F: Acceleration of block-matching algorithms using a custom instruction-based paradigm on a Nios II microprocessor. *EURASIP J. Adv Signal Processing* 2013, 2013: 118.

19. Gibson RM, Ahmadinia A, McMeekin SG, Strang NC, Morison G: A reconfigurable real-time morphological system for argumented vision. *EURASIP J. Adv Signal Processing* 2013., 134:

20. Chenini H, Derutin JP, Aufrere R, Chapuis R: Parallel embedded processor architecture for FPGA based image processing using parallel software Skeletons. *EURASIP J. Adv Signal Processing* 2013. in press

# Chapter 5

# A Fast Inspection of Tool Electrode and Drilling Depth in EDM Drilling by Detection Line Algorithm

**Kuo-Yi Huang**

*Department of Mechatronic Engineering, Huafan University, Taipei, Taiwan*

## ABSTRACT

The purpose of this study was to develop a novel measurement method using a machine vision system. Besides using image processing techniques, the proposed system employs a detection line algorithm that detects the tool electrode length and drilling depth of a workpiece accurately and effectively. Different boundaries of areas on the tool electrode are defined: a baseline between base and normal areas, a ND-line between normal and drilling areas (accumulating carbon area), and a DD-line between drilling area and dielectric fluid droplet on the electrode tip. Accordingly, image processing techniques are employed to extract a tool electrode image, and the centroid, eigenvector, and principle axis of the tool electrode are determined. The developed detection line algorithm (DLA) is then used to detect the baseline, ND-line, and DD-line along the direction of the principle axis. Finally, the tool electrode length and drilling depth of the workpiece are estimated via detected baseline, ND-line, and DD-line. Experimental results show good accuracy and efficiency in estimation of the tool electrode length and drilling depth under different conditions. Hence, this research may provide a reference for industrial application in EDM drilling measurement.

**Keywords:** Electrical discharge machining (EDM); Electrode length; Drilling depth; Detection line algorithm (DLA); Peak decision method

## 1. INTRODUCTION

Electrical discharge machining (EDM) is a nontraditional machining method usually employed in production of die cavities via the erosive effect of electrical discharges between a tool electrode and a workpiece. Its unique feature of using thermal energy to machine electrically conductive materials irrespective to their hardness and toughness make it applicable not only in the manufacture of die and mold components, but also in the fields of medicine, automotive and aerospace industry. The advantage with EDM is its ability to machine complex cavities, small parts with sharp internal or external radii, and fragile materials or workpieces requiring the creation and modification of very thin walls. However, the occurrence of tool electrode wear is unavoidable and is a very critical issue since tool shape degeneration directly affects the final shape of die cavity. To improve the machining accuracy in the geometry of a workpiece, methods to detect the tool electrode wear as well as compensate the wear of the tool electrode are required. Existing tool wear sensing methods such as offline wear prediction [1, 2] and real-time tool wear sensing approaches based on discharge pulse evaluation [3-5] are all indirect methods.

Optical measurement methods using machine vision techniques have been used for real-time tool wear evaluation in conventional machining processes [6-9]. Jurkovic *et al.* [6] used a machine system with a laser diode to measure the profile deepness of workpieces whereby a 3D image of a relief surface was obtained. Kim *et al.* [7]

developed a system with a CCD camera and an exclusive jig to measure the size of tool wear in a direct manner. Sortino [8] established a tool condition monitoring system which can detect the worn area of tool. Methods such as statistical, high pass, saturation, and normalization filters were used to detect the surface profile and worn area. Kwon and Fischer [9] proposed a machine vision system that can measure the worn area of cutting tool in lathe machining process.

Kaneko *et al.* [10] suggested an optical measurement method to measure the tool electrode deformation in the EDM process. The dielectric fluid droplet on the tool electrode had to be blown off first by compressed air after the electrode was pulled up to a position where the machine vision system operated. A shadow image of electrode was then acquired using a parallel light and the deformation of the tool electrode was estimated. Nevertheless, such method can only measure the deformation of tool electrode. The system is incapable of measuring the drilling depth in workpieces because the surface color of the electrode is dark under the parallel light source.

Currently, the drilling depth of a workpiece is not measured directly online in the EDM drilling process but, in fact, manually measured after dissecting the workpiece. To date, no studies have attempted to measure the drilling depth and the tool electrode length (with the dielectric fluid droplet on it) at the same time in EDM. Thus, this paper will present a new approach - a detection line algorithm that detects the electrode length with dielectric fluid droplet on it and the drilling depth in workpieces rapidly and effectively.

The organization of this paper is as follows. Section 2 describes the basic analysis and the proposed method for detecting the tool electrode length and drilling depth. Experimental results and discussions are given in Section 3 that confirm the effectiveness of the proposed method. Section 4 will present some concluding remarks.

# 2. MATERIALS AND METHODS

## 2.1 Image Acquisition System and EDM Drilling Machine

As shown in Figure 1, an EDM machine (JM-430, Jiten) and a controller (P-30, Jiten) were employed to drill workpieces to certain depths. In order to obtain tool electrode images on-line, a machine vision system is proposed. Images were acquired using a CCD (coupled-charge device) monochrome camera (WAT-902B, Watec) with a zoom lens (Zoom 6000 combinations, Navitar), a frame grabber (Meteor, Matrox Inc), and a personal computer (Intel Pentium 4 processor 2.4 GHz). Matrox Imaging Library (MIL 8.0, Matrox Inc) was linked to the programs to grab monochrome images of 640×480 pixels in size. The CCD camera was employed for image acquisition with forward lighting. Images were stored in the hard drive of the personal computer in tagged image file format (TIF). Image processing was performed using Visual C++ 6.0 programming.

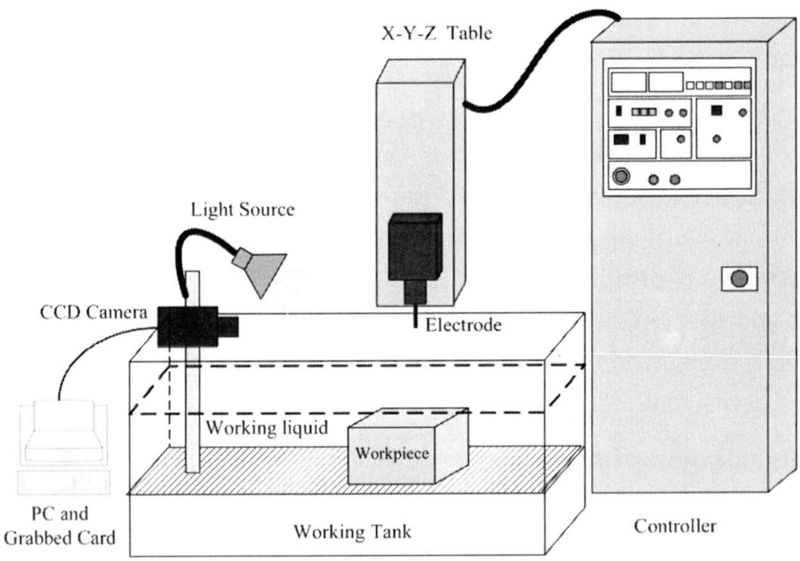


**Figure 1.** Experimental configuration

## 2.2 Electrode Length and Drilling Depth Detection

### 2.2.1 Electrode Image Extraction

Segmenting the tool electrode image is an essential procedure once the characteristics of the electrode have been extracted. The electrode image is extracted using thresholding, hole-filling, closing, and opening operators, as illustrated in Figure 2. Firstly, the principle axis of the tool electrode needs to be identified. By assuming the binary image of electrode is $f(x_i, y_i)$ (where $i=1, 2,\ldots N$, and the total number of pixels is $N$), the centroid is obtained as $\overline{X}=\frac{1}{N}\sum_{i}^{N}x_i, \overline{Y}=\frac{1}{N}\sum_{i}^{N}y_i$. The covariance matrix is defined as $C=\frac{1}{N}\sum_{i}^{N}V_iV_i^T-MM^T$, in which $V_i$ is the $i$'th coordinate vector of the image and $M=\frac{1}{N}\sum_{i}^{N}V_i$ is the mean vector. $T$ indicates vector transposition. A pair of orthogonal eigenvectors of the covariance matrix is calculated. The geometric features – the centroid and the principle axis of electrode, are then computed using eigenvectors, as shown in Figure 3.

(a) Original image. (b) Binary image.

**Figure 2.** Electrode image.

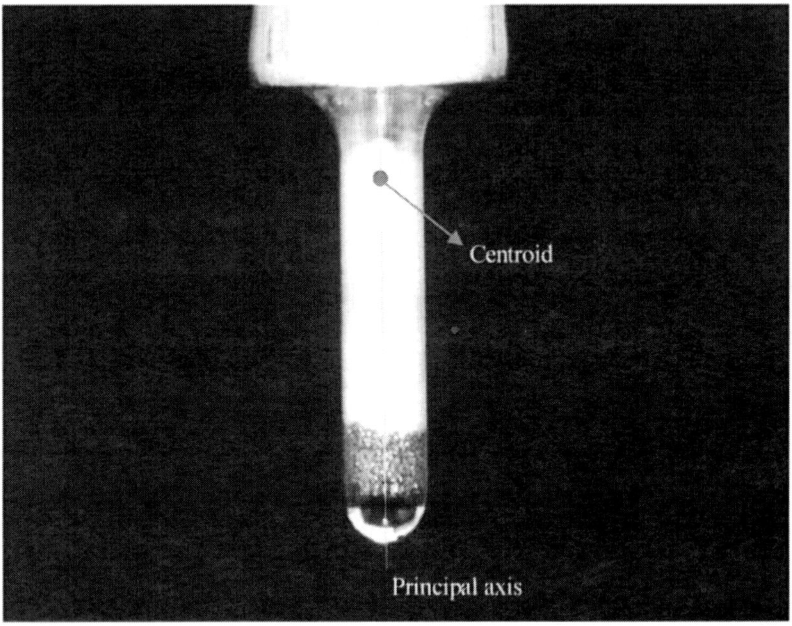


**Figure 3.** The principle axis and centroid of electrode.

### 2.2.2 Detection Line Algorithm

Before describing the detection line algorithm in detail, we first consider the basic analysis in a situation that the tool electrode image is well defined. As indicated in Figure 4, significant areas of the tool electrode include a base area, normal area, drilling area, and dielectric fluid droplet on the electrode tip. However, these areas are difficult to distinguish accurately and rapidly. Different area boundaries are defined: (1) a baseline between the base and normal areas, (2) a ND-line between the normal and drilling areas, and (3) a DD-line between the drilling area and dielectric fluid droplet.

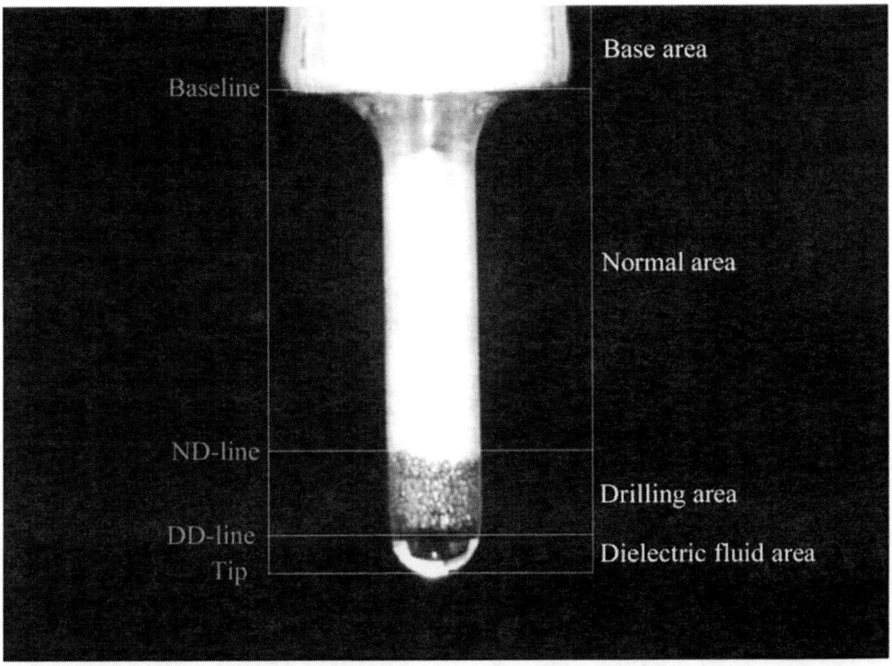


**Figure 4.** Baseline, ND-line, and DD-line

A prior experiment proceeded as follows. A detection line (100 pixels in length) is used to find gray levels along the direction of the principle axis from the centroid to the tip of the electrode section with scanning resolution in a pixel, as shown in Figure 5. There are different distribution forms of gray levels in different areas, as illustrated in Figure 6. The distributions of gray level are around 255 on the glossy normal area, as shown inFigure 6(a). In Figure 6(b), the distributions of gray level are between 100 and 255 because there are irregular texture images on the drilling area. As the electrode tip (with dielectric fluid droplet on it) is illuminated and thus causing a reflection of the dielectric fluid droplet, a dual peak appears in Figure 6(c), and the distributions of gray levels are between 0 and 255 on the dielectric fluid droplet. Therefore, a polynomial curve fitting method is adopted to fit the distributions of gray levels on detection lines. In Figure 7, the form of fitted curve is a single peak and the maximum value ($N_{max}$) is greater than 255 on the normal area. The fitted curve is also a single peak on the drilling area, but the maximum value ($T_{max}$) is far smaller than $N_{max}$. There is a special property – the dual peak on the dielectric fluid droplet area.

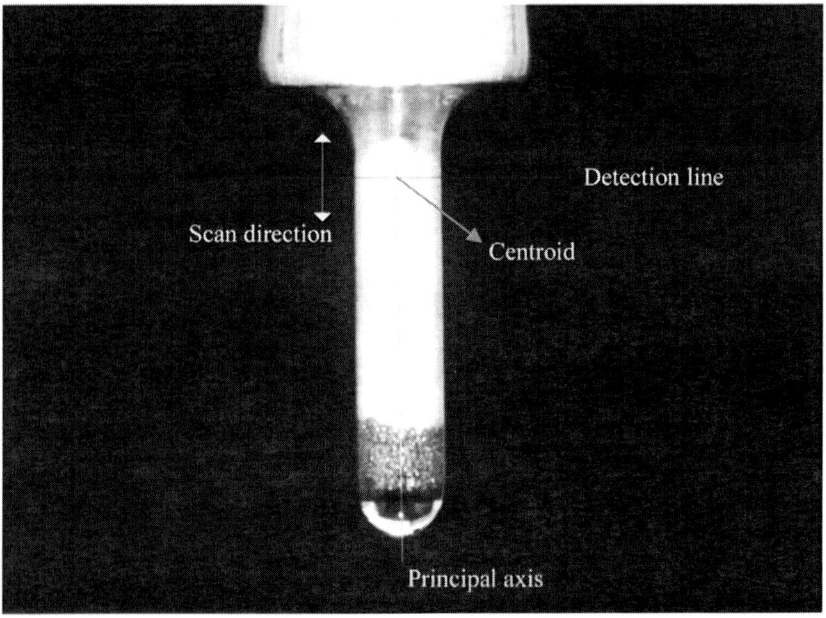


**Figure 5.** Scan direction of detection line on electrode.

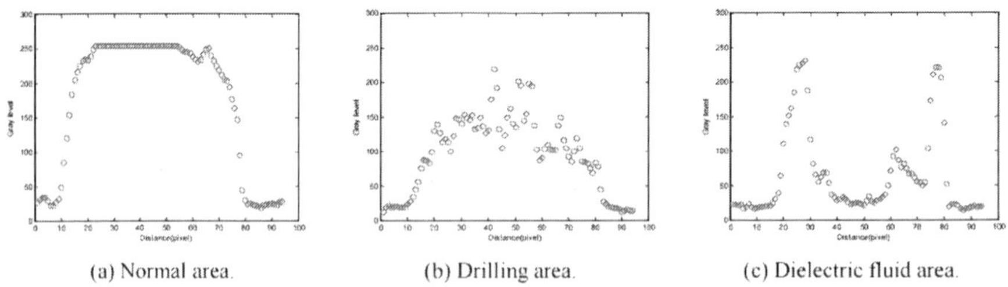


**Figure 6.** The distributions of gray levels on a detection line.

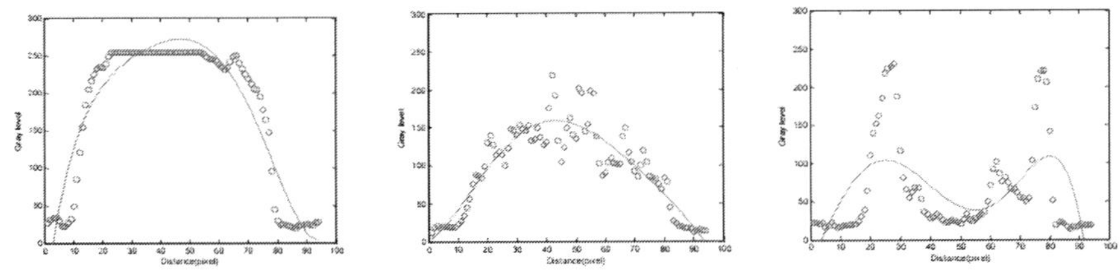

(a) Normal area. (b) Drilling area. (c) Dielectric fluid area.

**Figure 7.** Fitted curve for gray level on a detection line.

However, the distribution of gray levels method is not applicable in determining the position of the baseline because variations in gray levels along a detection line from normal to base areas are unobvious. For this reason, the baseline is determined using a detection line according to an obvious variation of the diameter from the normal area to the base area. Therefore, a novel method – the detection line algorithm (DLA) is proposed to find the positions of the ND-line, DD-line, and baseline. These boundary lines are then used to segment the base, normal, drilling areas, and dielectric fluid droplet on the tool electrode according to the above-mentioned contentions in this study. Thus, this method can be employed to estimate the tool electrode length with the dielectric fluid droplet remains on its tip effectively.

DLA is described as follows:

***Step 1***: Compute the distribution function of gray level defined as

$$g(p,t) = a_{0,p_i} + a_{1,p_i}t + a_{2,p_i}t^2 + a_{3,p_i}t^3 + a_{4,p_i}t^4 + a_{5,p_i}t^5, \quad (1)$$

by a polynomial curve fitting method [11], where $p = \{p_1, p_2, ..., p_n\}$ is a position parameter of the detection line along the principle axis of the tool electrode centroid and $t$ is a distance variable with the detection line.

***Step 2***: Find the local maximum value $g_{max}(p_i,t)$ according to $g(p_i,t)$. Further, the function of local maximize value $g_{max}(p,t)$ is established by obtaining $g_{max}(p_i,t)$.

***Step 3***: Determine the boundaries:

(1)Baseline

The diameter function of electrode $d(p)$ is established by a detection line. The first-order derivatives of$d(p)$ is defined as

$$d'(p) = \frac{\Delta d}{\Delta p} = \frac{d(p_{i+1}) - d(p_i)}{p_{i+1} - p_i} \tag{2}$$

Thus, the location of baseline is obtained at the point $p_{max}$ as maximum value of $|d'(p)|$. It means that an obvious variation of the diameter is at the baseline.

(2)ND-line

The slope variation $m(p_i,t)$ of $g_{max}(p_i, t)$ is defined as

$$m(p_i,t) = \frac{\Delta g_{\max}}{\Delta p} = \frac{g_{\max}(p_{i+1},t) - f(g_{\max}(p_i,t)}{p_{i+1} - p_i} \tag{3}$$

Therefore, the position of ND-line can be found at point $p_{ND}$ as the first obvious variation $|m(p_{ND},t)| \geq \delta$on scanning the tool electrode. $\delta$ is a positive constant.

(3)DD-line

The peak decision method (PD method) is based on the peak number (*PN*) of $g(p_i,t)$ moving along the tool electrode in this study. The location of DD-line is detected by PD method when *PN* is alternated from 1 (a single peak) to 2 (a dual peak). *PN* is defined as

$$PN = \begin{cases} 1, & then\ g(p_i,t) \in\ normal\ or\ drilling\ areas \\ 2, & then\ g(p_i,t) \in\ the\ drop\ of\ dielectric\ fluid \end{cases}, \quad (4)$$

***Step 4***: The tool electrode length and drilling depth are defined as:

(1) Tool electrode length is the distance between the baseline and ND-line.

(2) Drilling depth is the distance between the ND-line and DD-line.

The algorithms for the tool electrode length and detection and computation are developed using image processing techniques and DLA in this study.

## 3. RESULTS AND DISCUSSION

In this study, the electrode wear detection (EWD) software is written using image processing techniques, DLA in Visual C++ 6.0, and MIL 8.0 library, as shown in Figure 8. The EWD software extracts a binary tool electrode image (threshold value is 80), and identifies the centroid and principal axis of the electrode. Further, the EWD software can estimate the tool electrode length and drilling depth in a workpiece accurately and rapidly.

The distributions of gray levels from the centroid to the tip of the tool electrode using a detection line along the principle axis are illustrated in Figure 9.

In Figure 10, the gray level curves $g(p,t)$ are fitted by polynomial curve fitting which automatically uses the 5th order of polynomial function. The local maximum $g_{max}$ (p,t) have been found for $g(p,t)$, as shown in Figure 11(a). The slope $m(p_i,t)$ of $g_{max}(p,t)$ is obtained by Eq.(3). Thus, ND-line is determined in accordance with the first obvious variation of $|m(p_i,t)|$ as indicated in Figure 11(b) and 11(c).

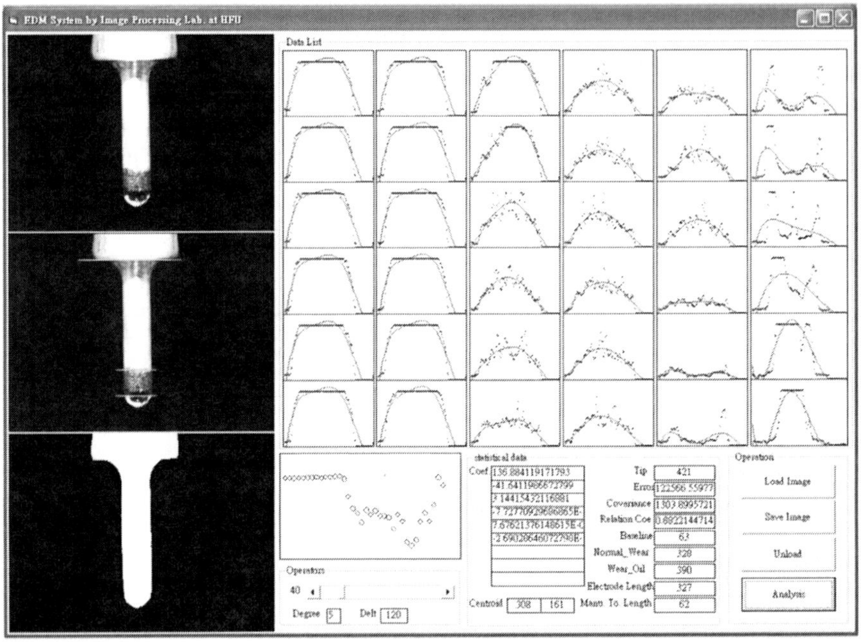


**Figure 8.** The EWM software interface.

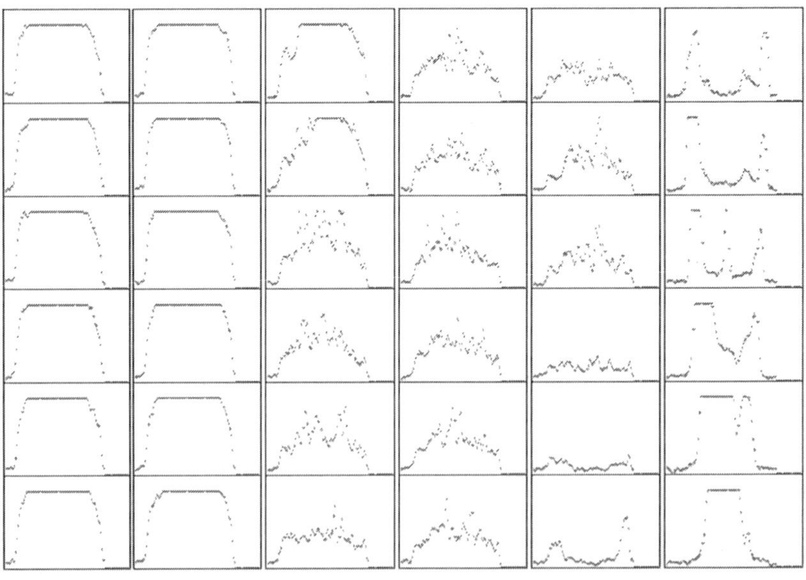

**Figure 9.** The gray level distributions on detection lines.

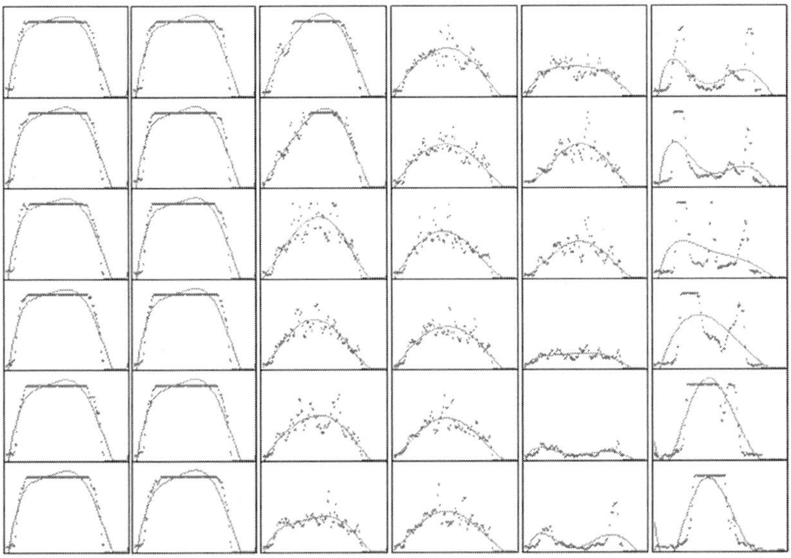

**Figure 10.** The gray level curves on detection lines.

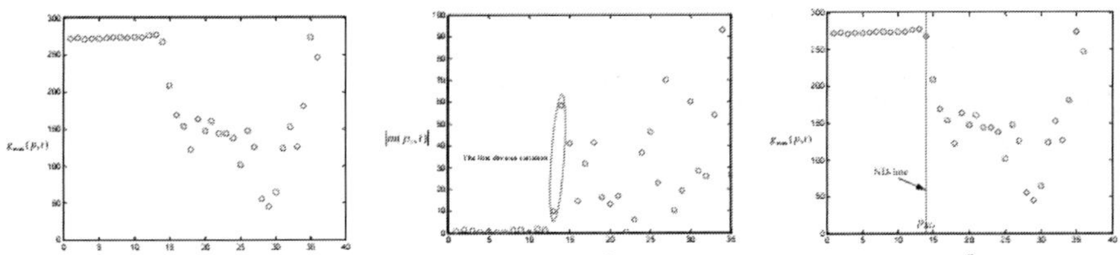

(a) The distribution of $g_{max}(p,t)$. (b) The distribution of $|m(p_i,t)|$. (c) The position of ND-line.

**Figure 11.** The ND-line detecting process. (with *p* as a position parameter)

The location of DD-line is estimated using PD method when the peak number (*PN*) is alternated from 1 (a single peak) to 2 (a dual peak). The peak number of gray level curve *g*(*p*,*t*) is shown in Figure 12. Although the gray levels of the drilling area scatter in distance-gray level space, the distribution of gray levels appears as a single peak curve. For the dielectric fluid droplet, the fitted curve is a dual peak. The shapes and maximum values of fitted curves are contributed to detections of the ND-line and DD-line positions.

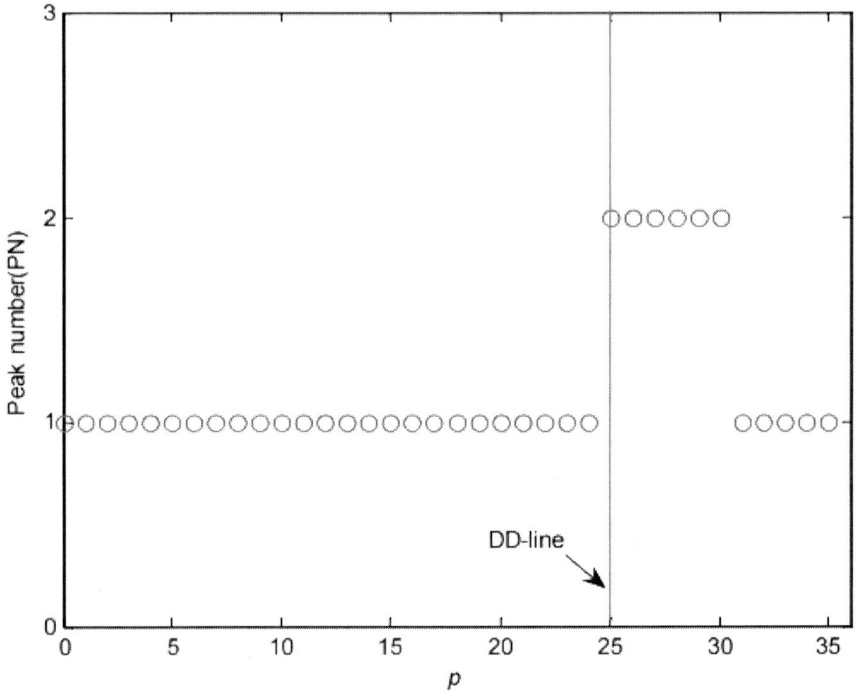


**Figure 12.** The distribution of peak number and DD-line using PD method (with *p* as a position parameter).

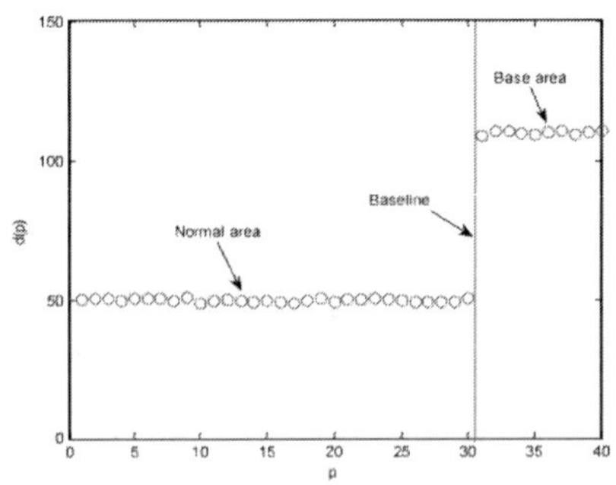


(a) The distribution of diameters $d(p)$ and baseline on base and normal areas.

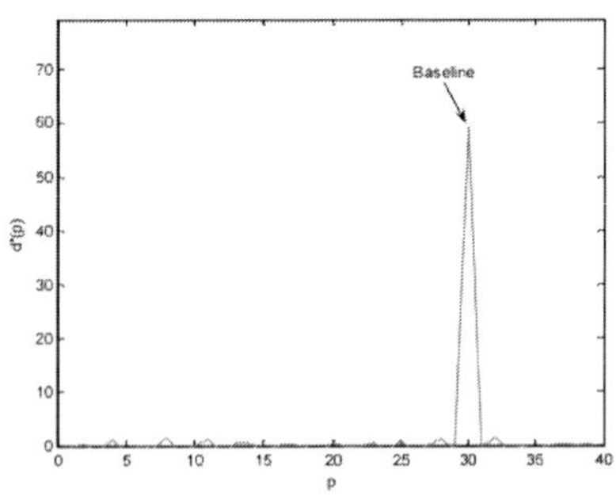


(b) The distribution of slopes $d'(p)$ and baseline on base and normal areas.

**Figure 13.** The baseline detecting process. (with *p* as a position parameter)

Finally, for the detection of the baseline, the diameter function of electrode $d(p)$ and its first-order derivative $d'(p)$ are obtained using DAL, as showed in Figure 13. Hence, the position of baseline is determined accurately.

Experimental conditions are shown in Table 1. Copper is used as the tool electrode anode, and the diameters of electrode are 1.5 mm (20 samples), 2.0 mm (20 samples), 2.5 mm (20 samples), and 3.0 mm (20 samples) respectively. A series of experiments with different machining parameters are performed and EDW is employed to estimate the tool electrode lengths and drilling depths. The workpieces are then cut open by WEDM (wire electrical discharge machine) manually for actual drilling depths measurement. The estimated values of electrode length and drilling depth are obtained using our machine vision system, and manually measured values are obtained by a tool-maker microscope. Figure 14 shows the machined holes, electrodes and cut section of the workpiece. Experimental results are given in Table 2. The drilling speed is increased with the peak current, but the electrode wear (i.e., the difference in electrode length before and after the drilling) is augmented simultaneously. For example, the average machined time is 28 minutes (electrode wear 0.062 mm) in a peak current of 6.0 A, but slowed down to 42 minutes (electrode wear 0.033 mm) in a peak current of 5.0 A with the same drilling depth (2.0 mm). The average error between estimated and manually measured electrode lengths is 0.075 mm, and for drilling depths is 0.245 mm. The accuracy of estimated drilling depth is reduced because the accumulating carbon on the electrode surface grown at the drilling area, and the size and shape of dielectric fluid droplet is uncertain. For this reason, the boundary between the normal and drilling areas is an irregular border. Moreover, another possible cause is the gap distance in EDM drilling. In general, the gap distance is an uncertain variable. However, under certain circumstances, the gap distance is more precise, and hence, overall accuracy can be increased. For example, a steady gap status is achieved when using the servo feed control in EDM drilling. Thus, the gap distance (about 0.05 mm) can be taken into account to estimate the drilling depth. The error of measured drilling depth is then reduced to 0.195 mm.

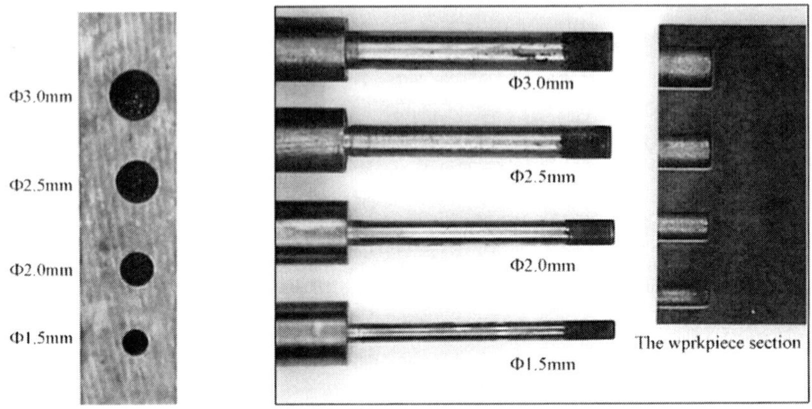


(a) Machined holes. (b) Machined workpiece section.

**Figure 14.** The drilled electrodes and a workpiece section.

**Table 1.** Experimental conditions.

| Parameters | Values |
|---|---|
| Electrode material | Copper |
| Peak current | 5.0A, 6.0A |
| Open voltage | 90 V |
| Pulse duration | 100 μs |
| Pulse interval | 100 μs |
| Diameter of tool electrode | ∅ 2.0, 2.5, 3.0 mm |
| Workpiece material | SKD11 |
| Gap distance | 0.05 mm |
| Dielectric flushing method | Static condition |
| Machined depth | 1.5, 2.0, 2.5, 3.0 mm |

**Table 2.** Estimated and manual results after EDM drilling.

| No. | Machining condition | | Electrode diameter | Ave. machining time (min.) | Ave. electrode length (mm) | | | Ave. Machined depth (mm) | | |
|---|---|---|---|---|---|---|---|---|---|---|
| | | | | | Manual | Estimated | Error | Manual | Estimated | Error |
| 1 | Setting depth | 2.0 mm | 1.5 mm | 42 | 19.85 | 19.76 | 0.09 | 2.08 | 1.95 | 0.13 |
| | | | 2.0 mm | 61 | 19.96 | 19.89 | 0.07 | 2.08 | 1.97 | 0.11 |
| | Peak current | 5.0 A | 2.5 mm | 117 | 19.93 | 19.94 | 0.01 | 2.12 | 1.96 | 0.16 |
| | | | 3.0 mm | 149 | 19.87 | 19.89 | 0.02 | 2.11 | 1.97 | 0.14 |
| 2 | Setting depth | 3.0 mm | 1.5 mm | 53 | 19.77 | 19.88 | 0.11 | 3.13 | 2.89 | 0.24 |
| | | | 2.0 mm | 99 | 19.91 | 19.94 | 0.03 | 3.17 | 2.87 | 0.30 |
| | Peak current | 5.0 A | 2.5 mm | 152 | 19.85 | 19.94 | 0.09 | 3.04 | 2.82 | 0.22 |
| | | | 3.0 mm | 199 | 19.91 | 20.04 | 0.13 | 3.14 | 2.87 | 0.27 |
| 3 | Setting depth | 4.0 mm | 1.5 mm | 60 | 19.78 | 19.92 | 0.14 | 4.19 | 3.85 | 0.34 |
| | | | 2.0 mm | 114 | 19.91 | 19.94 | 0.03 | 4.10 | 3.89 | 0.21 |
| | Peak current | 5.0 A | 2.5 mm | 163 | 19.78 | 19.84 | 0.06 | 4.21 | 3.81 | 0.40 |
| | | | 3.0 mm | 217 | 19.92 | 19.94 | 0.02 | 4.29 | 3.89 | 0.40 |
| 4 | Setting depth | 5.0 mm | 1.5 mm | 74 | 19.97 | 19.84 | 0.13 | 5.05 | 4.92 | 0.13 |
| | | | 2.0 mm | 133 | 19.88 | 19.90 | 0.02 | 5.10 | 4.96 | 0.14 |
| | Peak current | 5.0 A | 2.5 mm | 174 | 20.04 | 20.05 | 0.01 | 5.06 | 4.92 | 0.14 |
| | | | 3.0 mm | 242 | 20.03 | 19.94 | 0.09 | 5.08 | 4.97 | 0.11 |
| 5 | Setting depth | 2.0 mm | 1.5 mm | 28 | 19.92 | 19.94 | 0.02 | 2.14 | 1.88 | 0.26 |
| | | | 2.0 mm | 41 | 19.83 | 19.99 | 0.16 | 2.12 | 1.90 | 0.22 |
| | Peak current | 6.0 A | 2.5 mm | 72 | 19.95 | 19.89 | 0.06 | 2.13 | 1.86 | 0.27 |
| | | | 3.0 mm | 104 | 19.99 | 19.84 | 0.15 | 2.11 | 1.89 | 0.22 |
| 6 | Setting depth | 3.0 mm | 1.5 mm | 36 | 19.88 | 19.94 | 0.06 | 3.14 | 2.87 | 0.27 |
| | | | 2.0 mm | 65 | 19.86 | 19.84 | 0.02 | 3.19 | 2.88 | 0.31 |
| | Peak current | 6.0 A | 2.5 mm | 94 | 19.85 | 19.79 | 0.06 | 3.15 | 2.86 | 0.29 |
| | | | 3.0 mm | 134 | 19.84 | 19.89 | 0.05 | 3.22 | 2.90 | 0.32 |
| 7 | Setting depth | 4.0 mm | 1.5 mm | 54 | 19.87 | 19.89 | 0.02 | 4.17 | 3.84 | 0.33 |
| | | | 2.0 mm | 79 | 19.78 | 19.89 | 0.11 | 4.16 | 3.88 | 0.28 |
| | Peak current | 6.0 A | 2.5 mm | 115 | 19.87 | 19.79 | 0.08 | 4.18 | 3.91 | 0.27 |
| | | | 3.0 mm | 187 | 19.93 | 19.79 | 0.14 | 4.20 | 3.90 | 0.30 |
| 8 | Setting depth | 5.0 mm | 1.5 mm | 65 | 19.82 | 19.94 | 0.12 | 5.16 | 4.89 | 0.27 |
| | | | 2.0 mm | 107 | 19.87 | 19.84 | 0.03 | 5.19 | 4.92 | 0.27 |
| | Peak current | 6.0 A | 2.5 mm | 148 | 19.59 | 19.74 | 0.15 | 5.13 | 4.87 | 0.26 |
| | | | 3.0 mm | 213 | 19.73 | 19.84 | 0.11 | 5.15 | 4.90 | 0.25 |
| | | | | | Ave. error | | 0.075 | Ave. error | | 0.245 |

According to the above-mentioned results and discussion, the advantage of the proposed method is summarized as follows: the tool electrode length and the drilling depth of workpieces can be estimated effectively (no need of an air compressor to blow off the dielectric fluid droplet and cut open the workpieces).

However, the weak point of this study is that round corner of tool cannot be measured because of the retaining dielectric fluid droplet on the tip of tool electrode. Our expectancy is achieved according to the experimental results. The results of this study may be of interest to EDM industry attempting to develop an inspector and to increase efficiency.

## 4. CONCLUSIONS

The objective of this study is to propose a novel and efficient method for sensing electrode parameters in EDM drilling process. As presented in this paper, the conclusions can be summarized as follows: (1) the proposed detection line algorithm (DLA) can detect the tool electrode length and drilling depth accurately and effectively. DLA includes a polynomial curve fitting, slope variation, and PD methods, (2) our machine vision system is powerful and flexible under different experimental conditions on real time measurement, (3) our system can provide an important reference for EDM industry.

## REFERENCES AND NOTES

1. Yu, Z.; Masuzawa, T.; Fujiino, M. Micro-EDM for three-dimensional cavities-development of uniform wear method. *Ann. CIRP* **1998**, *47*, 169–172.

2. Tsai, Y.Y.; Masuzawa, T. An index to evaluate the wear resistance of the electrode in micro-EDM. *Journal of Materials Processing Tech.* **2004**, *149*, 304–309.

3. Dauw, D. On the deviation and application of a real-time wear sensor in EDM. *Ann. CIRP* **1986**, *35*, 111–116.

4. Bleys, P.; Kruth, J. -P.; Lauwers, B.; Zryd, A.; Delpretti, R.; Tricarico, C. Real-time tool wear compensation in milling EDM. *Ann. CIRP* **2002**, *51*, 157–160.

5. Bleys, P.; Kruth, J. -P.; Lauwers, B. Sensing and compensation of tool wear in milling EDM. *Journal of Materials Processing Technology* **2004**, *149*, 139–146.

6. Jurkovic, J.; Korosec, M; Kopac, J. New approach in tool wear measuring technique using CCD vision system. *International Journal of Machine Tools and Manufacture* **2005**, *45*, 1023–1030.

7. Kim, J.H.; Moon, D.K.; Lee, D.W.; Kim, J.S.; Kang, M.C.; Kim, K.H. Tool wear measuring technique on the machine using CCD and exclusive jig. *Journal of Materials Processing Technology* **2002**, *130*, 668–674.

8. Sortino, M. Application of statistical filtering for optical detection of tool wear. *International Journal of Machine Tools and Manufacture* **2003**, *43*, 493–497.

9. Kwon, Y.; Fischer, G.W. A novel approach to quantifying tool wear and too life measurements for optimal tool management. *International Journal of Machine Tools and Manufacture* **2003**, *43*, 359–368.

10. Kaneko, T.; Tsuchiya, M.; Kazama, A. Improvement of 3D NC contouring EDM using cylindrical electrodes and optical measurement of electrode deformation and machining of free-curves. *Proceedings of 10$^{th}$International Symposium for Electro Machining (ISEM-10)* **1992**, 364–367.

11. Foley, J.D.; Dam, A.D.; Feiner, S.K.; Hughes, J.F. Computer graphics: principles and practice. *Addison-Wesley* **1997**.

# Chapter 6

# Classification and Quality Evaluation of Tobacco Leaves Based on Image Processing and Fuzzy Comprehensive Evaluation

**Fan Zhang [1,2,★] and Xinhong Zhang [3]**

[1]*Institute of Image Processing and Pattern Recognition, Henan University, Kaifeng 475001, China*

[2]*College of Computer and Information Engineering, Henan University, Kaifeng, 475001, China*

[3]*Computing Center, Henan University, Kaifeng 475001, China*

## ABSTRACT

Most of classification, quality evaluation or grading of the flue-cured tobacco leaves are manually operated, which relies on the judgmental experience of experts, and inevitably limited by personal, physical and environmental factors. The classification and the quality evaluation are therefore subjective and experientially based. In this paper, an automatic classification method of tobacco leaves based on the digital image processing and the fuzzy sets theory is presented. A grading system based on image processing techniques was developed for automatically inspecting and grading flue-cured tobacco leaves. This system uses machine vision for the extraction and analysis of color, size, shape and surface texture. Fuzzy comprehensive evaluation provides a high level of confidence in decision making based on the fuzzy logic. The neural network is used to estimate and forecast the membership function of the features of tobacco leaves in the fuzzy sets. The experimental results of the two-level fuzzy comprehensive evaluation (FCE) show that the accuracy rate of classification is about 94% for the trained tobacco leaves, and the accuracy rate of the non-trained tobacco leaves is about 72%. We believe that the fuzzy comprehensive evaluation is a viable way for the automatic classification and quality evaluation of the tobacco leaves.

**Keywords:** Image analysis; Tobacco leaf; Fuzzy sets; Fuzzy comprehensive evaluation; Artificial neural network

## 1. INTRODUCTION

Because of the diversity and complexity of tobacco leaves, most of the classification and the quality evaluation of the flue-cured tobacco leaves are manually operated. It is a rigorous task. The tobacco leaves must be carefully classified by size, texture and color, all aided by a well-seasoned expert's feeling about the fine properties of the leaves. Errors often occur when the experts are tired, and the results of classification and quality evaluation relies on the judgmental experience of experts and many other factors, such as the emotion of experts, the human eyesight, the condition of illumination, *etc*. The grading process is extremely laborious, making the classification and the quality evaluation subjective and experientially based, while the efficiency and the stability of error rate are not satisfying enough. New technology and equipments are needed to automate the quality inspection process of tobacco leaves.

The criterion of the quality evaluation of flue-cured tobacco leaves usually include color, size, shape and disfigurement of flue-cured tobacco leaf, *etc*. Most of these properties relate to the human vision. Recently, image processing, machine vision, pattern recognition and fuzzy mathematics make a rapid progress with the development of the computer and multimedia technologies. The automatic classification method of tobacco leaves is likely to be enabled by these technologies. Some works on application of image processing to extract the features of tobacco leaves and works on the tobacco leaves classification have been presented. Zhang *et al.* presented a transformation technique from RGB signals to the Munsell system for the color analysis of tobacco leaves. Zhang *et al*. and Garcia *et al*. [1–3] introduced the development of a virtual expert for the classification of tobacco leaves. Zhang *et al*. [4] proposed an algorithm that extract the features of tobacco leaves based on neural network. There are also some other works that have been reported [5–8].

Fuzziness seems to pervade most human perception and thinking processes. It is the argument of this study, therefore, that the theory of fuzzy sets is highly suitable to the tasks of the classification and the quality evaluation of flue-cured tobacco leaves. In this paper, fuzzy comprehensive evaluation is used to classify flue-cured tobacco leaves. The aim of this study is to utilize the theory of fuzzy sets to demonstrate the applicability of fuzzy logic for grading of tobacco leaves.

The rest of this paper is organized as follows. Section 2 is a brief introduction about the mechanics of grading process of flue-cured tobacco leaves. In Section 3, a grading system based on image processing techniques is introduced, which automatically inspects and evaluates quality of flue-cured tobacco leaves. After we get the images of tobacco leaves from the image processing system, the features extraction of tobacco leaves is introduced in Section 4. In Section 5, we briefly introduce theory of fuzzy set and fuzzy comprehensive evaluation. Automatic classification of tobacco leaves is discussed in Section 6. The experimental results are shown in Section 7. The conclusions of this paper are drawn in Section 8.

## 2. TOBACCO LEAF GRADING

The quality inspection of tobacco leaves consists of two main aspects: internal and external examinations. The internal quality inspection is usually achieved by human sensory, smoking test or chemical analysis, while the external quality inspection is mainly achieved through human vision. It is costly and yet time-consuming to inspect internal quality since tobacco leaves contain too many ingredients to be handled. As an alternative, external quality examination is often used instead in the examination of internal quality of tobacco leaves, since external features are closely related to internal quality. The external quality inspection of tobacco leaves includes judgment of color, maturity, surface texture, size and shape. Human vision, which is inevitably limited by personal, physical and environmental factors, has been the predominant means of inspection.

The detailed grading standards of flue-cured tobacco leaves may vary from one country or even one tobacco strain to another, but the general method and the concerned external features of tobacco leaves are quite similar [9,10].

Tobacco leaves are classified as normal or abnormal leaves. Since the normal leaves are more common than the abnormal ones, they are discussed in this paper. The normal tobacco leaves are graded based on the position they grow on the stalk and the color they have. Three position categories (so-called large groups) are identified, that is, lugs (X), cutters (C) and leaf (B), corresponding to lower, middle and upper portion of a stalk. The judgment for growth position is mainly based on the color, surface texture, shape and vein condition of the tobacco leaves. Three hue categories (so-called small groups), lemon (L), orange (F) and red-brown (R), are specified. The groups are formed by combining the position and color categories, that is, lugs lemon (XL), lugs orange (XF); cutters lemon (CL), cutters orange (CF); leaf lemon (BL), leaf orange (BF) and leaf red-brown (BR). Each group is further divided into 3 or 4 grades based on the chroma, hue uniformity across the whole leaf, maturity (mainly judged from color), size and surface texture. The classification of tobacco leaves is symbolized as, for example, X2L, where X indicates that the leaf is from the lugs position, L denotes that the leaf is in the hue category of lemon yellow, and the 2 means that the tobacco leaf is at the second grade of this group. Three flue-cured tobacco leaves are shown as Figure 1.

**Figure 1.** Three images of tobacco leaves which are obtained from image processing system of tobacco leaves grading.

## 3. IMAGE PROCESSING SYSTEM

An image processing system of tobacco leaves grading is constructed (Figure 2). Actually, the lighted cabinet is the same one as Zhang has used [1], but all other equipments, such as computer and camera, has been updated. The image processing system is consisted of a color camera (Panasonic WV-CP470 0.8 Lux 752 × 582 1/3 inch CCD), an OK-C20B PCI Bus Frame Grabber (Chinese Automation Ltd., Beijing) with 512×512 pixel resolution and 24-bit color, a monitor, and a computer. A lighted cabinet with 800 × 800 × 700 mm (length, width and height) is constructed to control illumination. The chamber is illuminated by two LED lights.

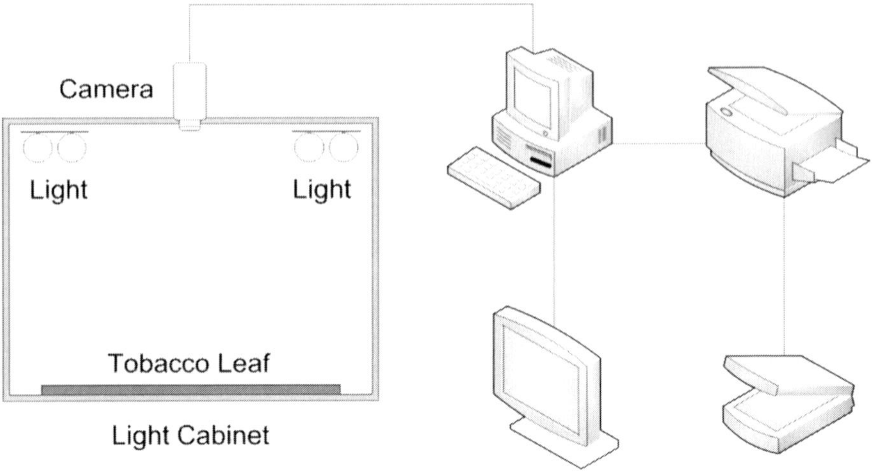


**Figure 2.** The image processing system of tobacco leaves grading.

LED lights are fixed on the top of the cabinet. Tobacco leaf is placed on a piece of white board that could slide into the cabinet. The digital color image of tobacco leaf is obtained by the color camera and sent to computer, in which it is saved as a pixel matrix. The images is composed of three sets of pixels for each color. The image's size is 512 × 512. Other equipments include a printer and a scanner. Delphi programming language is used to implement all algorithms.

## 4. FEATURES EXTRACTION

In this research, the digital image system process 24-bit color images of tobacco leaves. The size of tobacco leaves image is 512 × 512. Features of tobacco leaves can be extracted according to image processing, which include the shape, color, and texture features. These features are stored in a database in computer. The shape features include the surface area, surface perimeter and the disfigurement of tobacco leaf. The color features include the variance of red, green and blue channel of digital image of tobacco leaves. The texture features include the texture energy, texture entropy and texture contrast of digital image of tobacco leaves.

### 4.1. Color Features

Color is an important feature of tobacco leaves due to its close association with the perceived quality. It is a widely used parameter in the evaluation of their maturity, freshness, nutritional condition and growth factors.

There are a number of color systems, such as the RGB, CIE1931, HSI and Munsell [11], that can be used in machine vision for color evaluation. Each system has its own advantages and is used to satisfy different requirements. The color in most color systems is different from human color vision and cannot be intuitively understood. In order to a machine can simulate human color vision, the selected color system should possess the color spatial parameters and structure that are similar to human color sensation.

For the reason of economy in calculation, this research chooses the RGB color system to extract the color features of tobacco leaves. RGB images use three colors, red, green and blue to reproduce 16.7 million colors. Computer monitors display colors using this model. This research chooses three color features, they are the variance of red, green and blue channel of the digital image of tobacco leaves.

### 4.2. Shape Features

Image processing and machine vision techniques are used for the shape features extraction. Before the extraction of shape features, the edge data of the tobacco leaves should obtained firstly. Laplacian operator is used for the edge detection [12,13]. It is defined as follows,

$$\nabla^2 f(x,y) = \frac{\partial^2 f(x,y)}{\partial^2 x} + \frac{\partial^2 f(x,y)}{\partial^2 y}. \tag{1}$$

Laplacian operator is a quadratic derivative that is used to detect the abrupt zero-crossing of image intensity and often yields more exact edge detecting result. However, because of the presence of noises, the edge detection using Laplacian operator is not satisfying. This research chooses a Gaussian low-pass filter for the pre-smoothing. Gaussian low-pass filter is defined as follows,

$$g(x,y) = G(x,y) * f(x,y) = \frac{1}{2\pi\sigma^2} exp(-\frac{x^2+y^2}{2\sigma^2}) * f(x,y). \tag{2}$$

Laplacian operator and the Gaussian impulse response can be combined as a single Laplacian of Gaussian kernel,

$$\nabla^2 \frac{1}{2\pi\sigma^2} exp(-\frac{x^2+y^2}{2\sigma^2}) = -\frac{1}{\pi\sigma^4}(1 - \frac{x^2+y^2}{2\sigma^2}) exp(-\frac{x^2+y^2}{2\sigma^2}). \tag{3}$$

24-bit color image of tobacco leaves are transformed to binary image. After Laplacian of Gaussian filtering, a closed and connected contour is obtained when interior points are eliminated. Edge detection of a tobacco leaf using Laplacian of Gaussian filtering is shown in Figure 3.

The polygonal fitting is implemented to the edge curve when we get the edge data of the tobacco leaf. The aim of polygonal fitting is to substitute the smooth tobacco leaf edge to a polygonal edge. The polygonal fitting of edge of the tobacco leaf is shown in Figure 4. The vertexes in polygon is connected and formed some triangle. The sum number of pixels in each side of the fitted polygon is the approximate perimeter of the tobacco leaf. The hight, width and area of tobacco leaf can be calculated from the triangled polygon. The surface area of the fitted polygon is the approximate surface area of the tobacco leaf. We record the number of all the interior pixels of the fitted polygon, and record the number of all the interior pixels which color is same as the color of the background color. The ratio of two kinds of pixels is the disfigurement of the tobacco leaf.

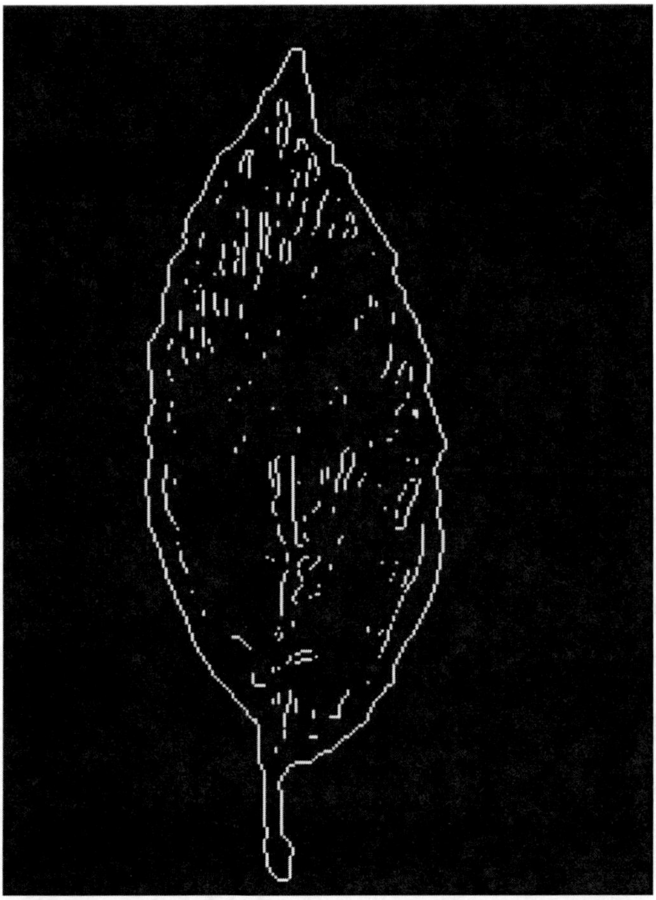

**Figure 3.** Edge detection of a tobacco leaf using Laplacian of Gaussian filtering.

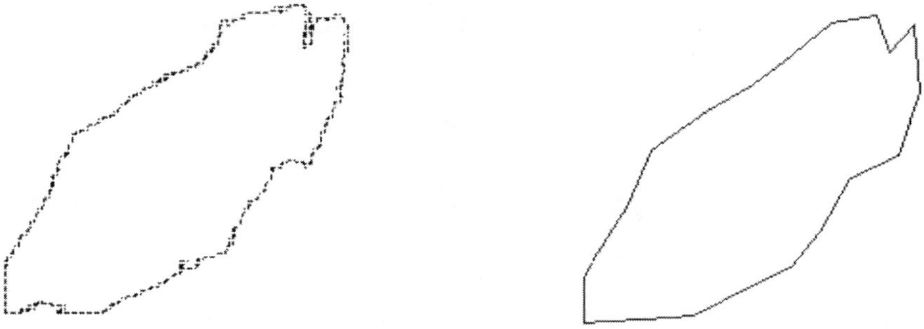

**Figure 4.** The polygonal fitting of edge of the tobacco leaf. The left image is the original tobacco leaf edge, the right image is the polygonal fitted edge.

## 4.3. Texture Features

The gray-level co-occurrence matrix (GLCM) is used for the extraction of texture features. The gray-level co-occurrence matrix can reveal certain properties about the spatial distribution of the gray-level in the texture image [14–16]. A gray-level co-occurrence matrix by calculating how often a pixel with the intensity (gray-level) value *i* occurs in a specific spatial relationship to a pixel with the value *j*. By default, the spatial relationship is defined as the pixel of interest and the pixel to its immediate right (horizontally adjacent), but we can specify other spatial relationships between the two pixels. Each element (*i, j*) in the resultant GLCM is simply the sum of the number of times that the pixel with value *i* occurred in the specified spatial relationship to a pixel with value *j* in the input image. For example, if most of the entries in the GLCM are concentrated along the diagonal, the texture is coarse with respect to the specified offset. The $N \times N$ co-occurrence matrix describes the spatial alignment and the spatial dependency of the different gray-level, whereas *N* is the number of gray-level in the image.

The dimension of gray-level co-occurrence matrix is same as the number of gray-level in images. In order to simplify calculation, firstly, we degrade the color image of tobacco leaf to a gray-level image. The maximal number of gray-level in this image is 256, so the maximal dimension of gray-level co-occurrence matrix is 256 × 256. But the 256 × 256 matrix is still too difficult to calculate, so we further degrade the 256 gray-level image to a 32 gray-level image, then the dimension of gray-level co-occurrence matrix is 32 × 32. During degrading the 256 gray-level image to 32 gray-level image, it will surely loss some subtle information in the image. This degradation is only used in the calculation of gray-level co-occurrence matrix, and will improve the computing efficiency greatly.

The gray-level co-occurrence matrix $p_\delta(i, j)$ is defined as follows,

$$p_\delta(i,j) = \{(x,y)|f(x,y) = i,\ f(x+DX, y+DY) = j\}. \quad (4)$$

The entry $(i, j)$ of $p_\delta(i, j)$ is the number of occurrences of the pair of gray-level $i$ and $j$ at inter-pixel distance $\delta = (DX, DY)$. Assume the size of image is $L \times L$, $(x, y)$ are the coordinate of pixels, $x, y = 0, 1, 2, \ldots, L-1$, $f(x, y)$ is the gray-level of pixels. Then the gray-level co-occurrence matrix of an image is as follows,

$$p_\delta(i,j) = \begin{pmatrix} p_\delta(0,0) & \ldots & p_\delta(0,N-1) \\ \ldots & p_\delta(i,j) & \ldots \\ p_\delta(N-1,0) & \ldots & p_\delta(N-1,N-1) \end{pmatrix} \tag{5}$$

Once the gray-level co-occurrence matrix is calculated, the texture features can be computed from it. In this paper, the texture features include the texture energy, texture entropy and texture contrast of the digital image of tobacco leaves. The formulae are as follows, the texture energy,

$$E = \sum_{i=1}^{N} \sum_{i=1}^{N} (p_{i,j})^2. \tag{6}$$

the texture entropy,

$$H = \sum_{i=1}^{N} \sum_{i=1}^{N} p_{i,j} \log p_{i,j}. \tag{7}$$

and the texture contrast,

$$H = \sum_{i=1}^{N} \sum_{i=1}^{N} (i-j)^2 p_{i,j}. \tag{8}$$

## 5. THEORY OF FUZZY SET

The fuzzy set theory is the extension of conventional (crisp) set theory. It handles the concept of partial truth and the truth values between 1 (completely true) and 0 (completely false). Zadeh introduced it in 1965 as a mean to model the vagueness and ambiguity in complex systems [17–20]. Fuzzy theory became popular after 1980s and were used mainly by researchers in electronics and computer engineering. Nowadays, an immense number of studies are carried out using this method.

The fuzzy set theory, provide a rich and meaningful addition to standard logic. The mathematics generated by these theories is consistent, and the fuzzy logic may be a generalization of classic logic. The applications which may be generated from or adapted to the fuzzy logic are wide-ranging, and provide the opportunity for modeling of conditions which are inherently imprecisely defined, despite the concerns of classical logicians. Many systems may be modeled, simulated, and even replicated with the help of the fuzzy systems, not the least of which is human reasoning itself. Areas in which the fuzzy set theory has been successfully applied include artificial intelligence, auto control, information processing, economics, psychology, *etc.*

Simple fuzzy classification (SFC), fuzzy similarity method (FSM) and fuzzy comprehensive evaluation (FCE), are all subtitles of fuzzy synthetic evaluation (FSE) and have been used recently by a number of researchers in various areas [21,22]. Fuzzy evaluation methods process all the components according to predetermined weights and decrease the fuzziness by using membership functions, therefore sensitivity is quite high compared to other index evaluation techniques.

Let $X$ is the set of objects, with elements noted as $x$. Thus, $X = x$. A fuzzy set $A$ in $X$ is characterized by a membership function $\mu_A(x)$, which maps each point in $X$ onto the real interval [0.0, 1.0]. As $\mu_A(x)$ approaches 1.0, the membership function of $x$ in $A$ increases.

$$A = \{x, \mu_A(x) | x \in X\}, \mu_A(x) : X \to [0, 1]. \quad (9)$$

The comprehensive fuzzy evaluation model is based on fuzzy set theory and the analytic hierarchical process which is developed by

Saaty [23]. Saaty advocated the use of deductive systems approach in the analysis of complex decision problem. Zadeh define fuzzy logic underlying models of reasoning which are approximate rather than exact. The fuzzy comprehensive evaluation (FCE), which provides a high level confidence in decision making by the fuzzy logic, is a branch of artificial intelligence. It would classify or distinguish things by means of analyzing the fuzzy information as much as possible. Before making a decision, the fuzzy decision engine (FDE) in corporate different information. The information is usually a fuzzy quantization feature or the evaluations of some objects. According to the factors, a matrix is constructed and then a weight vector is assigned. Based on the matrix and the weight vector, the fuzzy decision engine can reach a final decision after a comprehensive evaluation.

As mentioned above, classification, quality evaluation or grading of tobacco leaves is a fuzzy problem, so the fuzzy comprehensive evaluation can be used for the automatic classification.

## 6. AUTOMATIC CLASSIFICATION OF TOBACCO LEAVES

In this paper, nine features of the flue-cured tobacco leaves are extracted, which belong to three categories. The three classes of the flue-cured tobacco leaves are X1L, B4L and S1. The reason why we only choose three categories flue-cured tobacco leaves is that the process of classification, quality evaluation or grading need a lot of tobacco leaves which have been classified by experts. Getting all 40 categories is very difficult and very expensive. In fact, some categories of tobacco leaves are very rare. In this research, only 24 classified tobacco leaves are collected, and only eight categories have enough quantity (more than 100 pieces, we also need to divide them into two sets, training set and testing set) for the training of grading.

## 6.1. Mathematical Model

The comprehensive evaluation model gives a judgment to an object according to many factors in the fuzzy environment [24]. It gives a final judgment result. It is mainly made up by three essential factors, namely factor set, weight set and evaluation set.

Fuzzy comprehensive evaluation can be applied in three stages. Firstly, membership functions are determined. Then, using the membership functions, a fuzzy relationship matrix is formed. Lastly, the grading of tobacco leaves are given by fuzzy comprehensive evaluation.

In this paper, two-level fuzzy comprehensive evaluation is used for the classification of tobacco leaves. Firstly, we propose a mathematical model as follows.

1. The factor set

Assume that $U = \{U_1, U_2, . . ., U_m\}$ is a factor set, which is composed of $m$ kinds of factors. It represents some attributes of tobacco leaves. Each factor $U_i$ can be separated into several sub-factors $U_{ij}(i = 1, 2, . . ., m; j = 1, 2, . . ., n)$, and the sub-factors $U_{ij}$ form some factor subsets $U_i = \{U_{i1},U_{i2}, . . .,U_{in}\}$.

The factors which influence the classification of tobacco leaves are separated into three categories, $U = \{U_1,U_2,U_3\}$. The sub-factors of every subsets are, $U_1 = \{U_{11},U_{12},U_{13}\}$, $U_2 = \{U_{21},U_{22},U_{23}\}$, $U_3 = \{U_{31},U_{32},U_{33}\}$.

*$U_1$ = shape features, $U_2$ = texture features, $U_3$ = color features, $U_{11}$ = area, $U_{12}$ = perimeter, $U_{13}$ = disfigurement, $U_{21}$= texture energy, $U_{22}$ = textureentropy, $U_{23}$ = texturecontrast, $U_{31}$ = variance of red, $U_{32}$ = variance of green, $U_{33}$ =variance of blue.*

2. The weight set

(1) Sub-factor weight set

A weight $a_i(i = 1, 2, . . ., m)$ represents the different influence on the decision-marking of every factors, thus the weight set of sub-factor is $A = \{a_1,a_2, . . ., a_m\}$. According to the previous experiments, the most effective feature is the color features among the three features. We can effectively recognize the tobacco leaves according to the area of different color and the depth of color. The shape features are also very useful to the classification of tobacco leaves. While the texture features have less influence compares with the other two features. Therefore, we set $a_1 = 0.35$, $a_2 = 0.2$ and $a_3 = 0.45$.

(2) Factors weight set

We arranged the factors weight according to the membership function of sub-factor $U_{ij}$. The membership function comes from a great deal of experiments. $A_1 = \{0.3, 0.4, 0.3\}$, $A_2 = \{0.4, 0.3, 0.3\}$, $A_3 = \{0.3, 0.3, 0.4\}$.

3. The evaluation set

The test tobacco leaves belong to three classes, so the evaluation sets are $V = \{v_1 : X1L, v_2 : B4L, v_3 : S1\}$.

## 6.2. Computational Process

1. The sub-factor evaluation matrix.

A fuzzy set is fully defined by its membership function. How best to determine the membership function is the first question that has to be tackled. The approach adopted for acquiring the shape of any particular membership function is often dependent on the application. Because of the lack of a definite method for determining the membership function, we use artificial neural networks to determine it.

Back-propagation neural networks are probably the most well-known and widely applied of the neural networks today. In essence, the back-propagation net is a Perception with multiple layers, a different threshold function in the artificial neuron, and a more robust and capable learning rule.

Nine features are extracted from images of tobacco leaf. A back-propagation neural network is used to decide the membership of each feature in the fuzzy sets. The input layer of the BP neural network includes three neurons corresponding to the three features of a category of factors (shape, color or texture). The output layer includes three neurons corresponding to the membership function of three classes of tobacco leaves. A hidden layer is designed that includes five neurons. The structure of back-propagation neural network is shown as Figure 5.

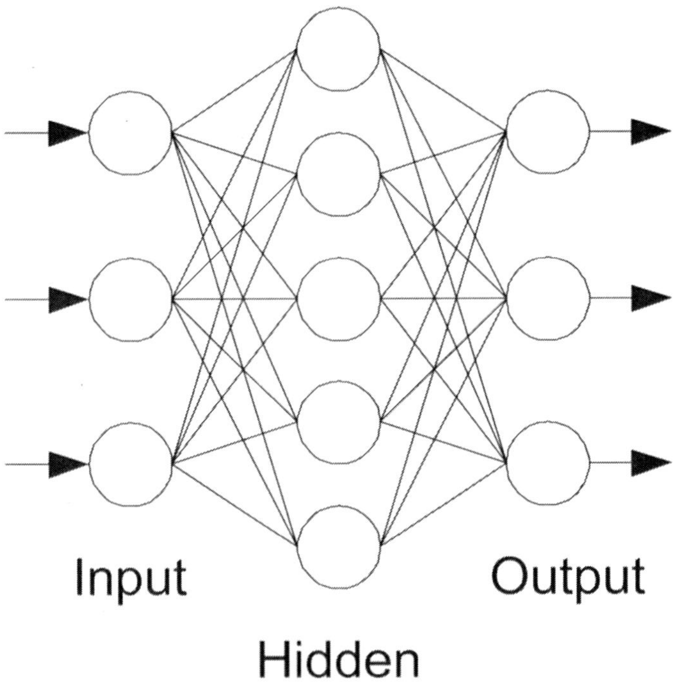


**Figure 5.** The structure of back-propagation neural networks.

In this paper, three features of a factors category (shape, color or texture) and the class of standard specimen tobacco leaves (The verdict of class is given by experts) are used in the training of neural network. For example, if a tobacco leaf belongs to X1L, then the output neuron corresponding to X1L is set to 1 and other two output neurons are set to 0. The training process is repeated until all the output is correct. Then we input three features of a factors category and get the membership of these features. The features of a factors category are normalized, $\sum_{j=1}^{n} r_{ij} = 1.$ According to the membership $r_{ij}(i = 1, 2, . . ., m; j = 1, 2, . . ., n)$, we get a sub-factor evaluation matrix $R_i$,

$$R_i = \begin{pmatrix} R_{11} & R_{12} & \dots & R_{1n} \\ R_{21} & R_{22} & \dots & R_{2n} \\ \dots & \dots & \dots & \dots \\ R_{m1} & R_{m2} & \dots & R_{mn} \end{pmatrix}. \tag{10}$$

2. The one-level fuzzy comprehensive evaluation matrix B.

$$B_i = A_i \cdot R_i. \tag{11}$$

$$B = (B_1, B_2, \dots, B_m)^T. \tag{12}$$

3. The two-level fuzzy comprehensive evaluation set *V*.

$$V = A \cdot B. \tag{13}$$

4. The evaluation set *V* and the class of the test tobacco leaves.

$$V_i = V_i / \sum_{i=1}^{3} V_i \tag{14}$$

$$\mu_A(x) = max(V_1, V_2, V_3) \tag{15}$$

## 7. EXPERIMENTAL RESULTS

In this research, 300 images of tobacco leaves are selected from the database, which include three classes of tobacco leaves—X1L, B4L and S1. Nine features are extracted from images of tobacco leaf, and these features are used for the learning of back-propagation neural network to get the membership of features in the fuzzy sets.

Three categories of factors (shape, color or texture) are extracted according to image processing and machine vision techniques. Experimental results of some tobacco leaves are shown in Tables 1–3.

**Table 1.** Shape features of some tobacco leaves.

| No. | Surface area (Number of pixels) | Surface perimeter (Number of pixels) | Disfigurement (%) |
|---|---|---|---|
| 1 | 40502 | 1080 | 1.28 |
| 2 | 48607 | 1308 | 0.56 |
| 3 | 39775 | 1013 | 3.96 |
| 4 | 57862 | 1406 | 3.01 |
| 5 | 18515 | 544 | 4.74 |
| 6 | 25924 | 956 | 1.90 |
| 7 | 10803 | 289 | 2.91 |
| 8 | 14435 | 419 | 3.12 |
| 9 | 59146 | 1750 | 2.16 |
| 10 | 30747 | 727 | 9.47 |
| 11 | 26838 | 625 | 1.47 |

Then, two group images of tobacco leaves are used in experiments. The first group includes 100 images, which comes from the images that have been trained by neural network. According to the results of the two-level fuzzy comprehensive evaluation, the accuracy rate of classification is 94%. The second group includes 50 images, which comes from the images that have been classified but have not been trained by neural network. After the two-level fuzzy comprehensive evaluation, the accuracy rate of classification is 72%.

Following is an evaluation process of a tobacco leaf. The average values of features from the three classes of standard specimen tobacco leaves are shown in Table 4. Table 5 shows the features of a test tobacco leaf. The grades of membership are shown in Table 6. We get the sub-factor evaluation matrix $R_i$ according to the membership, then calculate $B_i = A_i \cdot R_i$ and get the one-level fuzzy comprehensive evaluation matrix ***B***,

$$B = (B_1, B_2, \ldots, B_m)^T = \begin{pmatrix} 0.23 & 0.57 & 0.2 \\ 0.23 & 0.53 & 0.21 \\ 0.26 & 0.54 & 0.2 \end{pmatrix}.$$

After the two-level fuzzy comprehensive evaluation, we get the evaluation set *V*,

$$V = A \cdot B = (0.2345, 0.5575, 0.202).$$

We normalize the evaluation set, $V = \{0.2359, 0.5609, 0.2032\}$. According to the two-level fuzzy comprehensive evaluation, the grade of membership of test tobacco leaf is 0.2359 to the X1L, 0.5609 to the B4L and 0.2032 to the S1. Therefore this test tobacco is evaluated to fall in the B4L class of flue-cured tobacco leaves.

**Table 2.** Color features of some tobacco leaves (Dimensionless unit).

| No. | Variance of red | Variance of green | Variance of blue |
|---|---|---|---|
| 1 | 185.4286 | 150.7143 | 95.14286 |
| 2 | 185.5714 | 153 | 98.57143 |
| 3 | 183 | 154.3333 | 103 |
| 4 | 157.2857 | 123.1429 | 76.14286 |
| 5 | 162 | 132 | 87.14286 |
| 6 | 175 | 144.1667 | 94.33334 |
| 7 | 163.8571 | 129.1429 | 81 |
| 8 | 174 | 141 | 90.42857 |
| 9 | 132 | 102.6667 | 66.33334 |
| 10 | 157.5714 | 122.5714 | 77.71429 |
| 11 | 160 | 127.2857 | 82 |
| 12 | 167.2 | 136.6 | 88.4 |
| 13 | 162.8571 | 135.5714 | 88.85714 |
| 14 | 130.1667 | 100.3333 | 65.16666 |
| 15 | 141 | 110.4286 | 73.42857 |
| 16 | 129.2 | 102.6 | 69.4 |
| 17 | 120.625 | 94.25 | 65.125 |
| 18 | 114.5 | 91.75 | 67 |
| 19 | 119.7143 | 94.71429 | 68.28571 |
| 20 | 111.5714 | 91.42857 | 68.14286 |
| 21 | 170.4286 | 138.2857 | 89.42857 |
| 22 | 150.2857 | 116.1429 | 72.28571 |
| 23 | 142.7143 | 113.4286 | 75.42857 |
| 24 | 160.7143 | 126.4286 | 77.28571 |

**Table 3.** Texture features of some tobacco leaves (Dimensionless unit).

| No. | Texture energy | Texture entropy | Texture contrast |
|---|---|---|---|
| 1 | 47.85714 | 145 | 33.14286 |
| 2 | 45 | 150.2857 | 35.42857 |
| 3 | 51 | 135.8333 | 33.33333 |
| 4 | 44 | 144.5714 | 32.42857 |
| 5 | 57.28571 | 121.5714 | 31.28572 |
| 6 | 54 | 126.8333 | 27.83333 |
| 7 | 35 | 172.1429 | 41 |
| 8 | 48 | 143.8571 | 34 |
| 9 | 35.33333 | 158.6667 | 33.33333 |
| 10 | 38.28571 | 163.7143 | 39.85714 |
| 11 | 44.85714 | 146.5714 | 34.28571 |
| 12 | 61.6 | 110.4 | 27.4 |
| 13 | 71.57143 | 89.28571 | 25.42857 |
| 14 | 40 | 149.3333 | 32.33333 |
| 15 | 61.28571 | 106.5714 | 26.71428 |
| 16 | 69.2 | 85.4 | 21.8 |
| 17 | 52.25 | 121.25 | 27 |
| 18 | 64.75 | 94 | 24 |
| 19 | 46.42857 | 128.2857 | 25.57143 |
| 20 | 53.42857 | 113.8571 | 25.42857 |
| 21 | 42.57143 | 152.2857 | 35.57143 |
| 22 | 42.28571 | 153 | 37.71429 |
| 23 | 55.28571 | 120.4286 | 29.28572 |
| 24 | 39.14286 | 157 | 35.14286 |

**Table 4.** Features of three classes (X1L, B4L and S1) of the standard specimen tobacco leaves.

| $U_{11}$ | $U_{12}$ | $U_{13}$ | $U_{21}$ | $U_{22}$ | $U_{23}$ | $U_{31}$ | $U_{32}$ | $U_{33}$ |
|---|---|---|---|---|---|---|---|---|
| 2123 | 41937 | 0.011 | 0.48 | −1.43 | 33.14 | 887 | 696 | 575 |
| 941 | 16478 | 0.036 | 0.71 | −0.9 | 25.43 | 1027 | 826 | 593 |
| 2069 | 41242 | 0.08 | 0.42 | −1.53 | 35.57 | 633 | 612 | 523 |

**Table 5.** Features of a test tobacco leaf.

| $U_{11}$ | $U_{12}$ | $U_{13}$ | $U_{21}$ | $U_{22}$ | $U_{23}$ | $U_{31}$ | $U_{32}$ | $U_{33}$ |
|---|---|---|---|---|---|---|---|---|
| 820 | 18236 | 0.038 | 0.72 | −0.89 | 25.22 | 1032 | 853 | 698 |

**Table 6.** The grade of membership.

| | $U_{11}$ | $U_{12}$ | $U_{13}$ | $U_{21}$ | $U_{22}$ | $U_{23}$ | $U_{31}$ | $U_{32}$ | $U_{33}$ |
|---|---|---|---|---|---|---|---|---|---|
| X1L | 0.2 | 0.2 | 0.3 | 0.2 | 0.3 | 0.2 | 0.3 | 0.1 | 0.3 |
| B4L | 0.5 | 0.6 | 0.6 | 0.5 | 0.5 | 0.7 | 0.5 | 0.7 | 0.5 |
| S1 | 0.3 | 0.2 | 0.1 | 0.3 | 0.2 | 0.1 | 0.2 | 0.2 | 0.2 |

## 8. CONCLUSIONS

This paper proposes an automatic grading method of tobacco leaves based on the digital image processing and the fuzzy sets theory. A neural network is used to decide the membership function of the features of tobacco leaves in the fuzzy sets. The aim of this paper is to find a feasible method to realize the automatic grading of tobacco leaves. The experimental results of the two-level fuzzy comprehensive evaluation show that the accuracy rate of classification is about 94% for the trained tobacco leaves, and the accuracy rate of the non-trained tobacco leaves is about 72%.

Automatic grading of tobacco leaves is a very complex task. We think that 72% accuracy rate of the non-trained tobacco leaves is a challenging result. Even though this performance is not practically exciting, the experimental results show that fuzzy comprehensive evaluation is a viable way for the automatic classification or quality evaluation of tobacco leaves. In the future, more works will be done, *i.e.*, (1) the quality of standard specimen tobacco leaves should be improved, (2) more digital features will be extracted, which precisely express the properties of tobacco leaves, and (3) more categories of tobacco leaves will be dealt with.

## REFERENCES

1. Zhang, J; Sokhansanj, S; Wu, S; Fang, R; Yang, W; Winter, P. A trainable grading system for tobacco leaves.*Comput Electron Agric* **1997**, *16*, 231–244.
2. Zhang, J; Sokhansanj, S; Wu, S; Fang, R; Yang, W; Winter, P. A transformation technique from RGB signals to the Munsell system for color analysis of tobacco leaves. *Comput. Electron. Agric* **1998**, *19*, 155–166.
3. Garcia, M; Barreiro, P; Ruiz, AM; Alonso, R; Judez, L. Development of a virtual expert for color classification of tobacco leaves. *Proc. Sens. Decis. Support Syst. Agric. Food Ind. Environ* **1998**, *1*, 105–117.
4. Zhang, F; Fang, R; Cai, J. Study of getting tobacco leaf weight based on neural network. *Trans. Chin. Soc. Agric. Mach* **2000**, *31*, 61–64.
5. MacCormac, J. On-line image processing for tobacco grading in Zimbabwe. Proceedings of IEEE International Symposium on Industrial Electronics, Budapest, Hungary, 1–3 June 1993; pp. 327–331.
6. Zhang, F; Fang, R; Cai, J. Image retrieveal of standary tobacco leaf database. *Trans. Chin. Soc. Agric. Mach* **2001**,*32*, 66–67.

7. Zhang, H; Han, L; Wang, Z. A fuzzy classification system and its application. *Int. Conf. Mach. Learn. Cybern* **2003**,*4*, 2582–2586.

8. Ma, W; He, L; Xu, S; Chen, J; Wu, Z. Image segmentation based on transmission characteristics of flue-cured tobacco leaves. *Trans. Chin. Soc. Agricult. Eng* **2006**, *22*, 134–137.

9. United States Department of Agriculture. Official Standard Grades for Flue-Cured Tobacco U.S. Types 11, 12, 13, 14, and Foreign Type 92, 27 March 1989..

10. China Tobacco Corporation. *Training Handbook of Chinese Grading Criteria of Flue-cured Tobacco Leaves*; China Standards Publishing House: Beijing, China, 1992; pp. 1–38.

11. Agoston, GA. *Color Theory and its Application in Art and Design*; Springer-Verlag: New York, NY, USA, 1987.

12. Wang, X. Laplacian operator-based edge detectors. *IEEE Trans. Patt. Anal. Mach. Int* **2007**, *29*, 886–890.

13. Kamgar-Parsi, B; Rosenfeld, A. Optimally isotropic laplacian operator. *IEEE Trans. Image Proc* **1999**, *8*, 1467–1472.

14. Haralick, RM; Shanmugan, K; Dinstein, I. Textural features for image classification. *IEEE Trans. Syst. Man Cybern***1973**, *3*, 610–621.

15. Kerroum, M; Hammouch, A; Aboutajdine, D. Textural feature selection by joint mutual information based on Gaussian mixture model for multispectral image classification. *Pattern Recognition Lett* **2010**, *31*, 1168–1174.

16. Retrieval Abbadeni, N. Computational perceptual features for texture representation and retrieval. *IEEE Trans. Image Proc* **2011**, *20*, 236–246.

17. Zadeh, LA. Fuzzy sets. *Inform. contr* **1965**, *8*, 338–353.

18. Zadeh, LA. The concept of a linguistic variable and its application to approximate reasoning. *Inform. Sci* **1975**, *8*, 199–249.

19. Zadeh, LA. The Concept of A Linguistic Variable and Its Application to Approximate Reasoning. *Inform. Sci***1975**, *8*, 301–357.

20. Zadeh, LA. The concept of a linguistic variable and its application to approximate reasoning. *Inform. Sci* **1975**, *9*, 43–80.

21. Haiyan, W. Assessment and prediction of overall environmental qualityof Zhuzhou city. *J. Environ. Manage* **2002**,*66*, 329–340.

22. Lu, R; Lo, S. Diagnosing reservoir water quality using self-organizing maps and fuzzytheory. *Water Res* **2002**, *36*, 2265–2274.

23. Saaty, T. *The Analytic Hierarclcy Process: Planning, Priority, Resource Allocation*; McGraw-Hill: New York, NY, USA, 1980.

24. Wang, Y; Li, C; Zuo, Y. A selection model for optimal fuzzy clustering algorithm and number of clusters based on competitive comprehensive fuzzy evaluation. *IEEE Trans. Fuzzy Syst* **2009**, *17*, 568–577.

# Chapter 7

# Pose Measurement Method and Experiments for High-Speed Rolling Targets in a Wind Tunnel

**Zhenyuan Jia [1], Xin Ma [1], Wei Liu [1,*], Wenbo Lu [2], Xiao Li [1], Ling Chen [1], Zhengqu Wang [2] and Xiaochun Cui [2]**

[1]*Key Laboratory for Precision and Non-Traditional Machining Technology of the Ministry of Education, Dalian University of Technology, Dalian 116024, China*

[2]*AVIC Aerodynamics Research Institute, Shenyang 116024, China*

## ABSTRACT

High-precision wind tunnel simulation tests play an important role in aircraft design and manufacture. In this study, a high-speed pose vision measurement method is proposed for high-speed and rolling targets in a supersonic wind tunnel. To obtain images with high signal-to-noise ratio and avoid impacts on the aerodynamic shape of the rolling targets, a high-speed image acquisition method based on ultrathin retro-reflection markers is presented. Since markers are small-sized and some of them may be lost when the target is rolling, a novel markers layout with which markers are distributed evenly on the surface is proposed based on a spatial coding method to achieve highly accurate pose information. Additionally, a pose acquisition is carried out according to the mentioned markers layout after removing mismatching points by Case Deletion Diagnostics. Finally, experiments on measuring the pose parameters of high-speed targets in the laboratory and in a supersonic wind tunnel are conducted to verify the feasibility and effectiveness of the proposed method. Experimental results indicate that the position measurement precision is less than 0.16 mm, the pitching and yaw angle precision less than 0.132° and the roll angle precision 0.712°.

**Keywords:** Machine vision; Pose measurement; High-speed motion; Wind tunnel

## 1. INTRODUCTION

The pose measurement method has been widely used in many research fields such as aerospace, robots and medical science. In some cases, the improper separation of stores carried by a high-speed aircraft, such as bombs, auxiliary fuel tank, torpedoes and missiles, will greatly impact the performance of the mother plane and even threaten the safety of the pilot [1,2]. Simulative store separation experiments in wind tunnels provide valuable reference for the layout design and release parameters of the store. However, since wind tunnel models are usually small-sized and move and rotate at high speeds, traditional measurements fail to correctly measure their pose information. Vision measurement has proved its advantages such as being non-contact and high precision and the ability for real-time measurement. Therefore, pose measurement in wind tunnels based on vision measurement is of great importance [3,4].

Numerous approaches for measuring the pose parameters of targets have been studied by many scholars and research institutions. Watzlavick *et al.* presented the Optotrak™ measurement system by Canada's Northern Digital Inc. (Waterloo, ON, Canada). Three precisely calibrated linear CCDs are used as displacement sensors [5]. The 3D coordinates of each marker can be obtained in real time by capturing the near-infrared light given out by the active luminous markers. The precision and resolution of the system can reach 0.1

mm RMS and 0.01 mm, respectively. It has been successfully applied to the aerodynamic elasticity and angle measurement of the wind tunnel models of both Boeing and the NASA Ames Research Center. However, its low sampling frequency and big volume of embedded markers cannot satisfy high-speed pose measurement demand of small volume objects. Rock *et al.* combined the Carrier-Phase Differential Global Positioning System (CDGPS) and a binocular vision system to identify ground target images [6]. They used color object identification technology to process images captured by the left and right cameras, and employed two different images to locate the target projection. Finally, the aircraft pose parameters can be estimated according to stereo triangulation. Though this method is simple in calculation, the wireless signals in a complex environment are susceptible to be disturbed, so the measurement data are not stable. NASA LaRC developed a pose measurement system based on binocular vision for the wind tunnel model [7–10]. The model images are captured continuously and synchronously by two CCD cameras through the observation window. The pose parameters of the wind tunnel model can be calculated after measuring the 3D centroid coordinates of circular markers. However, this method has disadvantages due to the hidden phenomenon when the model is rolling. Murray *et al.* employed an Optical Tracking System based on Particle Image Velocimetry (PIV) to obtain the pitch angle, angular velocity and related pose information of a high-speed target [11]. Though high-speed measurements can be achieved, they cannot get the rolling angle utilizing this system. Chen presented a pose measurement method for experimental model based on active vision in a wind tunnel [12]. This method transforms the direct pose measurement of the target into an indirect measurement of spots on the wall, which amplifies the variation of the information. Thus, the resolution of the measurement system can be indirectly improved, and the maximum error of displacement of the cooperating target is 0.46 mm. However, its low precision cannot satisfy pose measurement requirements of small volume high-speed target and high-speed rolling motion. Fan *et al.* proposed an attitude and position tracking system for indoor carriers based on an integrated navigation fusion of INS/UWB information strategy [13]. The two subsystems (INS and UWB) are integrated by a feedback correction method. Then, the data fusion of the two subsystems can be realized by an optimal comprehension and filtering strategy. Though the position and attitude information can be obtained in real time, when it comes to small targets with high-speed rolling motion in a wind tunnel, the UWB technology can hardly meet the measuring environment demands. In summary, scholars have made different kinds of investigations on innovations in pose measurement under wind tunnel conditions, but the pose measurement speed is low and the hidden phenomenon of cooperation markers in the rolling procedure is ignored.

In this paper, a pose measurement method for high-speed rolling targets in wind tunnels is presented. The remainder of this paper is organized as follows: Section 2 will detail the vision theory and image acquisition method; Section 3 will describe the marker layout on the surface of target and the image matching method; Section 4 will present the pose information acquisition method from the constructed markers' 3D coordinates; Section 5 will show the results obtained from a set of testing scenarios. Finally, the paper ends with conclusions about the whole pose measurement method and the results obtained.

## 2. MEASUREMENT METHOD AND SYSTEM FOR HIGH-SPEED AND ROLLING TARGETS

### 2.1. Binocular Vision Theory

Vision measurement focuses on how to obtain 3D information from 2D image information. Two types of coordinate systems (*i.e.*, image and global coordinate systems) are involved in transforming the 2D image coordinates obtained from the camera into 3D global coordinate information, as shown in Figure 1.

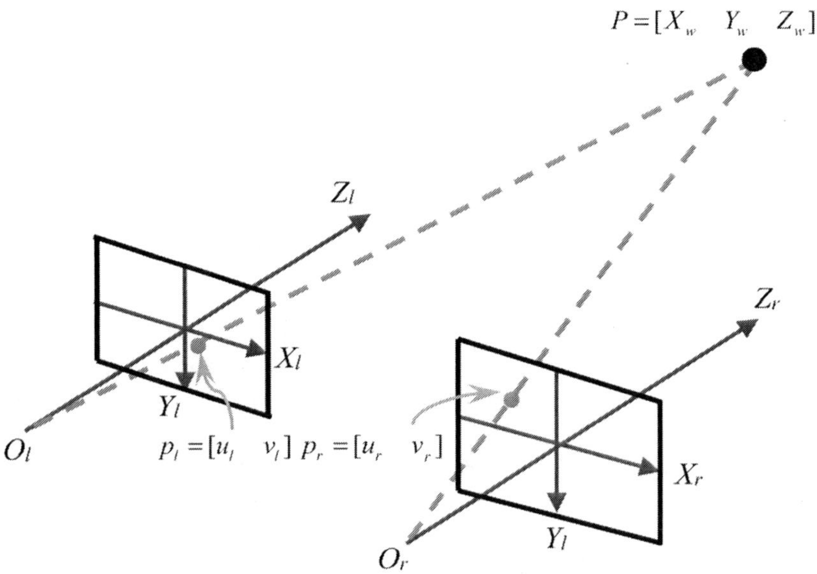


**Figure 1.** The principle of binocular stereo imaging.

In this study, the pinhole model is taken as the imaging model. However, due to some defects occurred in the manufacture and installation procedures of composite lenses, image distortion is unavoidable, resulting in aberration between the real and theoretical image points. Therefore, we introduce a non-linear imaging model considering the impact of aberration. The projection equation of the non-linear imaging model can be given by:

$$Z_c \begin{bmatrix} \hat{u}+\delta_x \\ \hat{v}+\delta_y \\ 1 \end{bmatrix} = M_1 \begin{bmatrix} R & T \\ 0^T & 1 \end{bmatrix} \begin{bmatrix} X_w \\ Y_w \\ Z_w \\ 1 \end{bmatrix} \tag{1}$$

where $p(\hat{u} \ \hat{v})$ represents the real point caused by image distortion; $(\delta_x \delta_y)$ stand for aberration, which are known already; $(X_w Y_w Z_w)$

represent the 3D coordinates of one point in the world coordinates; $Z_c$ is the scale factor; $M_1$represents the intrinsic parameter of the camera; rotation matrix $R$ and translation matrix $T$ are the extrinsic parameters.

Wide-angle lenses are used in our measurement system to obtain close shots with a large field of view, thus the main image distortion in our system is barrel distortion. To obtain a computation method with less complex and better stability, the first and second order distortion coefficients are employed in the aberration model, as shown below:

$$\begin{cases} \delta_x = k_1\hat{u}\left(\hat{u}^2+\hat{v}^2\right)+k_2\hat{u}(\hat{u}^2+\hat{v}^2)^2 \\ \delta_y = k_1\hat{v}\left(\hat{u}^2+\hat{v}^2\right)+k_2\hat{v}(\hat{u}^2+\hat{v}^2)^2 \end{cases} \tag{2}$$

where $k_1$, $k_2$ are the first and second coefficient of radial distortion.

**Figure 2.** Calibration targets taken in different angles.

Camera calibration is the preliminary step for establishing an accurate relationship between the image and the real world. In this paper,

Zhang's 2D calibration method is implemented to achieve a high precision calibration of the binocular vision measurement system with a wide field of 1 m × 1 m [14]. The calibration targets are shown in Figure 2.

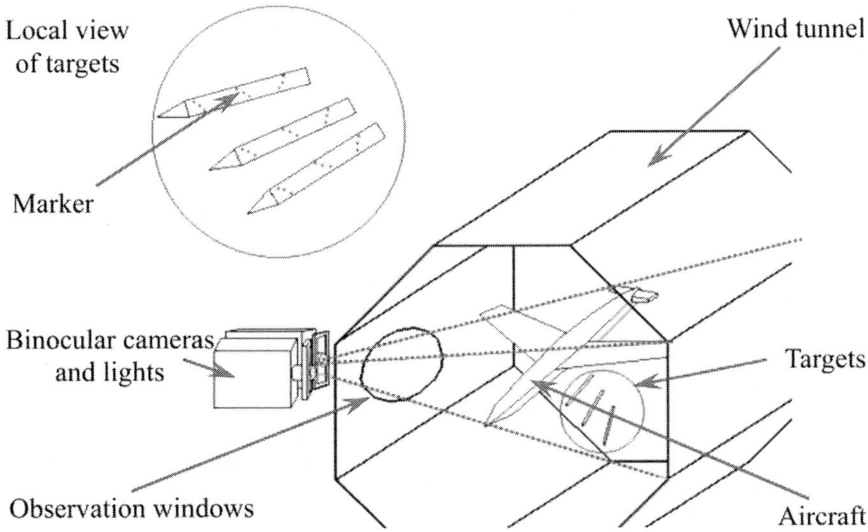


**Figure 3.** Camera-tunnel arrangement.

## 2.2. Measurement Method

In this paper, position and attitude parameters of high-speed and rolling targets can be achieved *via* analyzing image sequences of markers' moving trajectory which is captured in real time by a binocular vision measurement system. The measurement principle for position and attitude parameters of high-speed moving targets is depicted in Figure 3. Firstly, ultrathin retro-reflection markers are attached on the surface of target. Then, the left and right CCD cameras are used to capture the image sequences by applying the high-speed image acquisition technique. Moreover, the high-precision matching and recognition of the corresponding markers in the left and right images are facilitated based on spatial encoding, and then the 3D coordinates of the markers in the world coordinate system are reconstructed. Furthermore, the axis of the slender rolling target is fitted using Case Deletion Diagnostics. Finally, the pose information of the target is obtained by computing the 3D coordinates of the markers.

### 2.3. Ultrathin Retro-Reflection Markers for High-Speed Image Acquisition

The high speed image acquisition of rolling targets in a wind tunnel mainly has the following difficulties: (a) Owing to the limited size of the observation window and the high image acquisition speed, it is difficult to guarantee clear images; (b) Since the target is mostly a small-sized cylinder-like object of complicated shape, it is difficult to ensure the position accuracy of markers; (c) In order to guarantee the aerodynamic shape of the scaled model, the thickness of markers cannot exceed 30 um. However, normal markers are too thick (160 µm) to meet the requirements. To solve the aforementioned problems, an ultrathin retro-reflection markers fabrication technique based on a rolling-printed method is proposed to allow the high speed image acquisition of high-speed rolling target. Ultrathin retro-reflection markers are made by mixing glass microbeads, silver powder and resin according to the specific mixing ratio of 16:5:9. The thickness of the resulting ultrathin retro-reflection markers is only 20 µm, which guarantees the aerodynamic shape of the scaled model.

The diagram of the rolling-printed method is shown in Figure 4, where the screen plate that is designed according to the marker layout is placed atop the target. The ultrathin retro-reflection material is placed on top of the screen plate. When a process performs an operation on the device, the screen plate keeps in pure rolling contact with the target and moves continuously at a certain linear speed $V$ along the peripheral velocity direction. $V$ can be computed by $V = \omega r$, where $\omega$ and $r$ depict the angular velocity and radius of the rolling target, respectively. As a result, the ultrathin retro-reflection material in the mesh opening can be pumped or squeezed by the squeegee on the surface of the target. Figure 5 presents the finished target.

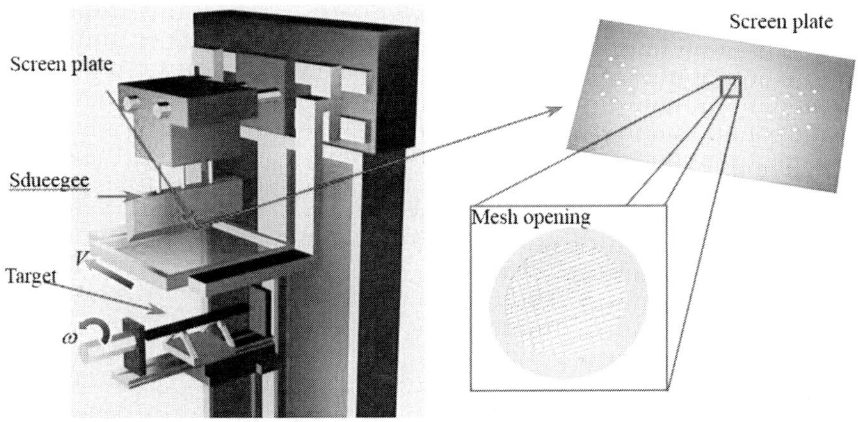


**Figure 4.** Diagram of the rolling-printed method and structure of the screen plate.

In this way, the thickness and the positioning accuracy of markers are ensured. Besides, images captured by the left and right cameras have higher signal-to-noise ratio and better brightness, and the image acquisition requirements can be satisfied under high shooting frequency conditions. As shown in Figure 6, the brightness of markers decreases while the shutter speed increases. However, markers are brighter and have higher signal-to-noise ratio at the 5000 shooting speed.

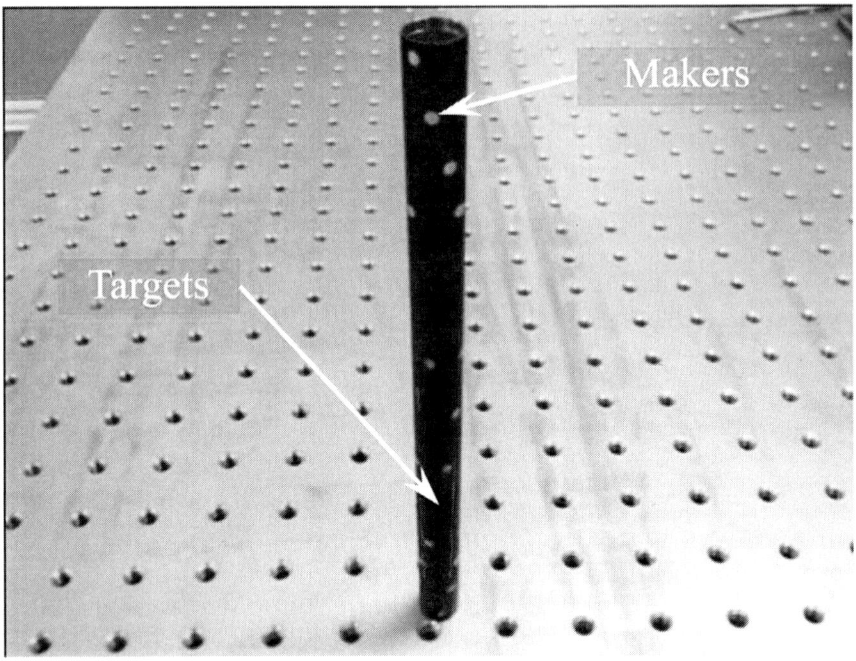


**Figure 5.** The finished target.

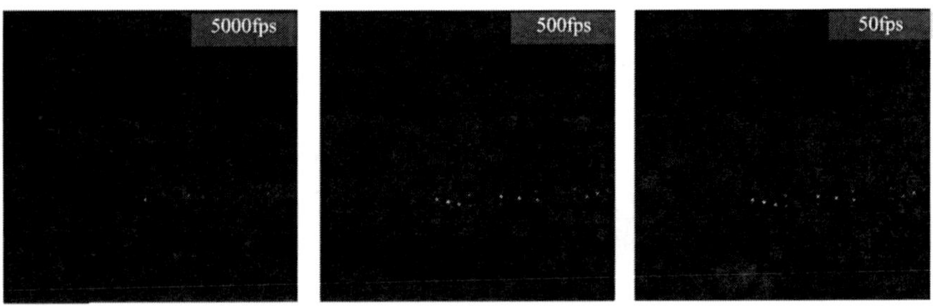


**Figure 6.** Shooting picture of ultrathin retro-reflection markers in different frames.

## 3. IMAGE PROCESSING

In this paper, cooperating markers are adopted to achieve rapid pose calculation of rolling targets. In order to improve the stability and precision of the results, it is necessary to attach more markers on the surface of the target. However, due to the small imaging area and lack of feature information, it is hard to match and recognize these markers. This section describes how to match and recognize markers with information loss.

### 3.1. Markers Layout of High-Speed Rolling Target

In order to calculate the pose parameters of the moving target quickly and accurately, the following problems must be solved: (1) it is difficult to acquire accurate matching and recognition of markers with less imaging area and inconspicuous motion features; (2) the high-speed rolling target in this paper is long and thin, making the target surface really small. Consequently, marker distribution is relatively dense, so that the recognition and matching of large number of markers would be very difficult; (3) markers' features (quantity, serial number, layout, *etc.*) are also difficult to be ascertained during the measuring process owing to the rolling motion of the target. To solve those problems, a spatial encoding method is presented in this paper.

Traditional encoding methods complete the encoding process by changing the shape of a single marker. Combining with dividing several markers into one group based on spatial relation, positional relationship between markers in the same group is used in the spatial encoding method proposed in this paper to realize encoding process [15]. As a result, the problem that small markers in larger field of view are difficult to encode is solved. As shown in Figure 7, each three markers are divided into one group which is called a spatial encoding group according to a linear constraint, and then the three markers can be ascertained through the distance ratio between them. The formula can be given by:

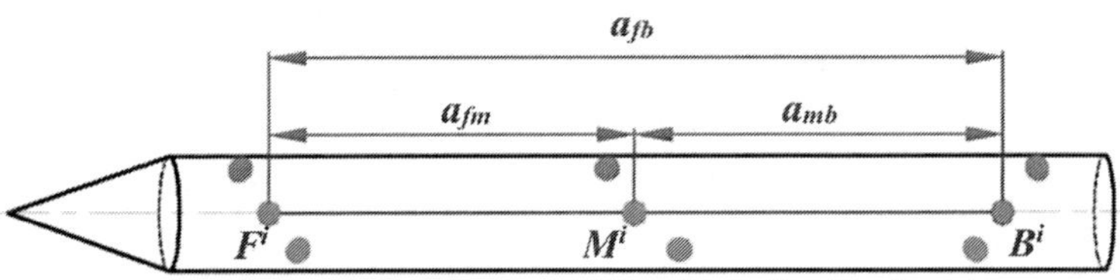


**Figure 7.** Markers distributed along the circumferential direction of the target.

$$\frac{a^{i}_{fm}}{a^{i}_{mb}} = c_{i}, \frac{a^{i}_{fm}}{a^{i}_{mb}} \neq \frac{a^{j}_{fm}}{a^{j}_{mb}} \tag{3}$$

$$\frac{a^{i}_{fm}}{a^{i}_{fb}} = l_{i}, \frac{a^{i}_{mb}}{a^{i}_{fb}} = n_{i}, \frac{a^{i}_{fm}}{a^{i}_{fb}} \neq \frac{a^{i}_{mb}}{a^{i}_{fb}} \tag{4}$$

where $a^i$ represents distance between the two space encoding markers in the same group of $i$; $f$, $m$ and $d$ stand for head, middle, tail part of the target, respectively; let $a^i_{fm}$ be the distance between two markers in the head and middle part of the target; $l_i$ is the distance ratio between $a^i_{fm}$ and $a^i_{fb}$, which can distinguish the $i$th group from all other groups; $c_i$ is the distance ratio between $a^i_{fm}$ and $a^i_{mb}$; $n_i$ is the distance ratio between $a^i_{mb}$ and $a^i_{fb}$; in this paper, we defined $V$ be encoding array, then the encoding array of group $i$ can be written as $V_i = [l_i c_i n_i]$, and the spatial encoding of markers can be accomplished by making the array elements in every encoding array unique.

To improve the precision and stability of the measurement system, it is necessary to increase the number of markers in the layout to satisfy the extraction precision. Moreover, a radial circular uniform distribution is adopted to solve the problem of the rolling motion of the target. To meet the requirements of image acquisition, a total of 12 spatial encoding groups are attached onto the target accurately according to the distance information of these three markers, as shown in Figure 8.

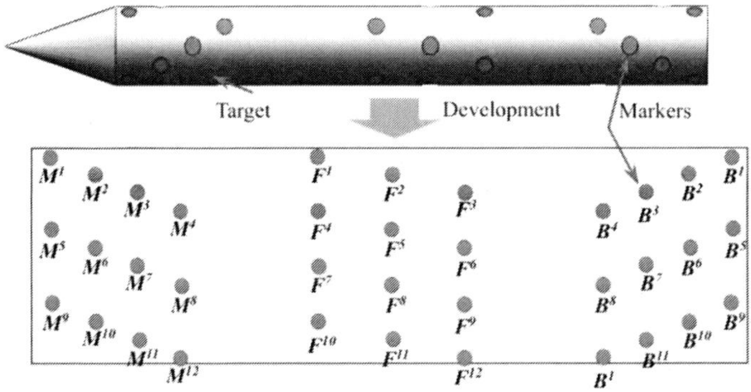


**Figure 8.** The markers layout.

In the process of measuring the pose of the target, at least three groups with a total of nine markers appear in the image simultaneously. The well-proportioned distribution of markers in the head, middle, and tail part of the target guarantees the number of markers as well as the pose estimation precision of the target.

### 3.2. Feature Extraction

In the complicated wind tunnel conditions, it is difficult to conduct the marker feature extraction due to such factors as small-sized model with large curvature change, large field of view and small imaging area of markers. Therefore, the gradient weighted method is employed to extract the center of the markers with high accuracy. Firstly, a convolution operation of the image is conducted based on a Gaussian first-order differential operator in order to obtain the gradient of each point in the image. The Gaussian first-order differential operator can be written as:

$$h'(x) = \frac{-x}{\sqrt{2\pi\sigma}} e^{-\frac{x^2}{2\sigma^2}} \tag{5}$$

Then, the gradient of image can be given by:

$$|G(x,y)| = \begin{bmatrix} F_x' \\ F_y' \end{bmatrix} = \begin{bmatrix} F(x,y) \otimes h_x' \\ F(x,y) \otimes h_y' \end{bmatrix} \tag{6}$$

The coordinates of gradient centroid of markers pattern can be expressed as:

$$c = \sum_{i=-h}^{h} \sum_{j=-w}^{w} \left[ |G(i,j)| \cdot P(i,j) / \sum_{i=-h}^{h} \sum_{j=-w}^{w} G(i,j) \right] \tag{7}$$

where *c* is the coordinates of the gradient centroid of the markers; $|G(i,j)|$ represents the weight of point $(i,j)$; *w* and *h* stand for the width and height of target image, respectively; $P(i,j)$ is the image coordinate of the point $(i,j)$.

### 3.3. Feature Matching between Two Views

Gray matching and feature matching are generally used for the classical and effective image matching. The gray matching method is a mathematical procedure based on the gray information and image technique, while features such as color, texture, shape, spatial position extracted from two or more images are used in feature matching. However, high-precision matching under extreme environment conditions cannot be achieved according to the gray and feature information due to the fact that markers captured by ultra high-speed cameras have a small area and the gray similarity between each one is big.

To solve the problem, spatial encoding markers are applied to transform the traditional matching method based on features into a problem according to spatial constraints between markers, as shown in Figure 9.

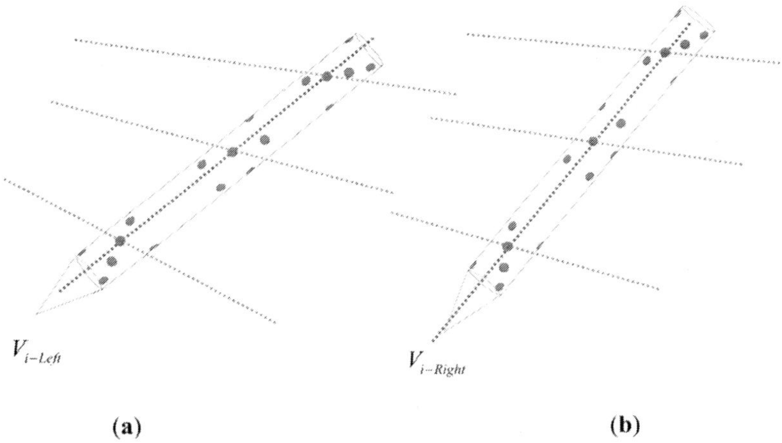


**Figure 9.** Matching between left and right images.

Firstly, spatial encoding markers in different groups are isolated by a collinear constraint, and then the matching relationship between the left and right images can be obtained through comparing $V_{i-Left}$ (obtained in Section 3.1) of the right image and $V_{i-Right}$ of left image. Moreover, based on the epipolar constraints, the corresponding marker matching is verified and the mismatched markers are removed.

### 3.4. The Recognition Method

The recognition process can be described as follows: (a) Reconstructed markers are grouped according to Section 3.3; (b) Recognition relationships can be obtained by comparing in turn each encoding array $V$ obtained by construction (Section 3.1) with the one $V_i$ ($i$=1,2...12) determined by markers layout, as shown in Figure 10.

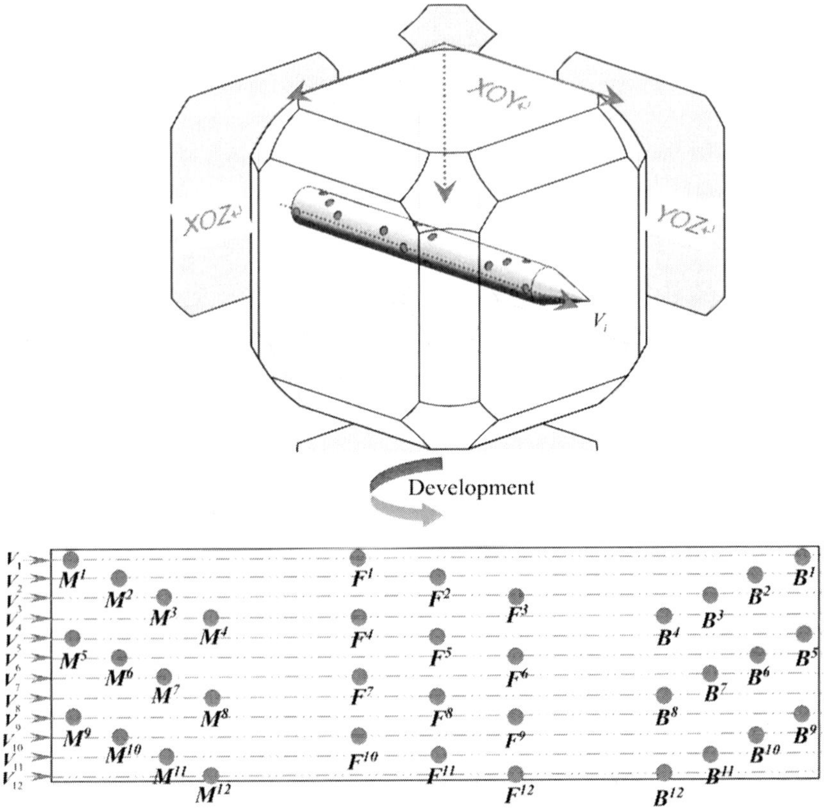


**Figure 10.** Spatial model of marker recognition.

# 4. POSITION AND ATTITUDE SOLUTION

The position and attitude parameters can be obtained by translating the coordinates from the local coordinate system on the slender rolling target to the world coordinate system through the translation and rotation matrix. Firstly, the axis of the slender rolling target is fitted by Case Deletion Diagnostics. Then the coordinates of the centroid can be solved based on the distance and axis constraint. Moreover, the absolute position method is applied to calculate the initial translation and rotation coordinate system which are used for the transformation, and at last the position and attitude information can be obtained.

## 4.1. Axis Fitting Based on Case Deletion Diagnostics

Errors caused by mismatching points have a great influence on the axis fitting solution. Thus, to guarantee the fitting precision, an axis fitting method based on Case Deletion Diagnostics is proposed to remove mismatched points. Case Deletion Diagnostic is commonly used to assess the influence of observations on the parameter estimators through subset deletion [16]. Utilizing the Case Deletion Diagnostic, the outlier or strong influence points are diagnosed by comparing the statistic difference between the deleted model and un-deleted model, thus the gross errors can be removed. Specifically, suppose that the data is $P=\{P_1,P_2,\ldots,P_n\}$, when removing the $i$th data point, if there is a difference between the deleted model and the un-deleted model, the outlier or strong influence points can be obtained, otherwise we can acquire the correct points which have little impact on statistical results.

Let the total number of the markers be $n$ and at least nine markers can be collected according to markers layout. Then the point set under the world coordinate system can be given by:

$$P=\{P_1,P_2,\cdots,P_n\} \tag{8}$$

$$P_i=(x_i,y_i,z_i),(i=1,2,\cdots,n) \tag{9}$$

where $(x_i,y_i,z_i)$ describe the 3D coordinates of point $P_i$ in the world coordinate system. $P$ stands for a point set. Case Deletion Diagnostic $M_w(\vartheta)$ for axis fitting can be set up as follows:

(1) The point set is applied to fit the axis equation *L* according to the theoretical radius *r* which represents the distance between markers and axis.

(2) The parameter estimators $\vartheta$ can be expressed as:

$$\theta = \sqrt{\sum_{i=1}^{n}\left(d\left(p_i\right)-r\right)^2} \tag{10}$$

where $d(p_i)$ is the euclidean distance from point $p_i$ to axis $L$; axis $\hat{L}$ for slender rolling target can be obtained after deleting the point $p_w$.

(3)

The estimated value $\hat{\vartheta}$ of parameter estimators can be given by:

$$\hat{\theta} = \sqrt{\sum_{i=1, i\neq w}^{n}\left(\hat{d}\left(p_i\right)-r\right)^2} \tag{11}$$

The judgment that whether the point $p_w$ is outlier or strong influence point can be expressed as:

$$\left|\hat{\theta}-\theta\right| \leq \varepsilon \tag{12}$$

where $\varepsilon$ represents the threshold defined above. When the above inequality is satisfied, we can get the result that point $p_w$ is a normal point, otherwise it is a strong influence point. The initial point set for Case Deletion Diagnostic $M_w(\vartheta)$ is all the markers collected. Every point is judged one by one, and a point within the set can be removed if it is outlier or strong influence point. Afterwards, the axis can be solved stably using the LM optimizing algorithm:

$$\begin{cases} \min \sqrt{\sum_{i=1}^{n} \left( d(p_i) - r \right)^2} \\ s.t. \quad \dfrac{x - x_0}{m} = \dfrac{y - y_0}{n} = \dfrac{z - z_0}{p} \\ d(p_i) = \dfrac{\sqrt{\begin{vmatrix} \dfrac{y_i - y_0}{n} & \dfrac{z_i - z_0}{p} \end{vmatrix} + \begin{vmatrix} \dfrac{z_i - z_0}{p} & \dfrac{z_i - x_0}{m} \end{vmatrix} + \begin{vmatrix} \dfrac{x_i - x_0}{m} & \dfrac{y_i - y_0}{n} \end{vmatrix}}}{\sqrt{m^2 + n^2 + p^2}} \end{cases} \tag{13}$$

where $P_0(x_0,y_0,z_0)$ stands for one point on the fitted axis; $L(m,n,p)$ is the direction vector of axis; $d(p_i)$ represents the distance between point $P_i(x_i,y_i,z_i)$ and the fitted axis.

## 4.2. Solution for Centroid Position Based on Distance Constraint

The centroid coordinates can be solved based on the distance constraint between markers. In this paper, about nine to twelve markers can be extracted according to the layout design. In order to improve the centroid coordinates' precision, optimization based on the distance between all markers captured and centroid are carried out. However, the aforementioned distance is different, and the extracted markers have different degrees of brightness and circularity. These factors have a different impact on the precision of the centroid coordinates. Thus, multi-points optimization based on setting weight for every point is presented. Since the centroid is on the axis, the centroid position can be optimized according to axis position calculated *via* Section 4.1. The optimization formula can be given by:

$$\begin{cases} \min\left(\sum_{i=1}^{n} \rho_i (Dc_i - dc_i)^2\right) \\ s.t. \quad \dfrac{x_c - x_0}{m} = \dfrac{y_c - y_0}{n} = \dfrac{z_c - z_0}{p} \end{cases} \tag{14}$$

where $\rho_i$ represents the weight value of each captured marker; $Dc_i$ stands for the measured distance between the centroid and the optimized markers; $dc_i$ is the real distance between the centroid and optimized markers; $C(x_c,y_c,z_c)$ is the centroid coordinate; $L(m,n,p)$ stands for the direction vector of the axis.

### 4.3. Absolute Pose Solution

In this paper, a pose acquisition method is carried out according to the aforementioned marker layout. Two coordinate systems–the initial reference coordinate system (IRCS) and the local coordinate system (LRCS), are established to acquire the pose information of the target through coordinate transformation. The IRCS represents the reference coordinate system set up at the first frame, while the LRCS means the local coordinate system set up at the frame of the measuring position.

As shown in Figure 11, when the axis fitting is finished (Section 4.1) and the centroid position determined (Section 4.2), the centroid of target $P_1$ is set as the origin of the reference coordinate system and the axis of the target is defined as the Y axis of the reference coordinate system.

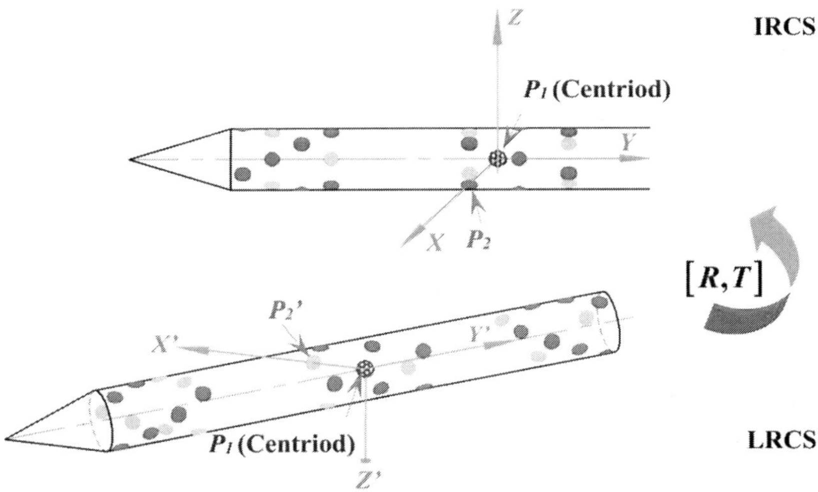


**Figure 11.** Schematic of the principal of absolute pose solution.

Moreover, since the X axis can be defined by any marker captured by cameras with high image quality, the optimum marker $P_2$ is chosen as the definition point. As a result, the space line through the centroid of the target parallel to the line through $P_2$ and perpendicular to the rotation axis of the target is defined as the X axis. Then, according to the right-handed coordinate system, the reference coordinate system can be set up.

To obtain the pose parameters, it is necessary to establish local coordinate system using the same marker $P_2$. However, marker $P_2$ may not be captured at the position measuring frame owing to the hidden markers phenomenon caused by the rolling movement. In order to establish the local coordinate system, the three-dimensional coordinates of all visible makers at the frame of the measuring position are reconstructed. Then, based on the recognition of visible markers and markers layout, the three-dimensional coordinates of the center of marker $P_2$ can be acquired. Afterwards, the local coordinate system can be obtained using the same establishment principle for the reference coordinate system.

The relationship between the point $p = (x \ \ y \ \ z)^T$ in IRCS and the corresponding $p' = (x' \, y' \, z')^T$ in LRCS can be written by:

$$\begin{bmatrix} x' \\ y' \\ z' \end{bmatrix} = R_{pt} \begin{bmatrix} x - x_0 \\ y - y_0 \\ z - z_0 \end{bmatrix} \tag{15}$$

where $(x_0 \ y_0 \ z_0)$ is the coordinates of the origin of the target in IRCS. Moreover:

$$R \begin{bmatrix} x \\ y \\ z \end{bmatrix} + T = \begin{bmatrix} x' \\ y' \\ z' \end{bmatrix} \tag{16}$$

where:

$$R = R_{\theta_Y} R_{\theta_X} R_{\theta_Z}$$
$$= \begin{bmatrix} \cos(\theta_Y)\cos(\theta_Z) - \sin(\theta_Y)\sin(\theta_X)\sin(\theta_Z) & \cos(\theta_Y)\sin(\theta_Z) + \sin(\theta_Y)\sin(\theta_X)\cos(\theta_Z) & -\sin(\theta_Y)\cos(\theta_X) \\ -\cos(\theta_X)\sin(\theta_Z) & \cos(\theta_X)\cos(\theta_Z) & \sin(\theta_X) \\ \sin(\theta_Y)\cos(\theta_Z) + \cos(\theta_Y)\sin(\theta_X)\sin(\theta_Z) & \sin(\theta_Y)\sin(\theta_Z) - \cos(\theta_Y)\sin(\theta_X)\cos(\theta_Z) & \cos(\theta_Y)\cos(\theta_X) \end{bmatrix} \tag{17}$$

As a result, the centroid position of the target in the world coordinate system can be represented by $T_{pb} = (x_0 \ y_0 z_0)$; $-\vartheta_Z$, $-\vartheta_X$, $-\vartheta_Y$ represent the three attitude parameters of the target in the world coordinate system: the yaw, pitch and roll. According to the coordinates of the chosen points mentioned above, the position and attitude parameters of the target can be computed.

## 5. EXPERIMENTAL ANALYSIS

Experiments on pose measurement of the target in a wind tunnel are conducted in this paper, as well as the precision verification test. In this section, the measurement precision of the three directions and three angles is verified.

### 5.1. Vision Measurement System

A wind tunnel is a dark narrow enclosure which can only be monitored by an observation window with a fixed shape. According to the actual wind tunnel structures, an ultra high-speed binocular vision measurement system is set up, as shown in Figure 12. The binocular vision measurement system contains two high-speed cameras (FASTCAM SA-X), two wide-angle lenses (Nikon 1735), two low angle lights, a shockproof platform, two electronic control platforms and a processing terminal. To minimize the influence of vibrations caused by the wind tunnel at runtime, the two cameras are placed symmetrically on a customized air flotation shockproof table. The camera system is installed on the electric control platform so that it can be translated and rotated as designed. The low angle DC lights are installed on the edge of the lenses to ensure the light requirements of images are met.

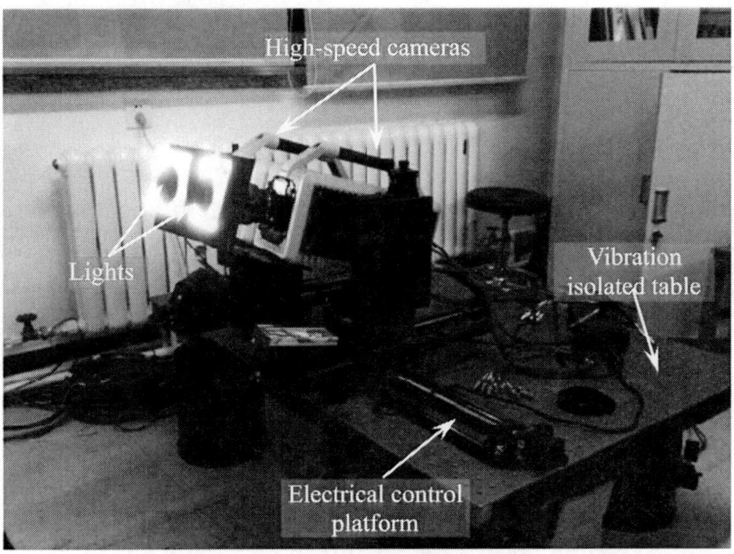


**Figure 12.** Mechanical support and hardware for cameras.

## 5.2. Measurement Experiment for Rotary Target in Wind Tunnel

As shown in Figure 13, the experimental facilities consist of a pose measurement system based on binocular vision, an ejection mechanism and a controlling system.

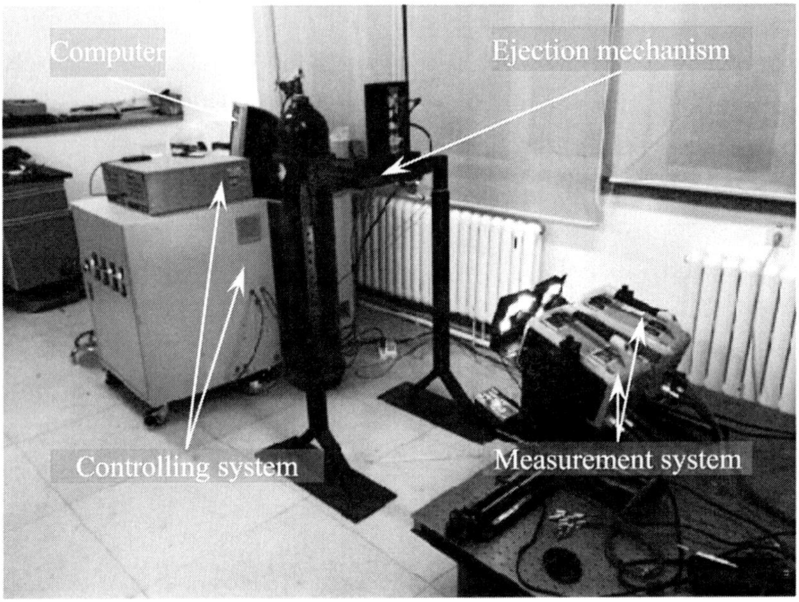


**Figure 13.** Layout of experimental facilities.

In the test with measurement field of 1 m × 1 m and measurement rate of 5000 fps, the ejection mechanism and controlling system are utilized to eject the target out of the tank with a particular velocity, angular velocity and angle. The vision measurement system is triggered to measure the pose information of the target synchronously. Based on the aforementioned method, the pose measurement resulte of the rolling target are verified.

To calculate the actual pose parameters of the target, experiments were conducted in a closed supersonic wind tunnel (FL-3). The facility layout for the wind tunnel tests is shown in Figure 14.

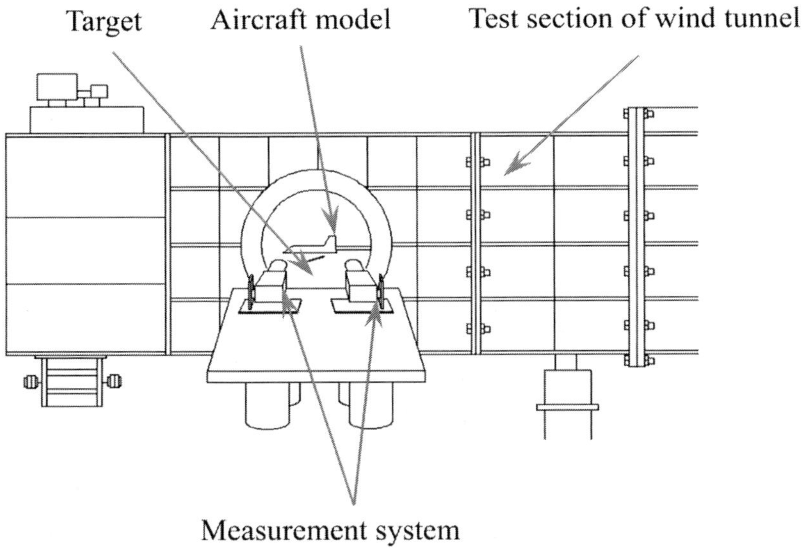


**Figure 14.** Facility layout for the wind tunnel test.

Specifically, an aircraft model is installed in the inner wall of the test section, and the ejection mechanism is installed in the ejection cabin of the aircraft model. Besides, the measurement system is arranged outside of the test section to measure the pose parameters of the object in real time through the observation window.

Quick pose measurements of the high-speed and rolling target with different inertia parameters under different Mach wind speeds are conducted. For instance, tests under 0.2 Ma, 0.4 Ma and 1.5 Ma, are completed in the transonic wind tunnel. Afterwards, the pose parameters can be given in the wind tunnel coordinate system, in which the *X*-axis and *Y*-axis are parallel to the airflow direction and the direction of gravity, respectively. Additionally, one point on the airplane cabin door is selected as the origin of the wind tunnel coordinate system and the *Z*-axis is established according to the right-handed system. The measured results for certain types of targets with 1.5 Mach speed are depicted in the following diagrams. The results of the position measurement are shown in Figure 15, and the results of the attitude measurement are shown in Figure 16.

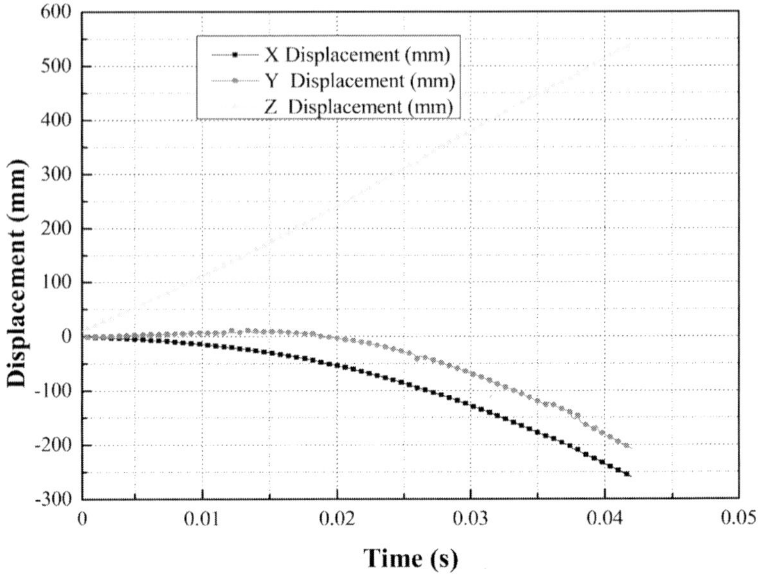


**Figure 15.** The results of the position measurement in the wind tunnel.

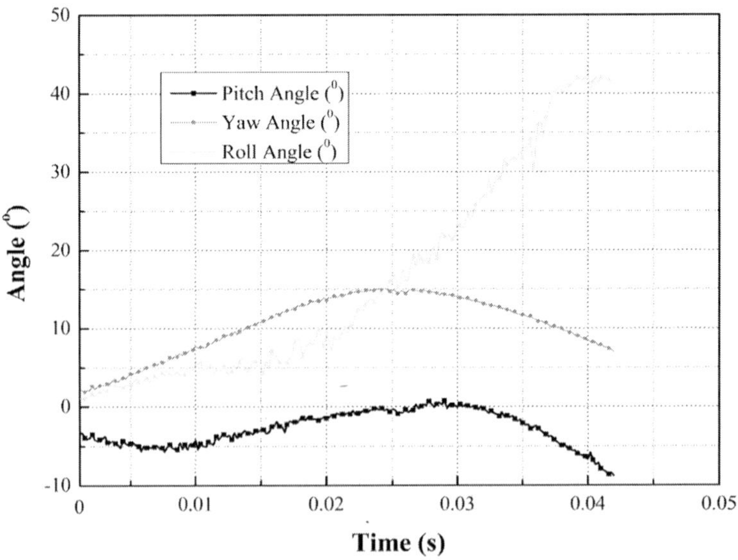


**Figure 16.** The results of the attitude measurement in wind tunnel.

Experimental results indicate that the quick intellectualized pose measurement of the target can be guaranteed by the proposed method and established measurement system. According to the experimental analysis, three main factors affect the pose measurement accuracy: (a) Problems such as large measuring range, limitation of the resolution of the ultra-high speed camera directly affect pose measurement precision of the target; (b) The extraction accuracy of the markers is affected due to factors such as small volume, surface profile of markers and random deformation during the rolling process.

## 5.3. Precision Verification Test in Laboratory

In this paper, targets are fixed on a high precision motion control stage. The *X, Y, Z* axis position measurement precision is verified through shooting the movement of targets when the motion control stage moves a fixed distance along the *X, Y, Z* axis direction with high precision. Then the attitude measurement precision of the measurement system is verified with the target rotating around the *X, Y, Z* axis with a fixed angle.

The experimental facilities are shown as Figure 17. For each camera, a high precision motion control stage combining a displacement platform and a rotary platform is built. With a position precision of 0.001 mm, the motion control stage is used to implement the specified moving distance of targets. Twenty four displacement accuracy verification test runs were conducted, and the target moved 20 mm in each run. Twenty four angle accuracy verification test runs were also conducted, where the target rotated five degrees around the three axes, respectively, in each run. The displacement measurement precision in each run is depicted in Figure 18. The measured angle precision in each run is shown Figure 19.

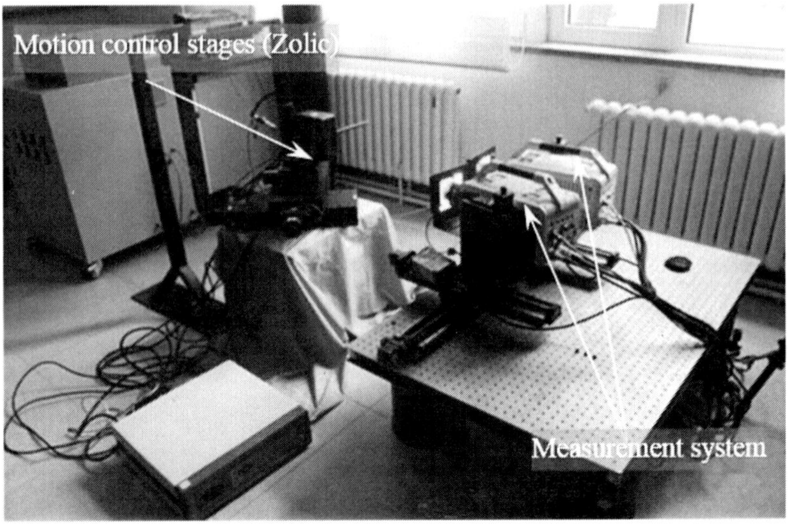


**Figure 17.** The calibration diagram of measurement system.

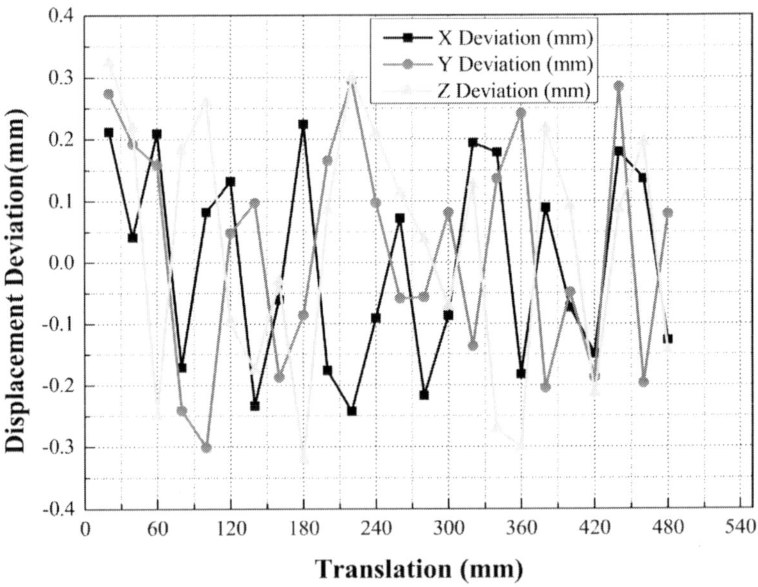


**Figure 18.** The position measurement precision.

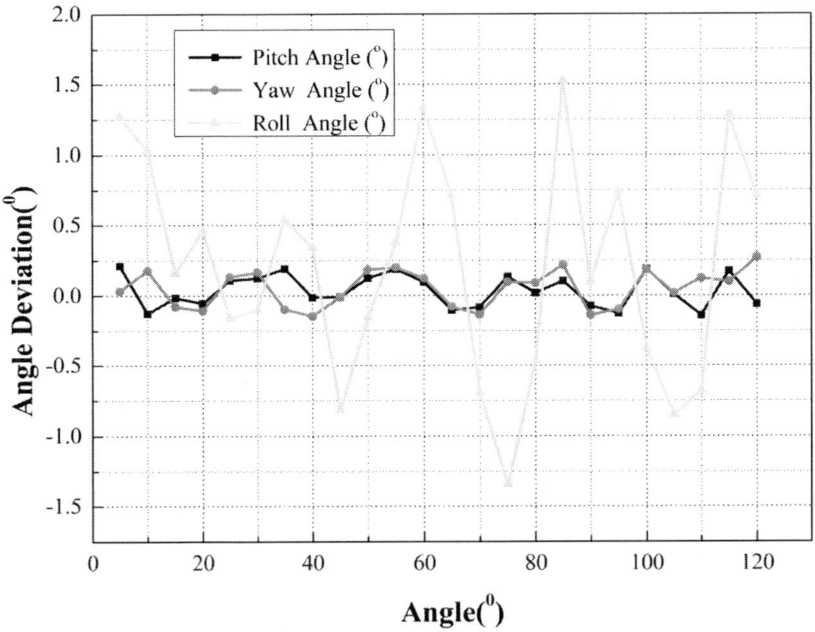


**Figure 19.** The angle measurement precision.

As shown in Figures 18 and 19, the mean square error of the displacement measurement in the X direction is 0.13 mm, while in the Y direction it is 0.14 mm, and in the Z direction 0.16 mm. The main errors mainly come from errors in the markers' center extraction and camera calibration. The mean square error of the pitching angle precision is 0.115°, and that of the yaw angle precision 0.132°. The high-precision solution of the measurement system for pitching angle and yaw angle results from the high-precision of axis fitting. The roll angle precision is 0.712°, mainly due to the small diameter of the object to be tested. In conclusion, the experimental results indicate that the proposed method can exhibit high accuracy for the position and attitude measurement of high-speed and rolling targets in a wind tunnel.

# 6. CONCLUSIONS

In this paper, we have presented a pose measurement method for wind tunnel tests to measure high-speed and rolling targets. A high-speed image sequence acquisition method based on ultrathin retro-reflection markers is presented to ensure high brightness and SNR. Ultrathin retro-reflection markers attached on the surface of a target by a rolling-printed method is as thin as 20 μm, guaranteeing the aerodynamic shape of the scaled model.

A novel marker layout on the basis of spatial coding is proposed to ensure that markers are distributed evenly on the target surface and to achieve high-accuracy pose information. This layout overcomes the problem of the information loss of markers when the target is rolling and ensures matching, so that accurate marker recognition can be obtained.

Moreover, a pose parameter computing method is proposed according to the markers' 3D coordinates. Besides, an axis fitting method based on Case Deletion Diagnostic can increase the stability of the measurement system and reduce the errors caused by mismatching.

The experimental results described above indicate that the proposed pose measurement system and method can achieve high accuracy and stability, and meets the requirements of wind tunnel tests. Finally, the rapid pose measurement with high precision for rolling targets is accomplished in a transonic wind tunnel environment, and good results are achieved. Our future research will focus on improving the pose measurement precision by algorithm optimization.

# ACKNOWLEDGMENTS

This paper is supported by the National Natural Science Foundation of China (Grant No. 51375075), and the Scientific Research Fund of Liaoning Provincial Education Department (Grant No. L2013035), and the Science Fund for Creative Research Groups of China (Grant No. 51321004).

## AUTHOR CONTRIBUTIONS

Zhenyuan Jia and Wei Liu developed the pose measurement method; Xin Ma proposed the ultrathin retro-reflection marker fabrication technique; Wei Liu was responsible for the recognition and matching of images; Xiao Li and Ling Chen participated in the design of the experimental facilities for the wind tunnel; Wenbo Lu, Zhengqu Wang and Xiaochun Cui carried out the wind tunnel tests and the most of the analyses. All authors wrote the paper together.

## CONFLICTS OF INTEREST

The authors declare no conflict of interest.

## REFERENCES

1. Lee, J.J.; Ho, H.N.; Lee, J.H. A. Vision-based dynamic rotational angle measurement system for large civil structures. *Sensors* **2012**, *12*, 7326–7336.

2. Marrón-Romera, M.; García, J.C.; Sotelo, M.A.; Pizarro, D.; Mazo, M.; Cañas, J.M.; Losada, C. Marcos, Á. Stereo vision tracking of multiple objects in complex indoor environments. *Sensors* **2010**, *10*, 8865–8887.

3. Newman, B.; Yu, S. *Development of a High Accuracy Angular Measurement System for Langley Research Center Hypersonic Wind Tunnel Facilities*; Langley Research Center: Hampton, VA, USA; August; 2003.

4. Park, H.S.; Kim, J.Y.; Kim, J.G.; Choi, S.W.; Kim, Y. A new position measurement system using a motion-capture camera for wind tunnel tests. *Sensors* **2013**, *13*, 12329–12344.

5. Watzlavick, R.L.; Crowder, J.P.; Wright, F.L. Comparison of model attitude systems—Active target photogrammetry, precision accelerometer, and laser interferometer. Proceedings of 19th Advanced Measurement and Ground Testing Conference, New Orleans, LA, USA, 17–20 June 1996.

6. Rock, S.M.; Frew, E.W.; Jones, H.; LeMaster, E.A.; Woodley, B.R. Combined CDGPS and vision-based control of a small autonomous helicopter. Proceedings of the American Control Conference, Philadelphia, PA, USA, 21–26 June 1998; pp. 694–698.

7. Jones, T.; Lunsford, C. Design and development of a real-time model attitude measurement system for hypersonic facilities. Proceedings of 43rd AIAA Aerospace Sciences Meeting and Exhibit, Reno, NV, USA, 10–13 January 2005.

8. Crawford, B.L.; Rhode, M.N. Miniature on-board angle of attack measurement system for hypersonic facilities. Proceedings of 25th AIAA Aerodynamic Measurement Technology and Ground Testing Conference, San Francisco, CA, USA, 5–8 June 2006.

9. Burner, A.W.; Fleming, G.A.; Hoppe, J.C. Comparison of three optical methods for measuring mode deformation. Proceedings of 38th Aerospace Sciences Meeting & Exhibit, Reno, NV, USA, 10–13 January 2000.

10. Graves, S.S.; Burner, A.W. Development of an intelligent videogrammetric wind tunnel measurement system. Processing of Optical Diagnostics for Fluids, Solids, and Combustion, San Diego, CA, USA, 29 July 2001.

11. Murray, E.N.; Jansen, J.B.; Gui, L.C.; Seiner, M.J.; Birkbeck, R. Measurements of store separation dynamics. Proceedings of 47th AIAA Aerospace Sciences Meeting including The New Horizons Forum and Aerospace Exposition, Orlando, FL, USA, 5–8 January 2009.

12. Chen, J.C.; Guo, M.; Ding, Z.L.; Yuan, F. Stereo vision based attitude measurement of aircraft model in wind tunnel. *J. Appl. Opt.* **2010**, *31*, 437–441.

13. Fan, Q.; Wu, Y.; Hui, J. Integrated navigation fusion strategy of INS/UWB for indoor carrier attitude angle and position synchronous tracking. *Sci. World J.* **2014**, *13*, 1–13.

14. Zhang, Z.Y. Camera calibration with one-dimensional objects. *IEEE Trans. Pattern Anal. Mach. Intell.* **2004**,*26*, 892–899.

15. Brown, L.G. A survey of image registration techniques. *ACM Comput. Surv.* **1992**, *24*, 325–376.

16. Christensen, R.; Pearson, L.M.; Johnson, W. Case Deletion Diagnostics for mixed models. *Technometrics***1992**, *34*, 38–45.

# Chapter 8

## Gradual Reduction in Sodium Content in Cooked Ham, with Corresponding Change in Sensorial Properties Measured by Sensory Evaluation and a Multimodal Machine Vision System

**Kirsti Greiff, John Reidar Mathiassen, Ekrem Misimi, Margrethe Hersleth, Ida G. Aursand**

*SINTEF Fisheries and Aquaculture, Trondheim, Norway, Department of Biotechnology, Norwegian University of Science and Technology, Trondheim, Norway*

### ABSTRACT

The European diet today generally contains too much sodium ($Na^+$). A partial substitution of NaCl by KCl has shown to be a promising method for reducing sodium content. The aim of this work was to investigate the sensorial changes of cooked ham with reduced sodium content. Traditional sensorial evaluation and objective multimodal *machine vision* were used. The salt content in the hams was decreased from 3.4% to 1.4%, and 25% of the $Na^+$was replaced by $K^+$. The salt reduction had highest influence on the sensory attributes salty taste, after taste, tenderness, hardness and color hue. The multimodal machine vision system showed changes in lightness, as a function of reduced salt content. Compared to the reference ham (3.4% salt), a replacement of $Na^+$-ions by $K^+$-ions of 25% gave no significant changes in WHC, moisture, pH, expressed moisture, the sensory profile attributes or the surface lightness and shininess. A further reduction of salt down to 1.7–1.4% salt, led to a decrease in WHC and an increase in expressible moisture.

## INTRODUCTION

A high consumption of sodium has been directly associated with a greater likelihood of increased blood pressure, which in turn has been directly related to the development of cardiovascular and renal diseases [1]. For these reasons, national and international bodies have set targets for a reduction in sodium consumption down to 2 g/day [2–4].

Due to the low fat content, cooked ham is a good source of animal protein in the diet. Usually when manufacturing cooked ham, the pork meat is coarsely ground into pieces that are tumbled with brine (containing water, salt, nitrite and other ingredients such as phosphate and polysaccharides). During the tumbling with brine, the salt- soluble myofibrillar proteins are extracted and they form a network. The network gels during the heating and chilling process [5], thereby solidifying the ham and minimizing cooking loss. Reducing salt contents in cooked ham increases cooking loss [6] and thereby the production costs.

Sodium chloride is added to a wide variety of foods to increase shelf life and palatability (e.g. in soups, meat products, bread, sauces and snacks). When it comes to sensory quality, sodium chloride contributes to saltiness and the overall flavor, while also suppressing bitterness [7]. Accordingly, the development of palatable sodium-reduced products is important in order to guide consumers towards more healthy food choices. Partial substitution of NaCl by KCl has shown to be one of the best alternatives for reducing sodium content [5, 8]. Studies have shown that KCl induces a bitter taste at high concentrations, in dry-cured loins [9], fermented sausage [10] and cooked ham [11]. Those results show that the maximum level of KCl replacement may vary among different type of product.

It is essential to characterize and understand the sensory effects of sodium reduction in foods. Sensory analysis is the most appropriate approach to fully describe the sensory perception of foods and descriptive profiling has been a popular sensory technique for cognitive descriptions of products in many years. These techniques give a complete sensory description of products and make it possible to identify underlying ingredient and process variables [12]. For measurement of flavor, no instruments currently exist, that can replace the human senses and describe the sensory perception. For appearance and texture attributes, the situation is different, as there are several examples of studies where instrumental data representing appearance and texture attributes, show a strong correlation with data from trained sensory panels [13–16].

In particular, classification of ham qualities (pork and turkey) is possible based on color and textural features extracted from digital color images. Logistic regression, used on these features, could to a large degree explain consumers' responses for visually-based sensorial attributes [13]. The qualities of pork ham could be distinguished based on visual texture characteristics extracted from fractal analysis of digital color images [16]. This showed that the fractal-based features are able to quantify quality-specific visual texture characteristics. A combination of geometric and texture features, extracted from digital color images, were input to multivariate classifiers, including artificial neural networks (ANNs), and were capable of predicting meat tenderness–as measured by shear force [17]. The eating quality of beef could be predicted from wavelet surface texture and other texture features extracted from digital color images. For the optical setup, a polarizer filter was placed on the lens and the meat pieces were surface-dried to mitigate some specular reflection [14]. Other machine vision approaches have been designed specifically to improve the objective analysis of color and texture in transclucent or semi-transparent muscle foods [18]. These works and others [15, 19] show that computer vision, with optimal illumination in combination with appropriate feature extraction and classifiers, can be used to predict sensorial properties from digital color images.

The effect of reduced salt/sodium content on cooked ham has previously been investigated by different authors [5, 20, 21], but nobody, to the best of our knowledge, has used the combination of sensorial Descriptive Analysis (DA) and multimodal *machine vision systemto* investigate the changes in the sensorial properties in cooked ham with effect of reduced salt/sodium content. In this paper, a proof-of-concept novel dual-polarization multimodal machine vision system is used, that is new to meat imaging [22].

The aim of this study was to investigate sensory quality of cooked pork ham containing gradually reduced salt/sodium content and a partial replacement of sodium ($Na^+$) by ($K^+$). The product quality parameters addressed were physicochemical and sensory properties obtained by sensory descriptive analyses and a multimodal *machine vision system*.

# MATERIALS AND METHODS

## Samples and Chemicals

*Cooked ham preparation.*

Eight different formulas of cooked hams were manufactured by Espeland AS, Ålgård, Norway 26–28 February 2013. Each of the formulas contained 20 kg of fresh coarsely grounded (perforated disc with hole size 30 mm), lean pork meat (*M. semimembranosus, M.adductor, M. semitendinosus, M. biceps femoris and M. psoas major)*, obtained from a local meat processing company (PrimaGruppen, Norway) four days after slaughtering. The samples are identified with sample IDs having the following codes: Na100, NaK100, NaK80, NaK60, NaK40, NaK20, which vary in the % of the amount of NaCl relative to the reference (Na100) and addition of potassium (NaK). See Table 1 for details. Reference cooked ham (Na100) had no added potassium, containing only potassium naturally occurring in the meat (approximately 330 mg $K^+$/100g). The amount of sodium in the reference (Na100) in the formulation was at same level as in a commercially cooked ham, 1.24 g $Na^+$/100g, corresponding to 3.1% salt. The mole ratio of sodium ($Na^+$) and potassium ($K^+$) was kept constant ($Na^+$: $K^+$ = 3:1) in all formulas containing potassium (NaK), were the contribution of all sodium and potassium in all ingredients were taken into account. The salt (NaCl) content (g/100g) was calculated as: added $Na^+$ (including natural sodium content in the meat) x 2.5 (recalculation factor for NaCl from $Na^+$), according on the provision of food information to consumers [23]. The amount of total salt content in the formulation was gradually decreased to 20% of the amount of the salt in the reference cooked ham, corresponding to 1.3% salt (NaK20). The brine solution for each formulation was prepared by dissolving 200 g commercial phosphate mixture (57% $P_2O_5$)(A. B. Corneliussen AS, Norway), 150 g gelatin (Gelita Sweden AB, Sweden), 60 g carrageenan (CEAMSA, Pontverda, Spain), 450 g Na-lactate (Purac Biochem, Gorichem, The Netherlands) and 150 g maltodextrin (Avebe U.A., The Netherlands) in 2.5 L tap water (t = 2–4°C). All formulas, excluding the reference ham (Na100), were added 3.3 g sodium nitrite (Merck, KGaA Darmstadt, Germany). Commercial food salt containing nitrite salt (Hoff Norske Potetindustrier, Gjøvik, Norway) was added to the reference ham (Na100). Sodium chloride (Hoff Norske Potetindustrier, Gjøvik, Norway) and potassium chloride (Culinar Lyckeby, Sweden) were added to the brine to achieve the expected $Na^+$ and $K^+$ content as shown in Table 1.

The brine was added to the pork meat in a tumbler (Fatosa, Barcelona, Spain) without vacuum and massaged for 2 x 25 min, stored 20 h at 2°C, and then tumbled for 15 more min. The meat matrix was stuffed in to a plastic casing (160 mm in diameter, Viscofan S. A., Navarra, Spain). Two parallel production batches of the hams with formulation NaK100 and NaK60 were prepared to control the reproducibility of the production. Seven hams (3.0 kg) from each formulation were produced. The hams were pressed in molds and kept at 0–2°C for 20 h before cooking. The hams were cooked in a cooking chamber (Fessmann, Germany) until they reached a core temperature of 78°C, chilled down in tap water and kept in a cold-storage chamber at 0–2°C. Two of the hams per formula were sliced in 20 slices (16 ± 1 g) 12 days after production, and alternate

**Table 1.** Sample ID, description of the sample, estimated sodium, potassium and NaCl content in the preparation of the eight cooked hams. E Each formulation varied in its amount of total salt. The reference cooked ham contained nitrite salt (Na 100 Reference). In the rest of the formulas (NaK100, NaK80, NaK60, NaK40 and NaK20) the amount of total salt content was gradually decreased to 20% of the amount of the salt in the reference cooked ham. To keep the mole ratio of sodium ($Na^+$) and potassium ($K^+$) constant ($Na^+$: $K^+$ = 3:1), all contribution of sodium and potassium from the raw material and the ingredients was added when calculation of the mole ratio.

| Sample ID | Description | Estimated sodium content (g/100 g ham) | Estimated potassium content (g/100 g ham) | NaCl** (%) | % reduction of sodium compared to the reference |
|---|---|---|---|---|---|
| Na 100 | Reference ham | 1.24 | 0.28 | 3.1 | 0 |
| NaK 100_1* | 100% of the amount of salt in the reference | 1.06 | 0.61 | 2.6 | 14 |
| NaK 100_2* | 100% of the amount of salt in the reference | 1.06 | 0.61 | 2.6 | 14 |
| NaK 80 | 80% of the amount of salt in the reference | 0.93 | 0.53 | 2.3 | 25 |
| NaK 60_1* | 60% of the amount of salt in the reference | 0.80 | 0.46 | 2.0 | 35 |
| NaK 60_2* | 60% of the amount of salt in the reference | 0.80 | 0.46 | 2.0 | 35 |
| NaK 40 | 40% of the amount of salt in the reference | 0.67 | 0.38 | 1.7 | 46 |
| NaK 20 | 20% of the amount of salt in the reference | 0.53 | 0.31 | 1.3 | 57 |

* Produced twice to control the reproducibility of the production

** The salt content (%) is calculated by using the formula: added sodium ($Na^+$), including natural $Na^+$ content in the meat x 2.5 (recalculation factor for NaCl from $Na^+$)

of the slices were subjected to sensorial evaluation and analysis of machine vision, respectively. Sensorial evaluation and machine v directly after slicing. The remaining cooked hams ision analyses were carried out were stored at 4°C for 15 days after production before chemical analysis. In addition, one slice (approximately 100 g) was used for further analysis.

## Chemicals.

Ammonium chloride ($NH_4Cl$), ammonium hydroxide ($NH_4OH$) and ammonium hydrogen fluoride ($NH_4FHF$ < 1%, $LD_{50}$ mg/kg not found) of analytical-reagent grade (Thermo Fisher Scientific, USA). Chemicals of food grade: sodium tripoly phosphate ($Na_5P_3O_{10}$) (A. B. Corneliussen AS, Norway), Na-lactate ($C_3H_5NaO_3$) (Purac Biochem, Gorichem, The

Netherlands) and sodium nitrite ($NNaO_2$)(Merck, KGaA Darmstadt, Germany).

## Imaging Setup and Image Acquisition

The imaging system consisted of a ColorRanger multimodal line-scan camera (SICK IVP AB, Linköping, Sweden), two high-intensity white LED linear array lights (Banner Engineering, Minneapolis, MN, USA), with polarizers on the LED arrays and in front of the camera lens. Additionally, a nematic liquid crystal industrial-grade polarization rotator (ARCoptix SA, Neuchâtel, Switzerland) was placed in front of the polarizer on the camera lens. The polarization rotator is controlled by the image acquisition PC and enables effectively to rotate the polarizer on the lens by means of an electric signal. The purpose of rotating the polarizer direction on the lens polarizer relative to the polarizer on the LEDs, was to be able to capture light reflected from the object for two polarization states.

The experiment sought to separately image the subsurface color and the surface color of the ham slices, in order to separately image the light that was scattered in the subsurface from the light that was directly reflected off the surface. Subsurface imaging revealed the bulk color of the ham near the surface, whereas surface imaging revealed the surface roughness, shininess and other effects such as "mother-of-pearl" appearance commonly seen in some hams. To separate the subsurface from the surface image, two images were acquired–an image $I_{\parallel}$ with LED and camera polarizers oriented parallel to each other, and an image $I_{\perp}$ with the polarizers oriented perpendicular to each other. Image $I_{\parallel}$ will image both the subsurface and the surface components, whereas $0049_{\perp}$ will image the subsurface components only, and hence the difference $I_{\parallel}—I_{\perp}$ between the two images will image only the surface components of the light. This principle of light interactions as a function of polarization state is illustrated in images in Fig 1.

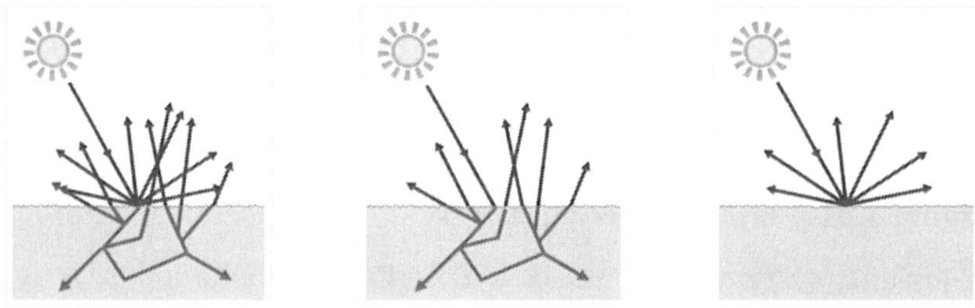


**Figure 1.** Illustration of the components of light interacting with the imaged raw material, imaged using parallel polarizers (left), crossed polarizers (middle) and the difference between the two (right).

The extracted imaging features were simply the mean of the red, green and blue ($r,g,b$) values, as acquired with the ColorRanger, over the entire ham slice and for both polarizer orientations. Thus, for each ham slice the ($r_{\parallel},g_{\parallel},b_{\parallel}$) and ($r_{\perp},g_{\perp},b_{\perp}$) values were obtained. The sum of ($r_{\perp},g_{\perp},b_{\perp}$) indicated the lightness of the sample and an increase either in $r_{\perp},g_{\perp}$ or$b_{\perp}$, indicated increased lightness. An average of nine slices per formulation of cooked hams, were used in the image acquisition experiment.

## Supplementary Image Acquisition

Image acquisition of the hams used for the sensory evaluation was done with a polycarbonate window in the imaging setup, which unfortunately affected the polarization of the imaged light. This resulted in suboptimal images. Therefore, only the blue channel images ($b_{\parallel}$ and $b_{\perp}$) were used for analysis and a supplementary image acquisition was done to obtain more optimal images. Here, the polycarbonate window was replaced with an optical grade AR-coated BK7 glass window. A supplementary production of cooked hams was conducted in the same manner as for the main experiment, and three formulation of cooked ham (Na100, NaK80 and NaK60) were manufactured for the supplementary image acquisition, solely for validation of *the multimodal imaging acquisition system*. The formulation, production process, and storage were similar to the cooked ham preparation as described above. An example set of images is seen in Fig 2. The images in Fig 2 are included in order to provide the reader with a visual understanding of the possibilities of using multi-modal imaging of cooked ham with dual polarization states.

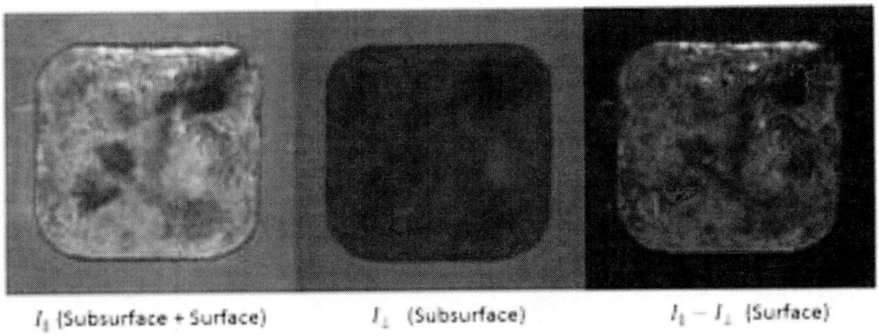


**Figure 2.** Images of a slice of ham, from supplementary Image Acquisition using parallel polarizers (left), crossed polarizers (middle) and the difference between the two (right).

## Chemical analysis

**Water activity** ($a_W$) was determined in cooked hams with a fast water activity-meter (GBX FAst/lab, Romans sur Isère Cedex, France). The **pH** measurements on light and dark muscle, in brine and cooked ham were carried out using a digital pH-meter WTW pH3110 (Weilheim, Germany) with a puncture electrode (WTW A 120513078, Weilheim, Germany). The **moisture** content was determined by drying three parallel samples of 5 g of minced cooked ham at 105°C for 24 hours [24]. **Water holding capacity (WHC)** was determined on minced cooked ham by low-speed centrifugation as described by Eide, Børresen [25] with a centrifugation force of 210 g. The WHC is expressed as the percentage of water retained in the mince after centrifugation for 5 min. The analyses were run in quadruplicate. **Sodium**contents in cooked hams were measured in an extract of the ham samples, using a Dual Star™ pH/ISE Meter (Thermo Fisher Scientific, Waltham, MA, USA) with a Na-selective electrode (Ross® Sodium Ion Selective Electrode, Thermo Fisher Scientific, Waltham, MA USA). For preparing the extract, 7.5g of ham was homogenized in ultra-pure water using an Ultra-turrax T-25 D (IKA, Labortechnik, Staufen, Germany) at 9000 rpm for 1 min. Then, samples were warmed up to 90°C for 30 min, cooled down to room temperature, transferred to a volumetric flask and diluted to 200 mL with ultra-pure water. Finally, samples were filtered through a cellulose filter paper (Whatman n° 1, Whatman International Ltd., Maidstone, UK). The Na-selective electrode method was a modification of the Kivikari [26] method. In this study the direct calibration method was used, whereas Kivikari, used the known addition method. A calibration curve was made by using three standards of analytical-grade NaCl from (Merck KGaA, Darmstadt, Germany) and Sodium ionic strength adjustor (Thermo Fisher Scientific, Waltham, MA, USA) was added to all solutions to ensure that samples and standards had similar ionic strength.

The modified method of Grau and Hamm [27] was used to measure **expressible moisture(EM)** for cooked hams. Samples were punched out with a hollow drill (25 mm in diameter) from cooked slices of hams (15 mm thick). Each sample was placed in the middle of ten filter papers (Whatman No. 1) and pressed down with a flat-ended cylindrical plunger (80 mm diameter), by single compression test mode and a test speed of 0.8 mm/s until 50% compression of total height, using a Texture Analyzer T.A.XT2 (Stable Micro System, Surrey, U.K.). Expressible moisture was determined as the amount of water released per gram of meat and was expressed in percentage.

## Sensory evaluation

Descriptive Analysis (DA) was conducted by a trained sensory panel according to Generic Descriptive Analysis as described by [12]. All assessors (n = 9) were selected and trained in accordance with ISO 8586–1 (ISO, 1993) and the test was done in a sensory laboratory designed in accordance with ISO 8589 (ISO, 2007). Each assessor evaluated all samples using EyeQuestion for direct recording of data (v3.8.7, Logic8, Elst(Gld), The Netherlands). A list of 21 attributes was generated from a brainstorming session with the assessors. This list included attributes representing appearance (color-hue, color intensity, whiteness, color evenness, shiny, marbling, cohesiveness, visible moist on surface), odor (sour, pork meat, metal), taste/flavor (sourness, sweetness, saltiness, bitterness, pork meat, metal, after flavor) and texture (hardness, juiciness, tenderness). Attributes were evaluated using a continuous, non-structured scale ranging from no intensity (1) on the left to high intensity (9) on the right. The assessors had previous experience with analyses of meat products including ham and were calibrated on selected attributes in a pre-test. DA was performed during 6 sessions on one day, in which 8 different hams were served in two replicates (totally 16 samples). The hams were sliced by a machine to a weight of 16 ± 1 g, and each assessor got one slice served per sample. Appearance attributes were evaluated on the surface of the ham slice, while the texture was evaluated biting over a rolled slice. The serving order was randomized across all sessions. All samples were expectorated and unsalted crackers and lukewarm water was available for rinsing.

## Data analysis

The influence of the different levels of sodium on physicochemical properties was studied through one-way analysis of variance (ANOVA), (Minitab 16, Minitab Inc.) In cases where the effect was defined as significant ($p<0.05$), the means were compared using Tukeys test to find the significant difference between the samples containing different amounts of salt.

PanelCheck 1.3.2 (www.panelcheck.com) was used to evaluate the panel performance in the pre-test. For determination of sensory attributes discriminating between samples, a two-way ANOVA with product as a fixed factor, panelist as a random factor and product x panelist as an interaction factor was performed. Tukey's Multiple Comparisons Test was applied to determine which products that was significantly different. The significance level was defined to $p<0.05$. (The ANOVA was run by SAS 9.2, SAS Institute, Inc., Cary, NS, USA).

# RESULTS AND DISCUSSION

## Chemical analysis

The results of the chemical analyses of cooked ham at different salt/sodium levels are summarized in Table 2.

**Table 2.** Water holding capasity (WHC), moisture, pH, sodium, salt and expressible moisture of cooked ham prepared with different levels of salt at constant $Na^+$: $K^+$ mole ratio 3:1. The reference cooked ham contained nitrite salt (Na 100 Reference). In the rest of the formulas (NaK100, NaK80, NaK60, NaK40 and NaK20) the amount of salt was gradually decreased to 20% of the amount of salt in the reference ham. Mean values ± SD (n3).

| | | | | | | |
|---|---|---|---|---|---|---|
| Na 100 | $78.45 \pm 1.03^{abc}$ | $74.58 \pm 0.23^{bc}$ | $6.16 \pm 0.02^{ab}$ | $1.35 \pm 0.17^{a}$ | $3.38 \pm 0.43^{a}$ | $0.96 \pm 0.30^{abc}$ |
| NaK 100_1 | $82.57 \pm 1.68^{a}$ | $73.63 \pm 0.26^{c}$ | $6.15 \pm 0.04^{ab}$ | $1.08 \pm 0.01^{b}$ | $2.70 \pm 0.03^{b}$ | $0.86 \pm 0.16^{ab}$ |
| NaK 100_2 | $80.59 \pm 0.50^{ab}$ | $73.67 \pm 0.15^{c}$ | $6.14 \pm 0.04^{a}$ | $1.03 \pm 0.04^{bc}$ | $2.58 \pm 0.10^{bc}$ | $0.84 \pm 0.16^{a}$ |
| NaK 80 | $81.55 \pm 1.13^{ab}$ | $74.40 \pm 0.14^{bc}$ | $6.19 \pm 0.02^{abcd}$ | $0.92 \pm 0.01^{cd}$ | $2.25 \pm 0.03^{cd}$ | $1.07 \pm 0.23^{de}$ |
| NaK 60_1 | $80.83 \pm 0.16^{ab}$ | $73.83 \pm 0.19^{a}$ | $6.21 \pm 0.02^{bcde}$ | $0.82 \pm 0.01^{de}$ | $2.05 \pm 0.03^{de}$ | $1.55 \pm 0.39^{de}$ |
| NaK 60_2 | $79.54 \pm 0.88^{abc}$ | $75.14 \pm 0.18^{ab}$ | $6.21 \pm 0.02^{bcd}$ | $0.81 \pm 0.01^{de}$ | $2.03 \pm 0.03^{de}$ | $1.12 \pm 0.17^{abcd}$ |
| NaK 40 | $76.31 \pm 0.25^{cde}$ | $75.43 \pm 0.28^{ab}$ | $6.24 \pm 0.02^{cdef}$ | $0.69 \pm 0.01^{ef}$ | $1.73 \pm 0.03^{ef}$ | $1.49 \pm 0.23^{cde}$ |
| NaK 20 | $72.71 \pm 1.83^{de}$ | $75.40 \pm 0.46^{ab}$ | $6.25 \pm 0.01^{def}$ | $0.55 \pm 0.01^{f}$ | $1.38 \pm 0.03^{f}$ | $1.96 \pm 0.35^{e}$ |
| p-value | 0.000 | 0.000 | 0.000 | 0.000 | 0.000 | 0.000 |

a-g Different upper-case letters within a column indicate significant differences ($p<0.005$) between different groups. Means that do not share a common letter are significantly different.

## Sodium content

The salt contents (%) in the cooked ham were calculated as measured $Na^+$-content multiplied with 2.5. The measured sodium content in the reference ham (Na 100 added as $Na^+$—ions only) was 1.35 g $Na^+$/100 g, this result was slightly higher than estimated in the formulation of the sample, 1.24 g $Na^+$/100g. The rest of the hams, were prepared with different levels of total salt including a constant $Na^+$:$K^+$ mol ratio of 3:1, and the measured sodium content were in good agreement with the estimated in the formulation.

## Water holding capacity (WHC)

As expected, a decrease in WHC was observed in hams where the salt content was reduced by 60% (NaK40) and 80% (NaK20) (on molar basis), corresponding to a measured salt content of 1.73 and 1.38% salt, respectively. These results are in accordance with Hamm (1972) and Offer & Knight (1988) who found that sodium chloride increases the water-binding of meat [28, 29]. Albarracín, Sánchez [30] explained that increased WHC in meat, resulting from increasing salt content, is due to the anions ($Cl^-$) preferentially binding to protein molecules. The moisture content in hams added a mixture of sodium and potassium salt without reduction of the total salt, 2.70% salt (NaK100) was significant lower than in cooked ham containing 1.38% salt (NaK20).

## pH

The pH in the raw material was within the range of 5.5–5.8. These pH values are similar to typical ultimate pH values in Norwegian pork [31]. The pH of the hams increased from pH 6.15 ± 0.02 to 6.25 ± 0.01 with decreasing sodium content. The pH in hams with the lowest levels of sodium, 1.73% salt (NaK40) and 1.38% salt (NaK20), were significant higher than the reference containing 3.38% salt (Na100) and the cooked ham with the mixture of sodium and potassium salt (NaK100). These findings are in accordance with Puolanne, Ruusunen [32], who found an average decrease, about 0.1 pH-units/%-units of salt, in cooked sausages.

## Expressible moisture

The expressible moisture increased with decreasing salt/sodium content, and those hams containing 1.38% salt (NaK20) had significantly higher expressible moisture than those containing 3.38% salt (Na 100).

## Water activity ($a_w$)

The $a_w$ decreased slightly from 0.97 to 0.96 with increasing salt content, although the differences were not significant (data not shown). According to Mossel, Corry [33], such levels of $a_w$ in cooked hams were too high to represent a hurdle for unwanted spoilage- and pathogenic microorganisms.

Compared to the reference ham (Na100), a replacement of $Na^+$-ions by 25% of $K^+$-ions gave no significant changes in WHC, moisture, pH or expressible moisture. This replacement results in a total sodium content of approximately 1.1 g /100g cooked ham. This finding is in accordance with Zanardi, Ghidini [34] who found no effects on pH and water activity in reduced sodium when replacing ($Na^+$) by a mixture of KCl, $CaCl_2$ and $MgCl_2$in Cacciatore salami compared to the traditional recipe.

### Descriptive sensory profile

Table 3 gives an overview of the mean values for the significant sensory attributes plus the attributes whiteness and shiny, as appearance attributes were most relevant for data from vision analysis. The table shows significance for 8 out of a total of 21 sensory attributes.

**Table 3.** Sensory properties in the cooked hams.

| | Apperance | | | | Taste and odour | | | | Texture | |
|---|---|---|---|---|---|---|---|---|---|---|
| Group | Colour hue | Cohesiveness | Whiteness | Shiny | Salty taste | Metal flavour | Metal odour | After taste | Tenderness | Hardness |
| Na 100 | $6.67^{abc}$ | $6.97^{ab}$ | $5.61^{ab}$ | 3.71 | $6.18^{abcd}$ | $4.74^{abc}$ | $4.94^{abc}$ | $5.92^{abc}$ | $5.36^{a}$ | $4.78^{ab}$ |
| NaK 100_1 | $6.84^{abc}$ | $7.12^{ab}$ | $5.59^{ab}$ | 4.21 | $6.53^{ab}$ | $5.12^{a}$ | $5.19^{a}$ | $6.21^{ab}$ | $5.02^{a}$ | $5.03^{a}$ |
| NaK 100_2 | $6.97^{ab}$ | $7.42^{a}$ | $5.49^{ab}$ | 3.76 | $6.58^{a}$ | $4.83^{abc}$ | $4.91^{abc}$ | $6.36^{a}$ | $5.11^{a}$ | $4.91^{ab}$ |
| NaK 80 | $6.97^{ab}$ | $7.18^{a}$ | $5.61^{ab}$ | 4.09 | $6.18^{abcd}$ | $4.92^{ab}$ | $4.84^{abc}$ | $6.14^{abc}$ | $5.09^{a}$ | $5.02^{a}$ |
| NaK 60_1 | $6.77^{abc}$ | $6.94^{ab}$ | $5.79^{ab}$ | 3.32 | $5.55^{bcde}$ | $4.76^{abc}$ | $4.94^{abc}$ | $5.52^{bc}$ | $5.40^{a}$ | $4.73^{ab}$ |
| NaK 60_2 | $6.49^{abcd}$ | $7.27^{a}$ | $5.72^{ab}$ | 3.98 | $5.26^{de}$ | $4.64^{abc}$ | $5.08^{ab}$ | $5.54^{bc}$ | $5.88^{abc}$ | $4.50^{abc}$ |
| NaK 40 | $6.77^{abc}$ | $6.66^{abc}$ | $5.91^{ab}$ | 3.76 | $4.90^{ef}$ | $4.34^{abc}$ | $4.63^{abc}$ | $5.73^{abc}$ | $6.13^{abc}$ | $4.06^{cd}$ |
| NaK 20 | $5.99^{d}$ | $6.01^{bc}$ | $6.20^{a}$ | 3.36 | $4.06^{f}$ | $4.03^{bc}$ | $4.28^{bc}$ | $4.73^{d}$ | $6.83^{bc}$ | $3.58^{de}$ |
| p-value | 0.0010 | 0.0013 | n.s. | n.s. | <0.0001 | 0.0065 | 0.0098 | <0.0001 | 0.0001 | <0.0001 |

$^{a-f}$ Different upper-case letters within a column indicate significant differences ($p<0.005$) between different groups. Means that do not share a common letter are significantly different. Non-significant: n.s.

## Appearance

Compared to the reference ham (Na100), a replacement of $Na^+$ ions by $K^+$ ions of 25% and reduction to 60% (NaK40) of total salt had no effect on the color hue. However, a reduction of total salt content by 80% and replacement of $Na^+$ ions by $K^+$ ions of 25% (NaK20) showed a significant lower color hue. There were significant differences between samples for cohesiveness, but there were no clear correlation between the salt content and the cohesiveness score. A possible explanation might be the test production. In small scale test production without vacuum, it can be difficult to avoid air and small gaps between the muscle pieces.

## Taste, flavor and odor

A reduction to 40% (NaK60) of total salt, corresponding to 2.04% salt, was possible without significantly influencing the salty taste. The changes in saltiness in this experiment correspond to another low-salt ham study, Ruusunen, Särkkä-Tirkkonen [5] found that hams with 1.4% salt were less salty than those containing 1.7–2.6% salt. The reduced saltiness can be explained by the reduced content of $Cl^-$—anions in the cooked ham since $Cl^-$ anions have an effect on the receptor cells and consequently on the perception of salt taste [35]. There were no significant differences in metal flavor and metal odor except for a higher value for metal flavor for one of the parallels of cooked ham containing the highest amount of potassium chloride (NaK100_1) compared to the cooked ham containing the lowest salt content (NaK20). These results indicate that a three to one replacement of $Na^+$ ions with $K^+$ions might be an acceptable level, regarding the issue of bitter (no significant differences between samples) and metallic flavor (NaK20 significant different from the other samples). Previous studies have shown that KCl may induce a bitter taste at high concentrations. In dry-cured loins [9] and fermented sausages [10], the maximum level was 40% replacement of sodium with potassium. In a study of cooked ham they showed that 2.0% NaCl had a higher score than a 50% replacement with KCl [11]. Another study found that it was possible to replace one-third of NaCl with KCl without altering the sensory properties of smoked salmon [36]. Those results show that the maximum level of KCl replacement may be dependent on product type.

Table 3 shows that a reduction to 60% (NaK40) of total salt had no effect on the after taste. However, a reduction of total salt content by 80% and replacement of $Na^+$ ions by $K^+$ ions by 25% (NaK20) gave a less pronounced aftertaste compared to all other hams. This can be explained by the fact that salt has a flavor enhancing effect in meat products [37], and the salt content can also effect on biochemical and enzymatic processes that in turn may impact flavor and/or structure of a product [30]. These findings are in accordance with Ruusunen,

Vainionpää [38], who found that ground meat patties with salt content down to 0.6% NaCl, had weak flavor intensity.

## Texture

Compared to the reference ham (Na100), a reduction down to 60% (NaK40) of total salt, corresponding to 1.73% salt, had no effect on tenderness or hardness in the cooked hams. However, a reduction of total salt content by 80% and replacement of $Na^+$ ions by $K^+$ ions of ¼ (NaK20), corresponding to a salt content of 1.38%, gave a more tender and less hardness on cooked ham. These results were as expected and in accordance with Ruusunen, Vainionpää [39], who found that more added salt increased the firmness in Bologna type sausages at 1.10, 1.35 to 1.60% added salt, Sofos [40] found that a reduction in salt content of more than 20% (<2.0% NaCl) in Frankfurters resulted in softer and less firm texture. It is important to keep in mind that the effects of proteins may differ in cooked ham where small pieces of lean meat are connected together whereas sausages have an emulsified fat protein network. In both cases the solubility and swelling of the myosin are nevertheless important. In cooked ham, molecular bonds are able to form inside the exudate matrix (gel cohesion) and between the exudate and the muscle [20], and when the salt concentration is reduced, the protein extractability is limited due to the solubility of the myosin [28, 29].

Compared to the reference ham (Na100), a replacement of $Na^+$-ions by $K^+$-ions of 25% gave no significant changes in sensory profile attributes. This replacement corresponds to a total sodium content of approximately 1.1 g /100 g cooked ham. These findings are in accordance with other studies [9–11, 36].

## Multimodal machine vision system

The main imaging experiment, using the multimodal machine vision system, was done using the same hams as with the chemical and sensorial measurements.

Machine vision was used to objectively study changes in color and texture in the surface. The change in lightness, as a function of reducing the salt content, is clearly seen in Fig 3A.

a)

b)

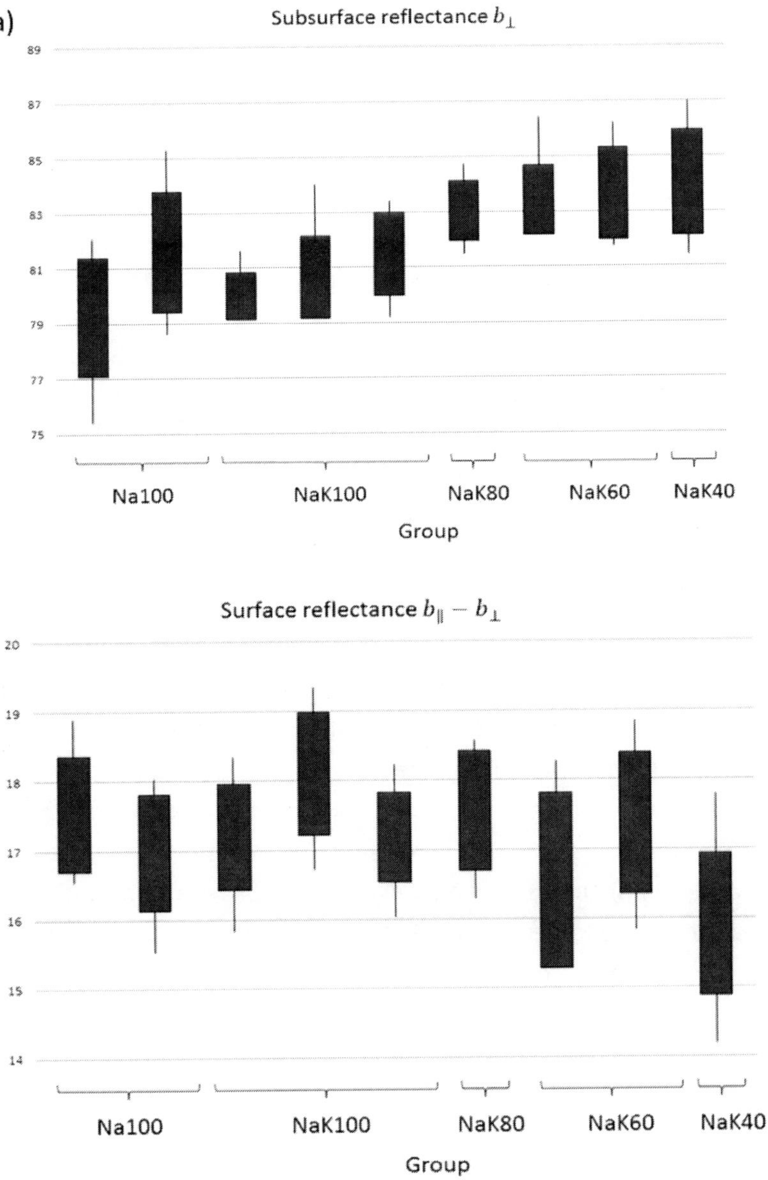


**Figure 3.** A, Mean subsurface reflectance b_⊥ for the hams with varying salt content. B, Mean surface reflectance b_∥−b_⊥ for the hams with varying salt content.

The intensity of the subsurface backscattered reflected blue light $b_\perp$ shows a clear increase as the salt content is reduced. This is confirmed by sensorial evaluation, indicating an increase in whiteness and decrease in color-hue with decreased salt content. A possible explanation for this behavior might be the decreased swelling of the salt soluble proteins and a weaker heat induced gel in cooked ham with 1.38% salt (NaK20) as discussed in above in section 3.3. Due to this theory, the surface of the cooked ham with less salt might be rougher, and the interaction of light will change, as has been shown previously [13]. Another explanation for the increased whiteness due to decreased salt content may be that salt affects the formation of heat stable nitric oxide myoglobin, the "cured meat color" [41].

A reduction in surface shininess, as measured by $b_\parallel - b_\perp$, using imaging, was only weakly linked to reduction in salt content, Fig 3B. Despite the challenges in the imaging setup in the main experiment, the improvements from the supplementary experiment in Fig 2 show that imaging with two polarization orientations can provide images that potentially can quantify subtle changes in visual appearance.

Since only simple features were used, namely the $(r_\parallel, g_\parallel, b_\parallel)$ and $(r_\perp, g_\perp, b_\perp)$ values computed as the mean over each slice, there is a greater potential in dual-polarization imaging if more advanced features such as those described in the literature [13–15, 17, 19] would be applied to dual-polarization images using the multimodal machine vision system described in this paper. Automatic segmentation, between the dark and light portions of the meat, may also help improve the quantification of the visual appearance characteristics, similar to how that human sensorial evaluators observe using their combined vision and decision processes.

## CONCLUSIONS

Compared to the reference ham (3.4% salt), a replacement of 25% $Na^+$-ions by $K^+$-ions gave no significant changes in WHC, moisture, pH, expressed moisture, the sensory profile attributes or the surface lightness and shininess. However, a reduction of salt content by 60% and 80% on molar basis or more (down to 1.7–1.4% salt) led to a decrease in WHC and an increase in expressible moisture. The salt reduction had highest influence on the sensory attributes salty taste, after taste, tenderness, hardness and color hue. To summarize, a reduction to 40% of total salt, corresponding to 2.04% salt, was possible without significantly influencing the salty taste. Further reduction down to 1.4% salt led to increased softness and reduced hardness in the cooked hams. When reduction of salt by more than 60% (down to 1.7% salt) together with a replacement of 25% $Na^+$-ions by $K^+$-ions, the low-salt ham manufacture procedure has to be modified. The multimodal machine vision system showed changes in lightness, as a function of reduced salt content.

## ACKNOWLEDGMENTS

The authors thank Marte Schei and Anne Blikra for their contribution in production and analyzing of the hams, MSc Aleksander Eilertsen and research scientist Morten Bondø for their assistance in setting up the electronics and programming of the machine vision system.

## AUTHOR CONTRIBUTIONS

Conceived and designed the experiments: KG JRM IGA. Performed the experiments: KG EM MH. Analyzed the data: KG JRM MH. Contributed reagents/materials/analysis tools: KG JRM EM MH. Wrote the paper: KG JRM EM MH IGA.

## REFERENCES

1. He FJ, MacGregor GA. Effect of modest salt reduction on blood pressure: a meta-analysis of randomized trials. Implications for public health. J Hum Hypertens. 2002;16(11):761–70.

2. WHO. Reducing salt intake in populations. Report of a WHO Forum and Technical Meeting. World Health Organization, Paris, 2006.

3. The Norwegian Directorate of Health. Strategy for the reduction of salt intake in the population. Recommendation from the National Nutrition Council. In: The Norwegian Directorate of Health, editor. Available:http://helsedirektoratet.no/folkehelse/ernering/strategier-og-satsninger/Documents/saltstrategi.pdf: The Norwegian Directorate of Health; 2011.

4. FSAI. Food Safety Authority of Ireland, Salt and health: review of the scientific evidence and recommendationsfor public policy in Ireland. 2005.

5. Ruusunen M, Särkkä-Tirkkonen M, Puolanne E. Saltiness of coarsely ground cooked ham with reduced salt content. Agricultural and food science in Finland. 2001;10:27–31.

6. Pietrasik Z, Gaudette NJ. The impact of salt replacers and flavor enhancer on the processing characteristics and consumer acceptance of restructured cooked hams. Meat Sci. 2014;96(3):1165–70.

7. Breslin PAS, Beauchamp GK. Suppression of Bitterness by Sodium: Variation Among Bitter Taste Stimuli. Chem Senses. 1995;20(6):609–23. pmid:8788095

8. Olson D. Salt for processing probably can be cut by only one quarter. The National Provisioner. 1982;7–10.

9. Gou P, Guerrero L, Gelabert J, Arnau J. Potassium chloride, potassium lactate and glycine as sodium chloride substitutes in fermented sausages and in dry-cured pork loin. 1996(0309–1740 (Print)).

10. Gelabert J, Gou P, Guerrero L, Arnau J. Effect of sodium chloride replacement on some characteristics of fermented sausages. Meat Sci. 2003;65(2):833–9.

11. Frye CB, Hand LW, Calkins CR, Mandigo RW. Reduction or Replacement of Sodium Chloride in a Tumbled Ham Product. J Food Sci. 1986;51(3):836–7.

12. Lawless HT, Heymann H. Sensory evaluation of food—principles and practices (2nd ed.). New York: Springer; 2010.

13. Iqbal A, Valous NA, Mendoza F, Sun D-W, Allen P. Classification of pre-sliced pork and Turkey ham qualities based on image colour and textural features and their relationships with consumer responses. Meat Sci. 2010;84(3):455–65.

14. Jackman P, Sun DW, Du CJ, Allen P. Prediction of beef eating qualities from colour, marbling and wavelet surface texture features using homogenous carcass treatment. Pattern Recognition. 2009;42(5):751–63.

15. Jackman P, Sun DW, Allen P. Prediction of beef palatability from colour, marbling and surface texture features of longissimus dorsi. J Food Eng. 2010;96(1):151–65.

16. Valous NA, Mendoza F, Sun D-W, Allen P. Texture appearance characterization of pre-sliced pork ham images using fractal metrics: Fourier analysis dimension and lacunarity. Food Res Int. 2009;42(3):353–62.

17. Chandraratne MR, Samarasinghe S, Kulasiri D, Bickerstaffe R. Prediction of lamb tenderness using image surface texture features. J Food Eng. 2006;77(3):492–9.

18. Alçiçek Z, Balaban MÖ. Development and application of "The Two Image" method for accurate object recognition and color analysis. J Food Eng. 2012;111(1):46–51.

19. Mendoza F, Valous NA, Allen P, Kenny TA, Ward P, Sun D-W. Analysis and classification of commercial ham slice images using directional fractal dimension features. Meat Sci. 2009;81(2):313–20.

20. Bombrun L, Gatellier P, Carlier M, Kondjoyan A. The effects of low salt concentrations on the mechanism of adhesion between

two pieces of pork semimembranosus muscle following tumbling and cooking. Meat Sci. 2014;96(1):5–13.

21. Aaslyng MD, Vestergaard C, Koch AG. The effect of salt reduction on sensory quality and microbial growth in hotdog sausages, bacon, ham and salami. Meat Sci. 2014;96(1):47–55.

22. Mathiassen JR, Misimi E, Bondø M, Veliyulin E, Østvik SO. Trends in application of imaging technologies to inspection of fish and fish products. Trends in Food Science & Technology. 2011;22(6):257–75.

23. Regulation EU no 1169/2011 of the European Parliament and the council of 25thOctober 2011. In Official Journal of the European Union L 304/18 22.11.2011.

24. AOAC. Official Methods of Analysis of the Association of Official Analytical Chemists. 15th ed. Arlington, Virgina: AOAC; 1990.

25. Eide O, Børresen T, Strøm T. Minced Fish Production From Capelin (Mallotus villosus). A New Method for Gutting, Skinning and Removal of Fat from Small Fatty Fish Species. J Food Sci. 1982;47(2):347–9.

26. Kivikari R. Analysis of sodium in meat products using an Na-selective eletrode. (In Finnish). Proc. of Meat Day Seminar 1996, Nr, 536. Proc. of Meat Day Seminar 1996. 1996.

27. Grau R, Hamm R. Eine einfache Methode zur Bestimmung der Wasserbindung im Muskel. Die Naturwissenschaften. 1953;40(1):29–30.

28. Hamm R. Koloidchemie des Fleisches: Parey, Berlin; 1972.

29. Offer G, Knight P. The structural basis of water-holding in meat. DimS- R.A. Lawrie, editor. Capters 3–4: London: Elsevier Applied Science; 1988.

30. Albarracín W, Sánchez IC, Grau R, Barat JM. Salt in food processing; usage and reduction: a review. Int J Food Sci Technol. 2011;46(7):1329–36.

31. Gjerlaug-Enger E, Aas L, Ødegård J, Vangen O. Genetic parameters of meat quality traits in two pig breeds measured by rapid methods. Animal. 2010;4(11):1832–43.

32. Puolanne E, Ruusunen MH, Vainionpää JI. Combined effects of NaCl and raw meat pH on water-holding in cooked sausage with and without added phosphate. Meat Sci. 2001;58(1):1–7. pmid:22061912 .

33. Mossel DAA, Corry JET, Struijk CB, Bair RM. Essentials of the Microbiology of Foods. A Textbook for Advanced Studies: John Wiley & Sons, Chichester, England; 1995.

34. Zanardi E, Ghidini S, Conter M, Ianieri A. Mineral composition of Italian salami and effect of NaCl partial replacement on compositional, physico-chemical and sensory parameters. Meat Sci. 2010;86(3):742–7.

35. Murphy C, Cardello AV, Brand JG. Tastes of fifteen halide salts following water and NaCl: Anion and cation effects. Physiology & Behavior. 1981;26(6):1083–95. pmid:7280070.

36. Almli V, Hersleth M. Salt replacement and injection salting in smoked salmon evaluated from descriptive and hedonic sensory perspectives. Aquaculture International. 2013;21(5):1091–108.

37. Desmond E. Reducing salt: A challenge for the meat industry. Meat Sci. 2006;74(1):188–96.

38. Ruusunen M, Vainionpää J, Lyly M, Lähteenmäki L, Niemistö M, Ahvenainen R, et al. Reducing the sodium content in meat products: The effect of the formulation in low-sodium ground meat patties. Meat Sci. 2005;69(1):53–60.

39. Ruusunen M, Vainionpää J, Puolanne E, Lyly M, Lähteenmäki L, Niemistö M, et al. Effect of sodium citrate, carboxymethyl cellulose and carrageenan levels on quality characteristics of low-salt and low-fat bologna type sausages. Meat Sci. 2003;64(4):371–81.

40. Sofos JN. Effects of Reduced Salt (NaCl) Levels on Sensory and Instrumental Evaluation of Frankfurters. J Food Sci. 1983;48:1692–9.

41. Honikel K-O. The use and control of nitrate and nitrite for the processing of meat products. Meat Sci. 2008;78(1–2):68–76.

# Chapter 9

# Number Determination of Successfully Packaged Dies Per Wafer Based on Machine Vision

**Hsuan-Ting Chang *, Ren-Jie Pan and Hsiao-Wei Peng**

*Photonics and Information Laboratory, Department of Electrical Engineering, National Yunlin University of Science and Technology, 123 University Road, Section 3, Douliou, Yunlin 64002, Taiwan*

## ABSTRACT

Packaging the integrated circuit (IC) chip is a necessary step in the manufacturing process of IC products. In general, wafers with the same size and process should have a fixed number of packaged dies. However, many factors decrease the number of the actually packaged dies, such as die scratching, die contamination, and die breakage, which are not considered in the existing die-counting methods. Here we propose a robust method that can automatically determine the number of actual packaged dies by using machine vision techniques. During the inspection, the image is taken from the top of the wafer, in which most dies have been removed and packaged. There are five steps in the proposed method: wafer region detection, wafer position calibration, dies region detection, detection of die sawing lines, and die number counting. The abnormal cases of fractional dies in the wafer boundary and dropped dies during the packaging are considered in the proposed method as well. The experimental results show that the precision and recall rates reach 99.83% and 99.84%, respectively, when determining the numbers of actual packaged dies in the 41 test cases.

**Keywords:** Automatic optical inspection; Wafer; Die; machine vision; IC packaging; Sawing line

## 1. INTRODUCTION

Machine vision has been widely used in various fields because only simple devices are required, and various solutions have been proposed for different kinds of applications, such as industrial measurement [1], text recognition [2], finger recognition [3], medical image analysis [4], face recognition [5], and human computer interfaces [6]. As for the industrial measurement in a semiconductor factory, the automatic optical inspection for wafer-related processes has been widely studied in recent years, such as detecting a die in the open circuit [7], wafer defect detection [8], the LED grading system [9], and rotation calibration in wafer packaging [10].

The number of packaged dies is important information for the manufacturer. In general cases, the number of dies per wafer can be determined by existing counting algorithms [11,12,13,14], which can be found on websites [15] and [16] as well. In these methods, the number of gross dies per wafer can be estimated by entering the parameters such as wafer size, die width, die height, horizontal and vertical spacing. In Reference [11], the variables required in the proposed algorithm include the die dimensions (width and length), the size and orientation of the wafer flat, the size of the non-yielding periphery zone, and the die array relative the center of the wafer. The use and evaluation of the yield models in IC manufacturing are discussed in Reference [12]. Several die-per-wafer yield models, which are derived from Poisson, Binomial, and exponential probability density functions, are reviewed. Moreover, de Vries pointed out that there are different formulas used by different semiconductor manufacturing companies [13]. He found that the accuracy of an exact count algorithm depends on the die area and the aspect ratio. All the above methods require the input of the dimensions of the die and wafer.

Recently, computer vision based methods have received great attention in terms of detecting wafer die defects [17,18]. However, there are few studies that focus on the automatic counting of the die number in the wafer images without providing the size and dimension information for the dies and wafers. In addition to our preliminary work [19], Xu *et al.* proposed a wafer die-counting algorithm using the geometric characteristics [20] in the wafer images. In this work, RANSAC (Random Sample Consensus) algorithms [21,22] are used to detect the wafer location and the sawing lines. The incomplete dies at the wafer rim strip containing the circle pixels can be easily detected and are then eliminated. Both high counting accuracy and good computational efficiency can be achieved. However, this method does not deal with cases of fractured and randomly dropped dies on the wafer.

In practical situations, some situations that could lead to incorrect counting results should be considered. For example, with the IC testing programs, some dies in a wafer that do not pass the test will not be packaged. The dies not being packaged are left on the wafer and thus a number of dies that different from those successfully packaged are obtained. General commercial equipment [23] could automatically calculate the number of dies in the above case. However, in the cases of the remaining dies that are broken, displaced, or rotated, they cannot be determined straightforwardly. Thus a manual calculation is required if the actual number is desired. It is very time consuming to obtain the precise number of successfully packaged dies through manual wafer inspection. This number should be exactly the same as that determined from the pick and place robot. The clients of the die-packaging factory can only estimate the number, assuming that no abnormal cases occurred during the process. However, this number is usually less than that of actual packaged dies. If the difference between the two numbers is large, the clients will not accept the result and will ask for an explanation. Therefore, in this study we propose a computer-vision-based method that can automatically determine the exact number of actual packaged dies in the residual wafer image. As opposed to existing methods, the wafer and die parameters such as size, width, and length are not required. In addition, the determined die-per-wafer number can be more accurate when abnormal cases occur during the packaging process.

The remaining part of the paper is organized as follows. In Section 2, the proposed methods with the required image processing algorithms are described. The experimental results are provided in Section 3. Finally, the conclusions are drawn in Section 4.

## 2. METHOD

Figure 1 shows the systematic block diagram of the proposed system, which consists of five stages in order to determine the number of packaged dies per wafer: (1) wafer region detection: detect the actual wafer region from the input image; (2) wafer position calibration: calibrate the rotation angle of the input wafer image; (3) die region detection: detect the packaged die region from the wafer region; (4) detection of die sawing lines: determine vertical and horizontal segmentation lines in the wafer region, and then use them to partition off the rectangular die regions; (5) die number counting: determine the exact number of actual packaged dies. The detailed procedures are described in later subsections.

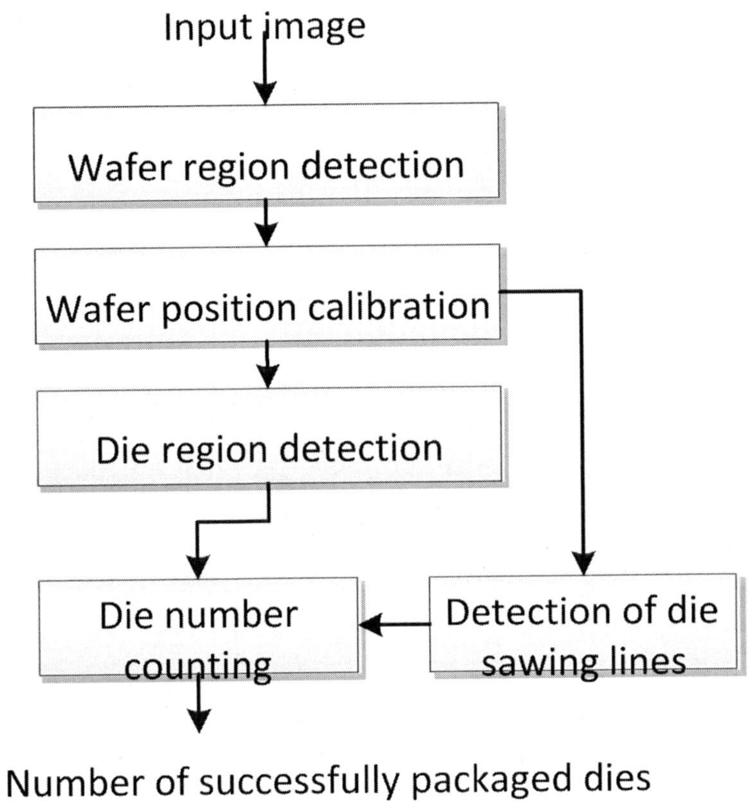


**Figure 1.** The system flowchart of the proposed method.

### 2.1. Wafer Region Detection

Figure 2a shows the input wafer image, which has redundant background information that should be removed for further processing. The detailed steps include: (1) color to grayscale transformation and binarization; (2) region labeling; (3) position calibration.

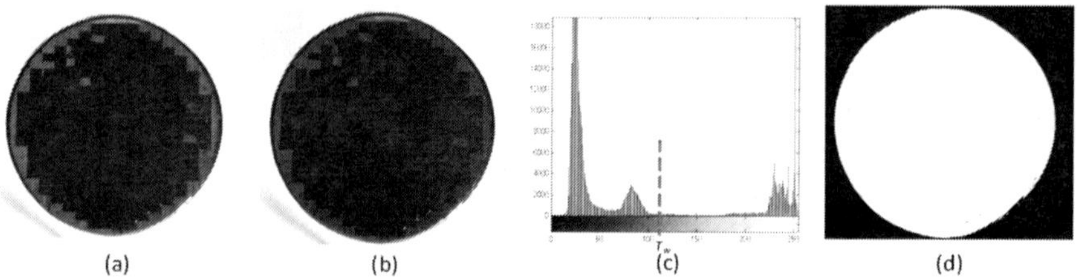


**Figure 2.** (**a**) Original image; (**b**) grayscale image; (**c**) histogram of the grayscale image; (**d**) binarized image.

### 2.1.1. Color-to-Grayscale Transformation and Binarization

A color image is composed of red, green, and blue components. Each component has a one-byte resolution, *i.e.*, 256 grayscale levels. A color image can be transformed to a grayscale image igray(x,y) by using the linear combination method shown in Equation (1).

$$i_{gray}(x,y) = 0.299 \times i_r(x,y) + 0.587 \times i_g(x,y) + 0.114 \times i_b(x,y) \quad (1)$$

where $i_r$, $i_g$, and $i_b$ denote the grayscale values in red, green, and blue components, respectively, and $(x,y)$ denotes the pixel coordinates.

The binarization process is often used in the object detection and segmentation framework in image processing. The main idea is to select a threshold $T_w$ and to force all the pixel values into two fixed grayscale values, 0 and 255, as shown in Equation (2).

$$w_b(x,y) = \begin{cases} 0, \text{ if } i_{\text{gray}}(x,y) > T_w \\ 255, \text{Otherwise} \end{cases} \quad (2)$$

where $w_b(x,y)$ is the pixel value after binarization. Figure 2b shows the grayscale image transformed from Figure 2a. Figure 2c shows the histogram of the image in Figure 2b. The threshold $T_W$ can be automatically determined by applying Otsu's method [24] on the histogram of the grayscale image. Figure 2d shows the binarized result ofFigure 2b, based on Equation (2). The white wafer region is well extracted from the black background.

### 2.1.2. Region Labeling

In order to remove the background and keep the wafer information simultaneously, the mask must conform to the sharpness of the wafer. In Figure 2d, there are certain small regions (black points) in the white region boundary and they should be removed. The connected component labeling method [25] is used to determine the small black regions and the size of each region. Only the largest black area can be retained with the operation shown in Equation (3).

$$w_b'(x,y) = \begin{cases} 0, \text{ if } w_{\text{label}}(x,y) = t \\ 255, \text{Otherwise} \end{cases} \quad (3)$$

where *t* is the label of the maximum black region and wlabel is a matrix that denotes the labeling result. Figure 3a,b show the mask w'b and the final wafer image w without the background information, respectively. As shown in Equation (4), the final wafer image is obtained as passing the input wafer image onto the mask w'b, *i.e.*,

$$w(x,y) = i(x,y) \cap w_b'(x,y) \quad (4)$$

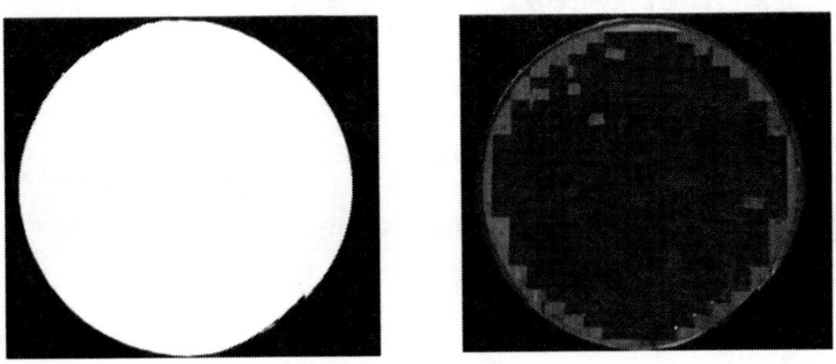

(a) (b)

**Figure 3.** (**a**) The mask of capturing the wafer image; (**b**) Wafer image with black background.

## 2.2. Wafer Position Calibration

Due to the possible deviation on the wafer placement, the die sawing lines could not be exactly horizontal and vertical in the image, which is necessary in order to accurately determine the die number in the following processing steps. Here, the Canny edge detection [26] and Fourier transform methods are used to determine the wafer rotation angle. First, a Canny edge detector is utilized to obtain the edge information we(x,y) in the wafer image shown in Figure 3b. Figure 4a shows that many horizontal and vertical sawing lines appear in this image. This edge information can be transformed into the frequency domain $W_e(u,v)$ by using the two-dimensional Fourier transform shown in Equation (5).

$$W_e(u,v) = \iint_{-\infty}^{\infty} w_e(x,y)e^{-j2\pi(ux+vy)}dxdy \tag{5}$$

Figure 4b shows the corresponding spectrum image, We(u,v), in which the major components appear at the nearly horizontal and vertical directions. In order to determine the angle θ rotated from the exact horizontal and vertical axes, the threshold *Tc* shown in Equation (6) is used to binarize the spectrum image We(u,v). Figure 4c shows the binary image Ct(u,v) derived from the image shown in Figure 4b.

$$C_t(u,v) = \begin{cases} 0, \text{if } W_e(u,v) > T_c \\ 255, \text{Otherwise} \end{cases} \tag{6}$$

To determine the rotation angle of the wafer, two points Ct(uh,vh) and Ct(ul,vl) located on the points in the nearly vertical direction in the image Ct(u,v) are selected. By using Equation (7), the deviation angle θ can be determined as

$$\theta = \frac{\pi}{2} - tan^{-1}\left(\frac{v_h - v_l}{u_h - u_l}\right) \tag{7}$$

The deviation angle θ can be used to calibrate the wafer image w(x,y) such that the sawing lines are as perfectly horizontal and vertical as possible. Equation (8) shows that the new coordinates ($x'$, $y'$) of the rotated image $W'(x', y')$ can be determined from the coordinates ($x$,$y$). However, if the coordinates ($x'$, $y'$) are non-integers, the bilinear interpolation is utilized to obtain the integer coordinates. Figure 5 shows the rotated image after using the position calibration.

$$\begin{bmatrix} x' \\ y' \end{bmatrix} = \begin{bmatrix} cos\,\theta & -cos\,\theta \\ sin\,\theta & sin\,\theta \end{bmatrix} \begin{bmatrix} x \\ y \end{bmatrix} \tag{8}$$

(a) (b) (c)

**Figure 4.** (**a**) Canny edge detection result of Figure 3b; (**b**) spectrum of the edge image shown in Figure 4a; (**c**) binary image in which the black points are corresponding to strong white points shown in Figure 4b.

### 2.3. Die region Detection

After the wafer region has been determined and its position has been calibrated in Subsection 2.2, the resident die regions, which are not taken away during packaging, are detected. In order to avoid the color saturation problem caused by the reflective points in the RGB color space, the YCbCr color space is utilized such that the brightness can be separated from its color components. Equation (9) shows the transformation function.

$$\begin{bmatrix} Y \\ Cb \\ Cr \end{bmatrix} = \begin{bmatrix} 16 \\ 128 \\ 128 \end{bmatrix} + \begin{bmatrix} 65.481 & 128.553 & 24.966 \\ -37.797 & -74.203 & 112 \\ 112 & -93.786 & -18.214 \end{bmatrix} \begin{bmatrix} R \\ G \\ B \end{bmatrix} \tag{9}$$

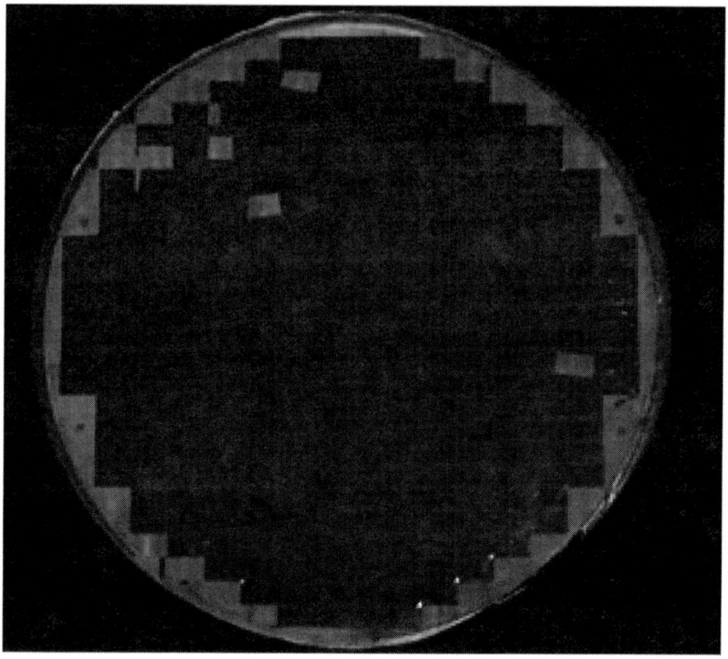

**Figure 5.** The wafer-region image after the position calibration.

Figure 6a–c show the Y, Cb, and Cr components of the wafer image in Figure 5, respectively. As shown inFigure 6b, the Cb component has a more obvious contrast than the other components and is nearly unaffected by reflection. To extract the regions of the resident dies, a binarization process defined in Equation (10) is used.

$$W_{\mathrm{dies}}(x,y) = \begin{cases} 255, \text{if } Cb(x,y) < T_{cb} \\ 0, \text{Otherwise} \end{cases} \quad (10)$$

where *Cb*(*x*,*y*) denotes the pixel value in the Cb component, $T_{cb}$ is the threshold value, which is determined by applying Otsu's method on the histogram of the Cb component image shown in Figure 7a; and Wdies(x,y)denotes the resident die image shown in Figure 7b.

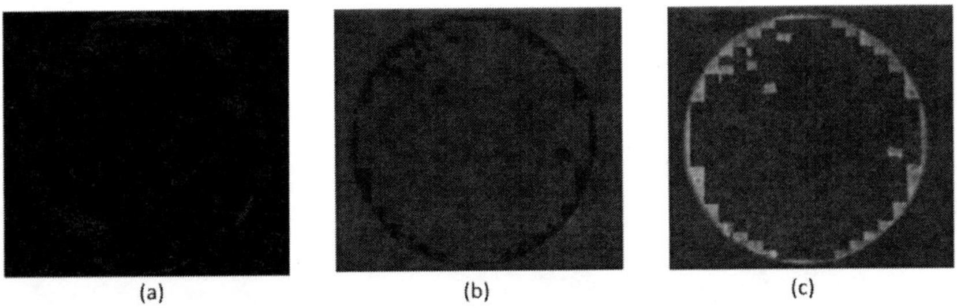


**Figure 6.** (**a**) The Y component image; (**b**) the Cb component image; (**c**) the Cr component image in the YCbCr color space.

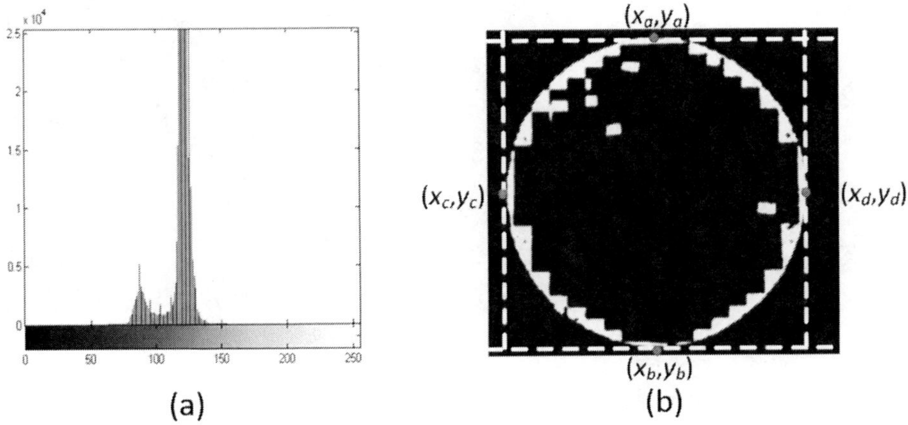


**Figure 7.** (**a**) Histogram of the Cb component; (**b**) the image of the resident die regions.

As shown in Figure 5, the rim strip of the wafer contains no dies and should be excluded to avoid possible confusion on die counting in further processing. In the third step, the area of the wafer region which does not include the rim strip is determined. The four non-zero value points $(x_a,y_a)$, $(x_b,y_b)$, $(x_c,y_c)$, and $(x_d,y_d)$ corresponding to the top, bottom, leftmost, and rightmost boundary points, respectively, are selected in the image Wdies shown in Figure 7b. The four points can be used to define an ellipse mask region WD using Equation (11).

$$W_D(x,y) = \begin{cases} 255, \text{if } \dfrac{(x-h)^2}{\alpha^2} + \dfrac{(y-k)^2}{\beta^2} \le 1 \\ 0, \text{Otherwise} \end{cases} \tag{11}$$

where

$$h = \frac{x_a + x_b}{2}, k = \frac{y_a + y_b}{2}, \alpha = \frac{x_d - x_c}{2}, \beta = \frac{y_a - y_b}{2}$$

Figure 8a shows a typical mask region, which is very close to a circle. By applying this mask onto the image inFigure 5, Figure 8b shows that the mentioned rim strip (shown in the white region) can be successfully removed.

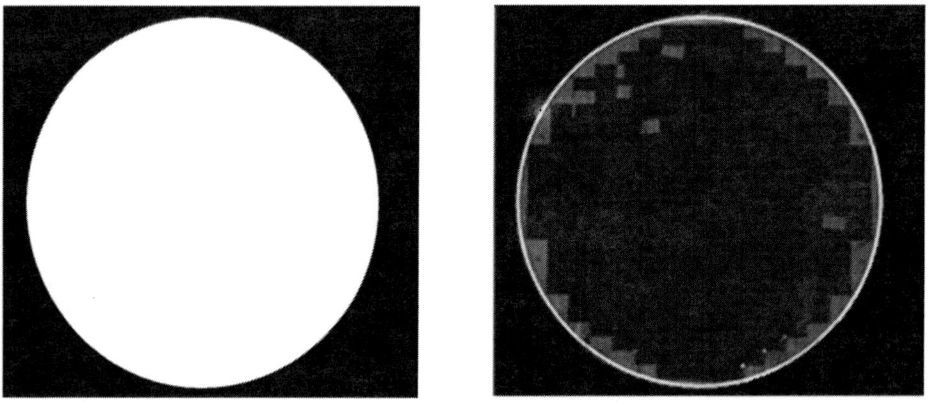

(a) (b)

**Figure 8.** (**a**) The mask of the wafer image; (**b**) the wafer image in which the region outside the white contour has been removed.

## 2.4. Detection of Die Sawing Lines

Prior to die counting, the geometrical information of a standard die, whose shape is rectangular and is defined by the sawing lines, should be derived. Therefore, detecting the die sawing lines in the wafer image is required. However, the sawing lines shown in Figure 9a are not obvious and thus are difficult to be easily detected. To overcome this problem, the histogram equalization method that can increase the global contrast in the image [27] is used. Figure 9b shows the enhanced result of Figure 9a. In this enhanced image e(x,y), the sawing lines have been intensified, thus they can be more easily detected. Equations (12) and (13) show that the pixel values of each column and row in the wafer image (Figure 9b) are accumulated to obtain the two vectors v(j) and h(i), respectively.

$$v(j) = \sum_x e(x, j) \tag{12}$$

$$h(i) = \sum_y e(i, y) \tag{13}$$

(a)

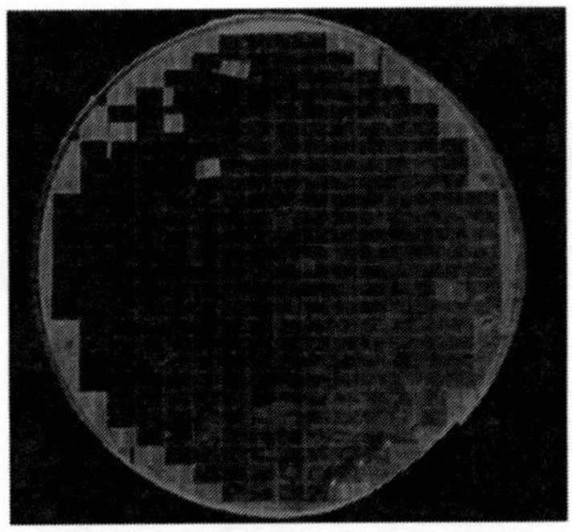

(b)

**Figure 9.** (**a**) The grayscale image obtained from Figure 3b; (**b**) the enhanced image $e(x, y)$ obtained by applying the histogram equalization on Figure 9a.

Figure 10a,b show the projections of the accumulated pixel values in the columns and rows, respectively. In both projections, many obvious peaks appear in accordance with the sawing line positions in the wafer image shown in Figure 9b, because the pixel values in the sawing lines are much larger than that in the die regions. In addition, the intervals between two consecutive peaks should be very similar in these two projections. However, due to the incomplete dies and the non-uniform illumination condition, the peak and non-peak values vary a lot. Therefore, the peaks cannot be detected by directly applying a fixed thresholding scheme. Figure 11 shows the flowchart of the proposed method to detect the peak positions $v_p(j)$ in the vertical direction. Here $j$ denotes the index of the detected peaks. The peak positions $h_p(i)$ in the horizontal direction can be detected with a similar strategy.

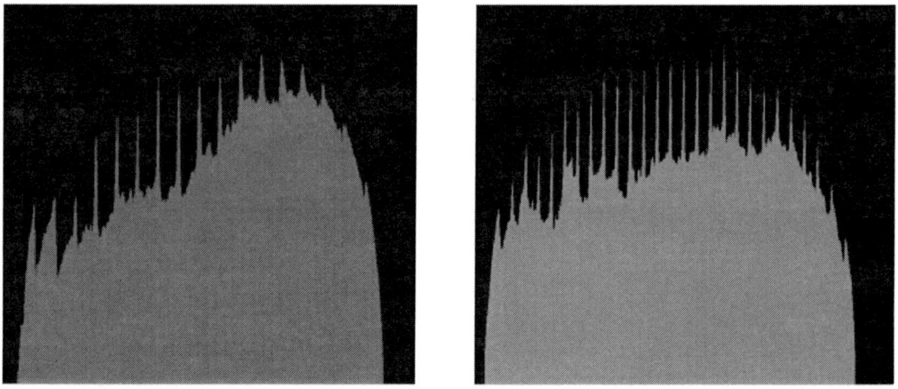

(a) (b)

**Figure 10.** The projections of the accumulated values in (**a**) the columns and (**b**) the rows.

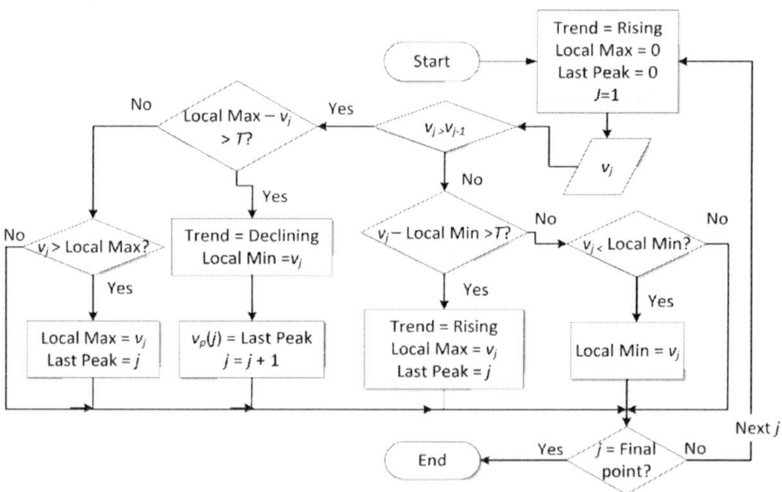


**Figure 11.** Peak detection flowchart in the vertical direction.

Figure 12 shows the detected die sawing lines in both the vertical and horizontal directions. The peak detection method described above shows that many incorrect sawing lines are detected. To solve this problem, the average line method is proposed to filter out the miss-detected sawing lines. Figure 13a,b show the depicted white lines representing the average values calculated by using Equations (14) and (15), respectively.

$$v'(j) = \frac{\sum_{j-l}^{j+l} v(j) + v(j)}{l+2} \tag{14}$$

$$h'(i) = \frac{\sum_{i-z}^{i+z} h(i) + h(i)}{z+2} \tag{15}$$

where v′ and h′ are the average values in the sliding windows of widths. Assume that l and w are the length and width of the die when the threshold *T* shown in Figure 11 is increased to a larger number in the peak detection method, respectively. As shown in Figure 11, a larger threshold *T* indicates a higher difference values between the two consecutive bins in the histogram. Figure 14a shows the detected peak positions with a large *T* value. The values *l* and *z* are calculated by using Equations (16)–(19), where we define the shortest distant between two peak positions to be length and width of the die in the histogram with a *T* value.

$$l = min\big(D_h(i)\big) \tag{16}$$

$$z = min\big(D_v(j)\big) \tag{17}$$

$$D_v(j) = \widehat{v_p}(j+1) - \widehat{v_p}(j) \tag{18}$$

$$D_h(i) = \widehat{h_p}(i+1) - \widehat{h_p}(i) \tag{19}$$

where vp^ and hp^ denote the detected peaks positions. Dv and Dh denote the distances between two consecutive peak positions in the vertical and horizontal directions, respectively. The die sawing lines $v_p$ and $h_p$ detected in the peak detection method are compared to the average values v' and h', respectively. If the condition $v_p(j) > v'(j)$ is satisfied, the new die sawing line is recorded as $v_r(k) = v_p(j)$. Figure 14b shows the detection result based on this average line method.

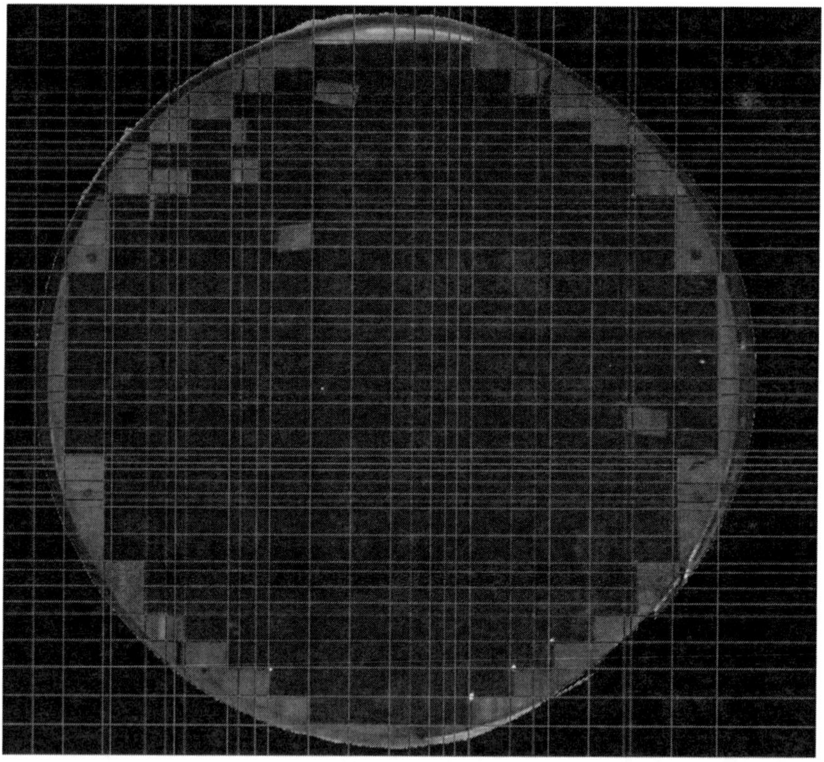

**Figure 12.** Result of the die sawing line detection.

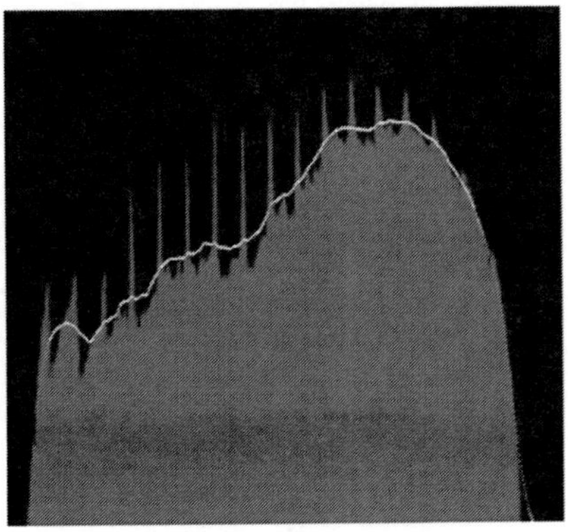

(a)

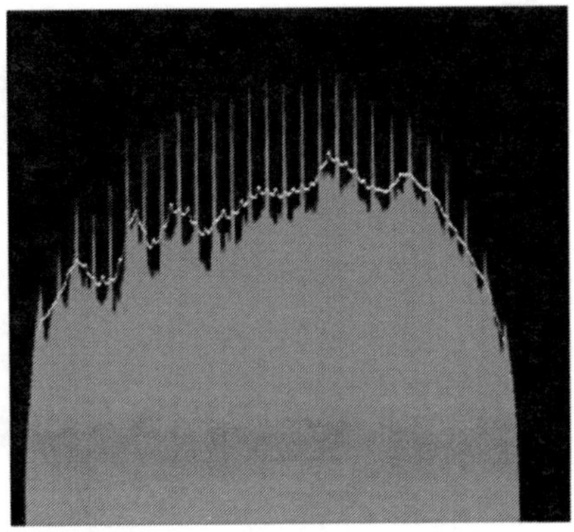

(b)

**Figure 13.** The result of the average line method: (**a**) average values shown on a white line in the vertical direction; (**b**) average values shown on a white line in the horizontal direction.

The last step is to guarantee that the distance between the adjacent real wafer saw lines $v_r(k)$ and $v_r(k+1)$ is greater than a predefined value $z$. Figure 15 shows the flowchart of this process and Figure 16 shows the final result of the die sawing lines.

## 2.5. Counting the Packaged Dies Number

With the detected die sawing lines shown in Figure 16, the exact number of successfully packaged dies can be determined. In a normal case, the dies that have been taken away from the wafer can be determined. In special cases, some dies are broken, rotated, or displaced during the wafer sawing, wafer probing, or packaging processes. In counting the number of regular rectangular dies, both the normal and special cases must be considered.

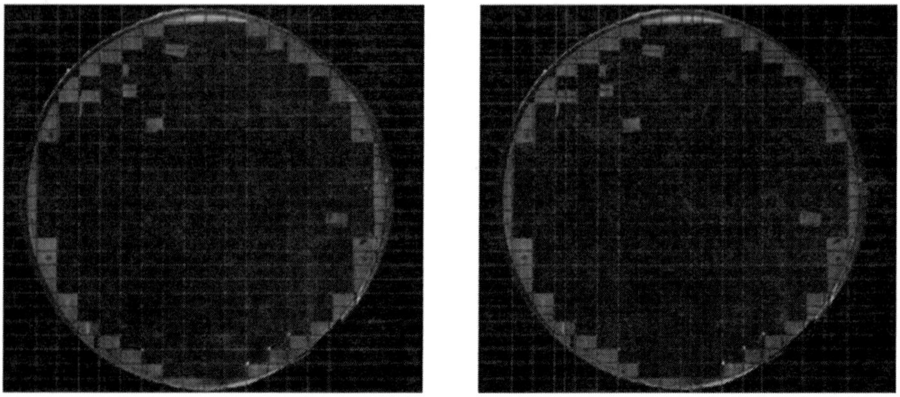

(a) (b)

**Figure 14.** (**a**) The result of the peak detection method with a *T* value; (**b**) the result of the average line method.

**2.5.1. Normal Cases**

Figure 17 shows that a matrix is constructed based on the die sawing lines. The binary entry value of the matrix is determined using Equation (20). The main idea is to evaluate the size of the wafer image WD in each corresponding local area, Nc(m,n) and to use the threshold Tn1 for judging whether the die in this location has been packaged or not.

$$N_c(m,n) = \begin{cases} 1, \text{if} \sum_{x=v_f(m)}^{v_f(m+1)} \sum_{y=h_f(n)}^{h_f(n+1)} \frac{W_D(x,y)}{255} > T_{n1} \\ 0, \text{Otherwise} \end{cases} \quad (20)$$

where the coordinate (*x*,*y*) denotes the pixel position in the image, the coordinate (*m*,*n*) denotes the entry position in the matrix, and $N_c$ denotes the area corresponding to the size of dies shown in Figure 18a. Some special dies, which should be taken away but in fact are not, or the opposite case, are also considered here. The information of the resident die image $W_{dies}$ is utilized to identify the actual die number *N* in the normal case. Equations (21) and (22) show

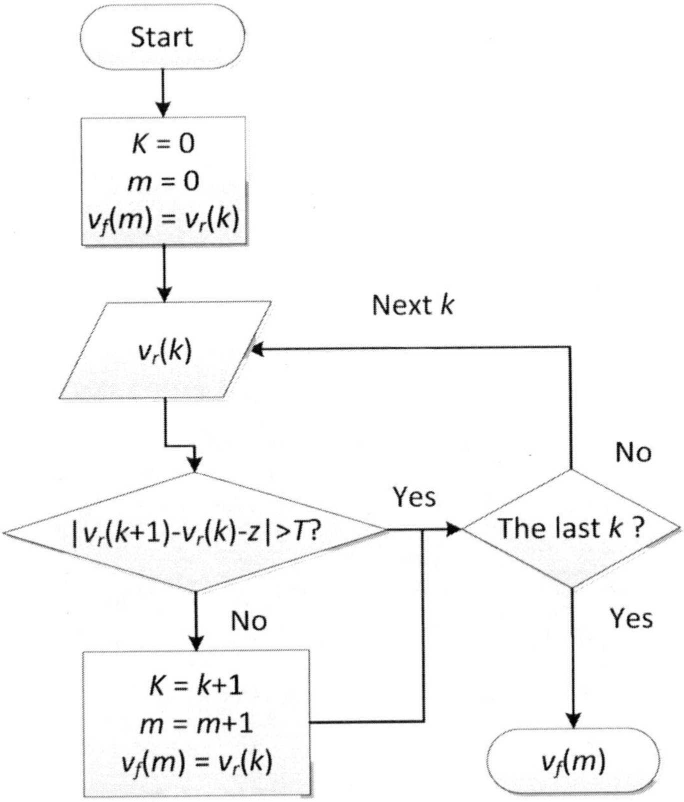


**Figure 15.** The flowchart of the last step.

the steps to determine the number *N*. Figure 19b shows the resultant image in which the incomplete dies have been discarded.

$$\widehat{N_c}(m,n) = \begin{cases} 1, \text{if } N_c(m,n) = 1 \text{ and } \sum_{x=v_f(m)}^{v_f(m+1)} \sum_{y=h_f(n)}^{h_f(n+1)} \frac{d(x,y)}{255} < T_{n2} \\ 0, \text{Otherwise} \end{cases} \quad (21)$$

$$N = \sum\nolimits_m \sum\nolimits_n \widehat{N_c}(m,n) \quad (22)$$

where Tn2 is the threshold used to judge the location of the die which has been packaged or not, *N* denotes the number of the packaged dies in the normal case, and d(x,y) denotes the calibrated wafer image shown in Figure 5.

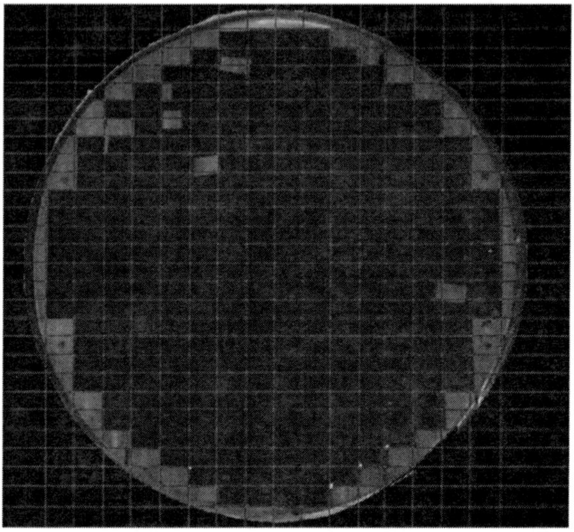

**Figure 16.** The final result of the detected die sawing lines.

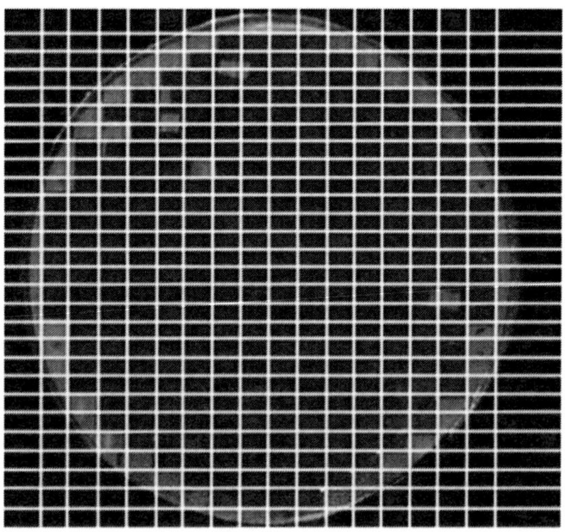


**Figure 17.** Wafer image mapped in the matrix defined by using the detected die sawing lines.

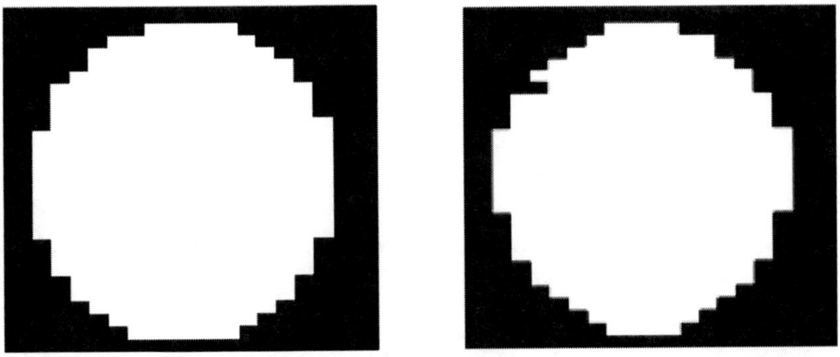

(a) (b)

**Figure 18.** (**a**) The area that is judged to be packaged; (**b**) actual packaged area in the normal case.

### 2.5.2. Abnormal Cases

If the resident dies are broken, rotated, or shifted from the normal position, they are abnormal cases, and should be treated in another way. Consider the calibrated wafer image shown in Figure 5. First, the intersection of the calibrated image and the actual packaged die image shown in Figure 18b is determined. The dies belonging to the abnormal case can be determined using Equation (23).

$$S_a(x,y) = d(x,y) \cap \widehat{N_c}(x,y) \tag{23}$$

where Sa denotes the image of the abnormal case shown in Figure 19a. It contains some deviation caused by the error introduced during the die sawing lines detection. Because the size of the deviation area is smaller than that of a normal die, the deviation could be removed by using the steps described in Equations (24) and (25).

$$S_c(m,n) = \begin{cases} 1, \text{if} \displaystyle\sum_{i=v_f(m)}^{v_f(m+1)-1} \sum_{j=h_f(n)}^{h_f(n+1)-1} S_a(i,j)/255 < T_{s1} \text{ and } S_n(m,n) = 1 \\ 0, \text{Otherwise} \end{cases} \tag{24}$$

$$S_n(m,n) = \begin{cases} 1, \text{if } \widehat{N_c}(m-1,n) < T_{n1} \; or \; \widehat{N_c}(m+1,n) < T_{n1} \\ or \; \widehat{N_c}(m,n-1) < T_{n1} \; or \; \widehat{N_c}(m,n+1) < T_{n1} \\ 0, \text{Otherwise} \end{cases} \quad (25)$$

here Sc denotes the result after removing the small deviation regions. The condition Sn(m,n)=1 indicates the position that contained the deviation value. Figure 19b shows the resultant image *Sn*.

(a) (b) (c)

**Figure 19.** (**a**) The dies with small deviation regions in the abnormal case; (**b**) the result after removing the small deviation regions; (**c**) the final dies in the abnormal case.

In the second step, the small areas are filtered and the number *S* of dies is calculated by utilizing the labeling method. The result is shown in Figure 19c. Finally, the number of the successfully packaged dies is obtained by using Equation (26).

$$P = N - S \quad (26)$$

## 3. EXPERIMENTAL RESULTS

In our experiments, a Microsoft LifeCam Cinema image sensor was used, and the computer specifications were as follows: CPU: Intel Core i5-3570K, RAM: DDR3 1600MHz 4G. The programming was implemented using Visual Studio 2008. Figure 20 shows the photographic environment. Two illumination sources were used in the experimental set up to reduce reflection effects in the captured images. According to the empirical tests in our experiments, the various threshold values in the proposed method are given as follows: both $T_w$ and $T_{cb}$ are automatically determined by using the Otsu method, $T_c$ = 185, $T$ = 25, $T_{n1}$ = 800, $T_{n2}$ = 700, and $T_{s1}$ = 450. The accuracy for evaluating the proposed method is defined in two aspects, the recall and precision rates, which are expressed as

$$\text{Precision rate} = \frac{\text{Number of correctly deteced dies}}{\text{Total number of detected dies}} \tag{27}$$

$$\text{Recall rate} = \frac{\text{Number of correctly detected dies}}{\text{Total number of dies}} \tag{28}$$

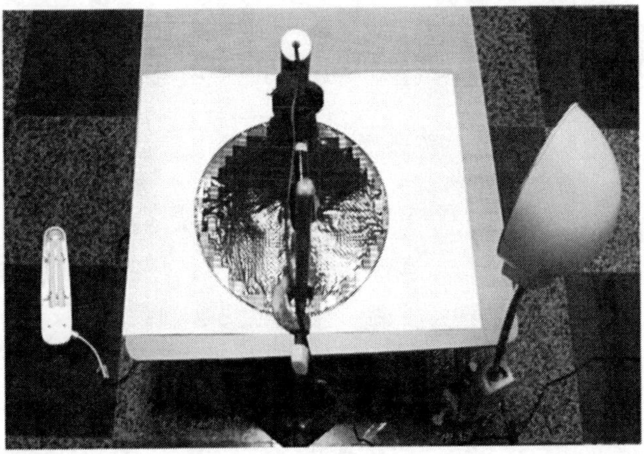

**Figure 20.** The experimental setup for taking the wafer images.

Figure 21a–j show ten samples of the all test wafer images in our experiments. Both normal and abnormal cases of the resident dies can be found in these images. Figure 22a–j show the corresponding detection results of the die regions. Figure 23a–j show the results of the detected die areas in the normal cases, while Figure 24a–j show the results of the detected dies area in the abnormal cases. Some tiny parts of the die, as shown in Figure 22b,c,f,g, can be discarded to prevent the inclusion of the number in the abnormal cases.

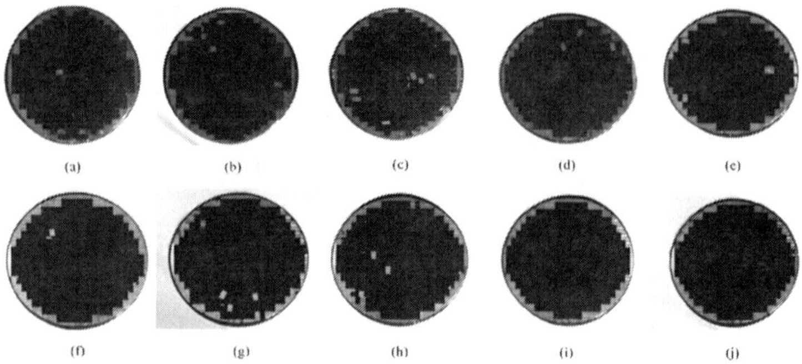


**Figure 21.** The ten test wafer images numbered from (a) to (j).

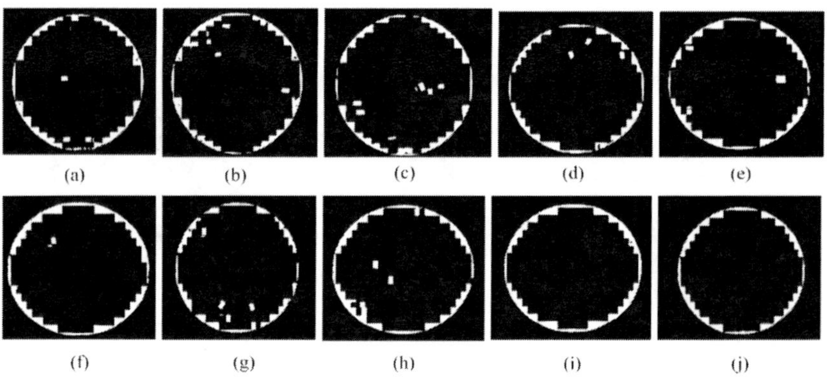


**Figure 22.** The results of the die region detection corresponding to the images shown in Figure 21a–j.

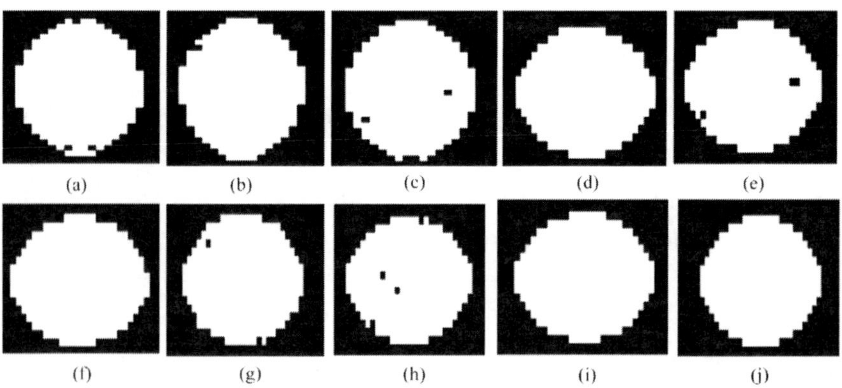


**Figure 23.** The packaged regions in the normal cases corresponding to the images shown in Figure 22a–j.

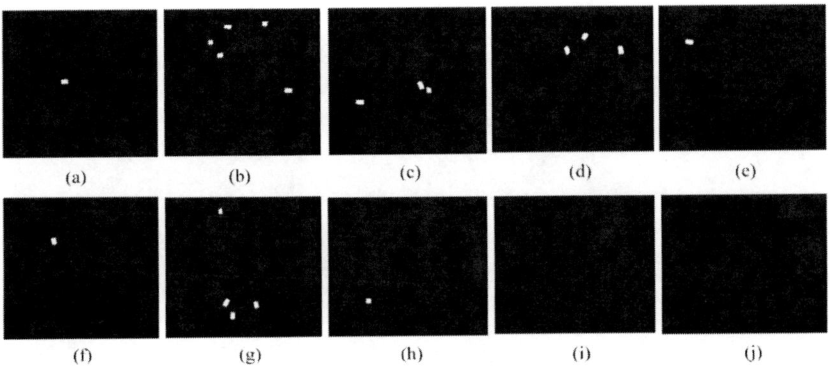


**Figure 24.** The results of the die regions in the abnormal cases corresponding to the images shown in Figure 22a–j.

There are 41 wafers images in total. The die numbers are divided into three situations: normal, abnormal, and packaged. As shown in this table, most of the dies in the abnormal cases can be correctly detected. Table 1summarizes the determined numbers in the normal, abnormal, and actual packaged cases. The recall and precision rates are provided as well. In this table, the precision and the recall rates are $(P/G) \times 100\%$ and 100%, respectively, when the detected number $P$ is greater than the ground truth number $G$. On the contrary, the precision and the recall rates are 100% and $(P/G) \times 100\%$, respectively, when the detected number $P$ is less than the ground truth number $G$. If the two numbers are equal ($P = G$), then both the precision and the recall rates are 100%. The recall and precision rates in the experimental results of the 41 test images achieve 99.82% and 99.84%, respectively. The computation time for each test image is around 0.7 s in average.

**Table 1.** The recall and precision results in the experiments.

| Wafer Image | Normal (*N*) | Abnormal (*S*) | Packaged (*P*) | Ground Truth (*G*) | Precision Rate |
|---|---|---|---|---|---|
| 1 | 315 | 3 | 312 | 311 | 99.68% |
| 2 | 315 | 3 | 312 | 311 | 99.68% |
| 3 | 315 | 5 | 310 | 309 | 99.68% |
| 4 | 310 | 10 | 310 | 309 | 99.68% |
| 5 | 323 | 13 | 310 | 309 | 99.68% |
| 6 | 314 | 6 | 308 | 309 | 100.00% |
| 7 | 313 | 3 | 310 | 310 | 100.00% |
| 8 | 314 | 4 | 310 | 310 | 100.00% |
| 9 | 318 | 4 | 314 | 314 | 100.00% |
| 10 | 321 | 7 | 314 | 314 | 100.00% |
| 11 | 326 | 11 | 315 | 314 | 99.68% |
| 12 | 326 | 11 | 315 | 315 | 100.00% |
| 13 | 312 | 1 | 311 | 311 | 100.00% |
| 14 | 323 | 10 | 313 | 311 | 99.36% |
| 15 | 324 | 12 | 312 | 311 | 99.68% |
| 16 | 315 | 3 | 312 | 311 | 99.68% |
| 17 | 312 | 1 | 311 | 311 | 100.00% |
| 18 | 313 | 1 | 312 | 311 | 99.68% |
| 19 | 319 | 7 | 312 | 311 | 99.68% |
| 20 | 321 | 6 | 315 | 316 | 100.00% |
| 21 | 320 | 5 | 315 | 316 | 100.00% |
| 22 | 320 | 2 | 318 | 318 | 100.00% |
| 23 | 321 | 4 | 317 | 318 | 100.00% |
| 24 | 312 | 1 | 311 | 311 | 100.00% |
| 25 | 319 | 7 | 312 | 311 | 99.68% |
| 26 | 313 | 1 | 312 | 311 | 99.68% |
| 27 | 317 | 8 | 309 | 311 | 100.00% |
| 28 | 317 | 7 | 310 | 311 | 100.00% |
| 29 | 302 | 4 | 298 | 311 | 100.00% |
| 30 | 317 | 6 | 311 | 312 | 100.00% |
| 31 | 313 | 0 | 313 | 313 | 100.00% |
| 32 | 315 | 2 | 313 | 313 | 100.00% |
| 33 | 315 | 2 | 313 | 313 | 100.00% |
| 34 | 316 | 3 | 314 | 313 | 99.68% |
| 35 | 322 | 7 | 315 | 313 | 99.37% |
| 36 | 318 | 2 | 316 | 316 | 100.00% |
| 37 | 325 | 9 | 316 | 316 | 100.00% |
| 38 | 330 | 11 | 319 | 316 | 99.06% |
| 39 | 320 | 3 | 317 | 316 | 99.68% |
| 40 | 319 | 2 | 317 | 315 | 99.37% |
| 41 | 316 | 1 | 315 | 315 | 100.00% |

# 4. CONCLUSIONS

This paper presents a machine-vision-based method to automatically determine the number of successfully packaged dies in a wafer image. The most significant contribution of the proposed method is that it can handle all the cases of the residual dies, including those in the wafer boundary, broken dies, fractured dies and dropped dies in the wafer. The precision and recall rates achieved were 99.82% and 99.84%, respectively, in the 41 test wafer images.

Figure 21a–j show that the brightness and position of each wafer image are slightly different. It is influenced by the ambient light and non-fixed photographic environment. In the future work, we will improve the image capture environment such that the number of system parameters can be reduced to make the system simpler. In addition, more test images will be collected to make the proposed method more robust in the various abnormal cases.

# ACKNOWLEDGMENTS

This research is partially supported by the Ministry of Science and Technology (MOST), Taiwan under contract numbers MOST 103-2221-E-224-019 and MOST 103-2221-E-224-035 MY2. The authors thank for the reviewers' valuable comments and the English revision made by Resta S. Cheng.

# AUTHOR CONTRIBUTIONS

Hsuan-Ting Chang has been responsible for the whole system modeling and the evaluation of the experimental results. Ren-Jie Pan and Hsaio-Wei Peng have been responsible for the experimental setup and the system implementation with Matlab coding.

## REFERENCES


1. Driels, M.R.; Pathre, U.S. Vision-based automatic theodolite for robot calibration. *IEEE Trans. Robot. Autom.* **1991**, *7*, 351–360.

2. Madhvanath, S.; Govindaraju, V. The role of holistic paradigms in handwritten word recognition. *IEEE Trans. Pattern Anal. Mach. Intell.* **2001**, *23*, 149–164.

3. Kumar, A.; Yingbo, Z. Human Identification Using Finger Images. *IEEE Trans. Image Process.* **2012**, *21*, 2228–2244.

4. Lin, Y.S.; Lee, T.C.; Chang, H.T.; Peng, S.J.; Huang, J.W.; Wang, H.P.; Hung, C.W. A computer-aided method for automatic localization and thickness measurement of peritoneum in ultrasound images. In Proceedings of the Annual International Conference of the IEEE Engineering in Medicine and Biology Society, MA, USA, 30 August–3 September 2011; pp. 8005–8008.

5. Gao, Y.S.; Leung, M.K.H. Face recognition using line edge map. *IEEE Trans. Pattern Anal. Mach. Intell.* **2002**,*24*, 764–779.

6. Hackenberg, G.; McCall, R.; Broll, W. Lightweight palm and finger tracking for real-time 3D gesture control. In Proceedings of the IEEE Virtual Reality Conference (VR), Singapore, Singapore, 19–23 March 2011; pp. 19–26.

7. Zeng, Z.; Dai, S.; Mu, P.A. Wafer defects detecting and classifying system based on machine vision. In Proceedings of the International Conference on Electronic Measurement and Instruments, Xi'an, China, 16–18 August 2007; pp. 4-520–4-523.

8. Wu, H.H.P.; Yang, J.G.; Hsu, M.M.; Wu, C.J. Automatic measurement and grading of LED dies on wafer by machine vision. In Proceedings of the IEEE International Conference on Mechatronics, Kumamoto, Japan, 8–10 May 2007; pp. 1–6.

9. Wang, G.; Li, D.; Wu, L.; Deng, Y.; Liu, R. Machine vision recognition of disconnection failure of IC wafer. In Proceedings of the International Conference on Electronic Packaging Technology, Shanghai, China, 26–29 August 2006; pp. 1–4.

10. Sharma, G.; Kumar, A.; Rao, V.S.; Soon, W.H.; Kripesh, V. Solutions strategies for die shift problem in wafer level compression molding. *IEEE Trans. Compon. Packag. Manuf. Technol.* **2011**, *1*, 502–509.

11. Croft, G.D.; Lomenick, R.L.; Youngblood, D.L.; Johnston, J.M. Die-counting algorithm for yield modeling and die-per-wafer optimization. *SPIE* **1997**, *3216*, 186–196.

12. Cunningham, J.A. The use of evaluation of yield models in integrated circuit manufacturing. *IEEE Trans. Semicond. Manuf.* **1990**, *3*, 60–71.

13. De Vries, D.K. Investigation of gross die per wafer formulas. *IEEE Trans. Semicond. Manuf.* **2005**, *18*, 136–139.

14. Magee, M.R.; Beer, M.D.; Erck, W.R. Computation of Die-Per-Wafer Considering Production Technology and Wafer Size. United States Patent US 6,529,790, 4 March 2003.

15. Die Per Wafer Calculator 1.00. Available online: http:// mrhackerott.org/semiconductor-informatics/ informatics/toolz/ DPW Calculator/ Input.html (accessed on 6 April 2015).

16. Die-per-Wafer Estimator. Available online: http://www.silicon-edge.co.uk/j/ index.php/resources/die-per-wafer (accessed on 6 April 2015).

17. Mital, D.P.; Teoh, E.K. Computer based wafer inspection system. In Proceedings of the 1991 International Conference on Industrial Electronics, Control and Instrumentation, 28 October–1 November 1991; pp. 2497–2503.

18. Su, C.T.; Yang, T.; Ke, C.M. Neural-network approach for semiconductor wafer post-sawing inspection.*IEEE Trans. Semicond. Manuf.* **2002**, *15*, 260–266.

19. Chang, H.T.; Pan, R.J. Automatic counting of packaged wafer die based on machine vision. In Proceedings of the 2012 International Conference on Information Security and Intelligent Control (ISIC 2012), Douliu, Taiwan, 14–16 August 2012; pp. 274–277.

20. Xu, S.; Cheng, Z.; Gao, Y.; Pan, Q. Visual wafer dies counting using geometrical characteristics. *IET Image Process.* **2014**, *8*, 280–288.

21. Wafer Chip Counter—IVC12. Available online: http://www.ivtech.com.tw/ (accessed on 6 April 2015).

22. Fischler, M.A.; Bolles, R.C. Random sample consensus: A paradigm for model fitting with applications to image analysis and automated cartography. *Commun. ACM* **1981**, *24*, 381–395.

23. De la Fraga, L.G.; Dominguez, G.M.L. Robust detection of several circles or ellipses with heuristics. In Proceedings of the IEEE Congress Evolutionary Computation, New Orleans, LA, USA, 5–8 June 2011; pp. 484–490.

24. Otsu, N. A threshold selection method from gray-level histograms. *IEEE Trans. Syst. Man Cybern.* **1979**, *9*, 62–66.

25. Gonzalez, R.C.; Woods, R.E. *Digital Image Processing*, 2nd ed.; Prentice-Hall, Inc.: New Jersey, NJ, USA, 2002.

26. Canny, J. A computational approach to edge detection. *IEEE Trans. Pattern Anal. Mach. Intell.* **1986**, *PAMI-8*, 679–698.

27. Kim, Y.T. Contrast enhancement using brightness preserving bi-histogram equalization. *IEEE Trans. Consum. Electron.* **1997**, *43*, 1–8.

# Chapter 10

# Objective Definition of Rosette Shape Variation Using a Combined Computer Vision and Data Mining Approach

**Anyela Camargo, Dimitra Papadopoulou, Zoi Spyropoulou, Konstantinos Vlachonasios, John H. Doonan, Alan P. Gay**

*Institute of Biological, Environmental and Rural Sciences, Aberystwyth University, Gogerddan, Aberystwyth, Ceredigion, United Kingdom*

## ABSTRACT

Computer-vision based measurements of phenotypic variation have implications for crop improvement and food security because they are intrinsically objective. It should be possible therefore to use such approaches to select robust genotypes. However, plants are morphologically complex and identification of meaningful traits from automatically acquired image data is not straightforward. Bespoke algorithms can be designed to capture and/or quantitate specific features but this approach is inflexible and is not generally applicable to a wide range of traits. In this paper, we have used industry-standard computer vision techniques to extract a wide range of features from images of genetically diverse *Arabidopsis* rosettes growing under non-stimulated conditions, and then used statistical analysis to identify those features that provide good discrimination between ecotypes. This analysis indicates that almost all the observed shape variation can be described by 5 principal components. We describe an easily implemented pipeline including image segmentation, feature extraction and statistical analysis. This pipeline provides a cost-effective and inherently scalable method to parameterise and analyse variation in rosette shape. The acquisition of images does not require any specialised equipment and the computer routines for image processing and data analysis have been implemented using open source software. Source code for data analysis is written using the R package. The equations to calculate image descriptors have been also provided.

## INTRODUCTION

The goal of this study was to use a computer vision and data mining approach to compare the rosette shapes of the founders of a Multiparent Advanced Generation Inter-Cross (MAGIC) population. A genetic analysis of the same population was performed and reported previously [1]. Objective computer-aided phenotyping has been proposed as a solution to the genotype-phenotype bottleneck [2], but there remain numerous technical challenges with regard to its implementation at the whole organism level. However, there has been little exploration of the ability of computer vision techniques to define and discriminate between phenotypes.

We chose *Arabidopsis* rosettes as our experimental material for three main reasons. First, the rosettes in this species (under our growth conditions) grow close to the ground and can be treated essentially as 2-D objects, simplifying image acquisition and processing. Second, previous studies indicate that there is significant shape variation between accessions. Natural variation in continuously varying traits has been shown for morphological traits and for responses to stimuli. Examples of the former are morphological comparisons during development between Ler-0, Col-0 and Ws-0 ecotypes [3], quantitative trait loci (QTL) analysis of leaf and floral organ size of 162 recombinant inbred lines (RIL) from a reciprocal cross between Ler and Cvi [4] and seed size of the *iku*2-1, *fis*2-1, *arf*2,*pAP*1::*ARF*2 mutants and Col-0 and

Ler-0 ecotypes [5]. Examples of the latter are the effects of drought, low temperature and differing levels of UV-B on chlorophyll-fluorescence on growth [6] and the natural variability of 23 accessions in response to nitrogen [7]. Third, *Arabidopsis* is a widely used model system with sophisticated genetic and genomic resources [8] available for dissecting biological processes. Forward genetic approaches have been used to study mutants with strong phenotypic effects providing insight into the underlying molecular functions. While this approach is extremely useful as a research tool, commercial plant breeding often requires exploitation of continuous variation. Analysis of continuous variation in breeding populations is more demanding, but effective automation of the phenotype measurements would have huge advantages for crop improvement and food security. *Arabidopsis* is also a good model for studying continuous variation, with the advantage of thoroughly investigated genomics [9], [10]. The native range is North-Western Eurasia and it has recently colonised other parts of the world during the Columbian Exchange [11]. Local populations have often diverged, to a degree depending on factors such as time of separation and differential selection. The species is therefore a useful model to study natural variation, its underlying genetic basis and its consequences.

Natural variants provide material for studying genome evolution and the genetic dissection of complex traits. The *Arabidopsis* lines used here are the inbred parental lines of a MAGIC mapping population, which have been selected from a wide range of locations and cover a range of genetic diversity [12]. The MAGIC population contains several hundred recombinant inbred lines (RILs) descended from the 19 founder lines, via a series of defined intercrosses. These RILs and the 19 founders have been genotyped and previously scored for development-related traits such as flowering time [1].

High throughput methods that are suitable for measuring continuous variation have been applied to *Arabidopsis*. For example, a single time point study characterised *Arabidopsis*plants grown in vitro by analysing rosettes, leaves and leaf cells in 111 mutants and three wild-type accessions [13]. In another study, rosette areas of ecotypes were analysed across developmental stages using an automated phenotyping pipeline [14]. Responses to soil water deficit of natural accessions have been reported from the PHENOPSIS platform [15]. Similarly, GROWSCREEN investigated growth potential of starch-free mutants of *Arabidopsis* [16]. These approaches often use non-destructive image analysis as an element of growth measurements. However, for complex biological objects there is no generally accepted method of parameterising shapes, which makes quantification of change and determination of significance of differences difficult, particularly for characters subject to continuous variation. In *Arabidopsis* some aspects, such as leaf shape [17], [18]have been studied in detail, but usually by destructive methods. Also, the technique used (principal component analysis of points on the leaf margin) is difficult to apply to overlapping composite structures that change in shape as the plant grows, as in*Arabidopsis* rosettes (Figure 1).

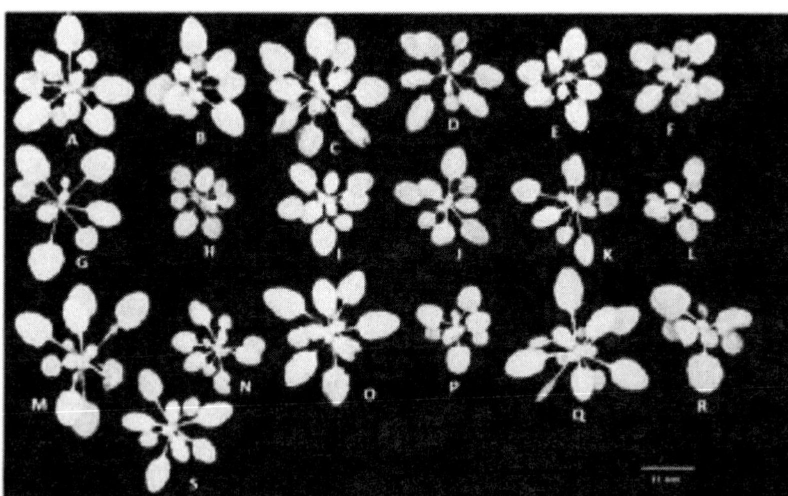

**Figure 1.** Images of representative plants of the 19 parental lines [1] at 28 DAS. (A) EDi-0, (B) Can-0, (C) WS-0, (D) Hi-0, (E) Zu-0, (F) Po-0, (G) Sf-2, (H) Wil-2, (I) Oy-0, (J) Kn-0, (K) Ct-1, (L) Wu-0, (M) Tsu-0, (N) Col-0, (O) Rsch-4, (P) No-0, (Q) Bur-0, (R) Ler-0 and (S) Mt-0.

Using the 19 parental lines as a test population, we investigate the ability of a range of morphological descriptors developed for image analysis [19] to discriminate rosette images, an exercise not previously reported for *Arabidopsis*. We used machine-vision methods to analyse shape descriptors extracted from segmented images of rosettes [20] and provided a wider range of parameters with definitions of their calculations than previously reported. This method does not require any specialised equipment for image capture and is therefore generally applicable. Two different commercially available software packages were evaluated and used to extract descriptors. This allowed us to compare the accessions according to their phenotypic diversity and to address the following questions: 1) Are shape descriptors time-dependent, ecotype-dependent or both? 2) What are the most important descriptors of rosette shape among the set tested? 3) Do shape descriptors differ between the ecotypes? 4) If shape descriptors change with time, is the direction and amount of change similar in all ecotypes? We show that shape descriptors can be used to parameterise and determine significant differences between rosette shapes of *Arabidopsis*lines and we discuss the potentially wider role of these characters. We also compare our data with that of a previous study in different media and at a single time point [13], to assess the generalizable ability of these results This provides a cost-effective, scalable method to parameterise shape that can be used non-destructively on whole plants.

## MATERIALS AND METHODS

### Plant material

Seeds of 19 genetically contrasting but individually uniform ecotypes [12] (EDi-0, Can-0, WS-0, Hi-0, Zu-0, Po-0, Sf-2, Wil-2, Oy-0, Kn-0, Ct-1, Wu-0, Tsu-0, Col-0, Rsch-4, No-0, Bur-0, Ler-0, Mt-0) of *Arabidopsis thaliana* were sown on moist Levington F2 compost (Scotts UK Professional, Bamford, Suffolk, UK) in 24 pot (each pot 51 by 47 by 47 mm) trays kept at 4C for one week before moving to a controlled environment room (CER) at 23°C day/20°C night, day/night

(8/16 h) and 110 µmol $m^{-2}$ $s^{-1}$ PPFD (Sylvania VHO fluorescent tubes). These conditions were chosen to be reasonably similar to the conditions recommended in a laboratory manual for the growth of *Arabidopsis* (16–25°C, 120–150 µmol $m^{-2}$ $s^{-1}$ PPFD), with a day length of less than 12 hours to avoid acceleration of reproductive development[21]. Twelve replicates were grown per ecotype and trays were watered with a conventional watering can. Trays were also moved and rotated regularly to randomise local environmental variables and watering. No further nutrients were supplied during the course of the experiment.

## Data acquisition

Photographs of rosettes were taken using a Panasonic DMC-G1 camera mounted horizontally on a tripod at a resolution of 3000×4000 pixels on 17, 22, 25, 28 and 30 days after stratification (DAS), $t_1$ to $t_5$ respectively. Images were taken between 10.20 am and 11.20 am in the growth chamber where light and temperature were kept constant. A composite image of typical plants on 28 DAS is shown in Figure 1. Using an internal length reference, a scaling factor was calculated (average 7.31 pixels per mm SEM 0.104) and applied to each image to compensate for any slight variation in the position of the tray relative to the camera and to convert pixel-based measurements to dimensions to facilitate comparisons with other work. All measurements were made in the early stages of plant development, before significant floral development, when it was reasonable to analyse the rosette as a two dimensional structure.

## Image analysis

Image processing was performed using LemnaGrid software from LemnaTec [22] in the following sequence: 1) Nearest neighbour foreground/background colour separation was used to classify pixels. Two sets of colour intensities, corresponding to foreground (target) and to background (non target) are selected. RGB pixels matching selected

**Figure 2. Example features extracted from one plant of EDi-0.** (A) normsmallpax and lormlargepax, (B) vrectsizex and vrectsizey, (C) maxdiam, (D) outline of convex hull, from which convhullcirc and convhullarea are determined (E) minrectarea, (F) mincirclediam.

intensities are mapped into the image. A search around mapped pixels is performed to identify pixels with similar intensities that might be part of the foreground/background regions. Once the search is performed, the image is converted to binary, where 1 is the target (plant) and 0 the background (compost, tray, etc). 2) Morphological techniques were then applied to deal with pixels incorrectly classified [19]. First, morphological erosion was applied to remove small and isolated pixel regions incorrectly classified as plant. Second, morphological dilation was applied to correct for those pixels located in the border of the images that were incorrectly classified as background. 3) A final filter operation used the area of the pots to mark approximately the region occupied by each plant in the tray, and foreground pixels outside this region were deleted. Once the images were segmented, 20 image features (Table 1 shows the list of features - descriptors) describing the geometry, shape and size of rosettes were extracted. Some of these features are illustrated in Figure 2 (an example set is shown in Figure S1). Table S2 shows the values corresponding to the descriptors highlighted in Figure S2. In Methods S2 further details of the specific calculations used, their labels in the Lemna Tec software, their equivalents in Matlab [23] and the complete data table of image features are provided.

**Table 1.** Shape descriptors extracted from segmented *Arabidopsis* rosettes.

| Id[1] | Name | Description | Group[2] | Trans[3] | Unit |
|---|---|---|---|---|---|
| 1 | Mincirclediam | Diameter of the smallest circle the rosette would pass through without touching. | A | $\log_e$ | mm |
| 2 | Normsmallpax | Ratio of the Sum of distances of all pixels from smaller axis in direction of the larger axis normalised to rosette area | N | | Ratio |
| 3 | Normlargepax | Ratio of the Sum of distances of all pixels from the larger axis in direction of the smaller axis. normalised to rosette area | N | | Ratio |
| 4 | Minrectarea | Area of smallest rectangle of any orientation covering rosette | A | $\log_e$ | $mm^2$ |
| 5 | Mindistcenbdy | The distance between the centroid and the nearest point on the rosette boundary | N | | mm |
| 6 | Vrectsizey | Height of the smallest vertical rectangle covering the rosette. | A | $\log_e$ | mm |
| 7 | Vrectsizex | Width of the smallest vertical rectangle covering the rosette | A | $\log_e$ | mm |
| 8 | Compactness | Rosette Area/Conhullarea | N | | Ratio |
| 9 | Normrotmo | Moment of inertia of rosette around centroid | N | | Ratio |
| 10 | Area | Area of rosette | A | $\log_e$ | $mm^2$ |
| 11 | Paxratio | Normlargepax/Normsmallpax | N | | Ratio |
| 12 | Circumference | Perimeter of rosette excluding holes | A | $\log_e$ | mm |
| 13 | Excentricity | Ratio of Normlargepax to Normsmallpax | N | | Ratio |
| 14 | Maxdiam | Maximum distance between two points on the rosette boundary | A | $\log_e$ | mm |
| 15 | Roundness | $Circumference^2$/Area | N | | Ratio |
| 16 | Bdryround | $Bdrycount^2$/area. | N | $\log_e$ | Ratio |
| 17 | Bdrycount | Boundary of rosette including perimeter and holes | A | $\log_e$ | mm |
| 18 | Bdrytoarearatio | Bdrycount/Area | N | | $mm^{-1}$ |
| 19 | Conhullcirc | Length of convex hull, the line with no concave sections surrounding the rosette | A | $\log_e$ | mm |
| 20 | Conhullarea | Area included in Conhullcirc | A | $\log_e$ | $mm^2$ |

[1]id is index to descriptors used in Figure 5
[2]Indicates whether descriptor is in the Area (A) or non-Area group (N)
[3]Indicates if data were transformed using a loge scale.

The features used to describe shape can be grouped into two classes, those with a simple meaning and definition and those whose interpretation is more complex. For example, comparing 'Area' and 'Roundness': 'Area' is the pale green region comprising the rosette within the rectangle in Figure 2; 'Roundness', indicating circularity of the object, is more complex as it is given by the ratio of $Circumference^2$ to Area, where 'Circumference' is the total length of the lines forming the outside of the rosette. Simple and complex features are necessary to give a complete description of the shape of the object and will be used to quantify variation between shapes of parental lines. The relationship between the shape descriptors over a range of rosette shapes is illustrated in Figure S1. In addition, Relative Rosette Area Growth Rate (RRAGR) was calculated as:

$$RRAGR = \frac{\log\left(Area_{t_{i+1}}\right) - \log\left(Area_{t_i}\right)}{t_{i+1} - t_i} \quad (1)$$

where $Area_{t_i}$ is the rosette area at time $t_i$, with $t_i$ as defined above. RRAGR were plotted and analysed at the mean time for RRAGR calculation.

## Data processing and analysis

The descriptors were loaded into a dataset and after Shapiro normality tests appropriate $\log_e$ transformation were applied when necessary to produce normality (Table 1). The Bonferroni Outlier Test was applied to identify and remove outliers that could bias the results. A linear mixed effect (lme) model for repeated measurements [24] was fitted for each character (Eq. 2). This modelling approach was favoured against other alternatives as it is appropriate when dealing with time series, when the variances of the observations are unequal or when there is a degree of correlation between measurements.

$$Y_{ij} = \beta_1 x_{1ij} + \ldots + \beta_p x_{pij} + b_{i1} z_{1ij} + \ldots + b_{iq} z_{qij} + \varepsilon_{ij} \quad (2)$$

$$\varepsilon_{ij} \sim N\left(0, \sigma^2 \lambda_{ijj}\right), Cov\left(\varepsilon_{ij}, \epsilon_{ij'}\right) - \sigma^2 \lambda_{ijj'}$$

Where $Y_{ij}$ is the response variable for the $j$th of $n_i$ observations in the $i$th of $M$ ecotypes

$x_{1ij}, \ldots, x_{pij}$ are the fixed-effect regressors for observation $j$ in group $i$

$b_{i1}, \ldots, b_{iq}$ are the random-effect coefficients for group $i$, $i=1, \ldots, q$ number of groups

$z_{1ij}, \ldots, z_{qij}$ are the random-effect regressors

$\beta_i$, ..., $\beta_p$ are the fixed-effect coefficients, $i=1, .., p$ number of effects

$\varepsilon_{ij}$ is the error for observation $j$ in group $i$

$\sigma^2\lambda_{ijj'k}$ are the covariances between errors in group $i$. If the observations in a group represent longitudinal data on a single individual (e.g. observations collected over time), then the structure of the λ's is specified to capture autocorrelation among the errors.

The post-hoc Tukey test was applied to perform pairwise analysis over the fitted models P-values were adjusted using the Bonferroni multiple test correction ($P<0.05$).

ReliefF [27] and Principal Component Analysis (PCA), two contrasting methods of determining the relative importance of multivariate characters were used to compare variability of shape descriptors. ReliefF estimates the quality of attributes in classification problems with strong interdependencies and PCA (with variables scaled to zero mean and unit variance) was used to determine underlying grouping variables which summarise variability in the data. All statistical analysis were carried out using the R [25] and the Weka[26] packages.

## RESULTS

The evaluation of time courses of ecotype shape descriptors proceeded in three stages: Firstly, differences in shape parameters between the ecotypes (an ecotype effect) were determined. Secondly, changes with time were across all ecotypes (a time effect) were assessed, and thirdly differences in the changes with time between ecotypes (an interaction effect e.g. time x ecotype) were checked. Inspection of plots of the shape descriptors across time and ecotype were used to establish general characteristics of the data (see Figure 3 for an example plots and the full set in Figure S2). They also helped design statistical models for each descriptor. These plots clearly fall into two groups (Table 1), one whose time course was continually rising similar to that of Area (Area group) and those whose time courses were much more variable in slope and direction (the NonArea group). More details of these groups are in the 'Analysis of descriptors over time' section below. The Area Group characters have a quadratic time course, suggesting that a quadratic effect of time should be included in any statistical model. However, we recognise this is a simplification of the complete growth curve, possibly sigmoid, for which we have partial data only. The same plots also showed that shape descriptors, for both groups: a) changed over time (not horizontal lines across the time), suggesting time dependency; b) were significantly different between ecotypes (lines touched or overlapped), suggesting ecotype dependency and c) were time and ecotype dependent.

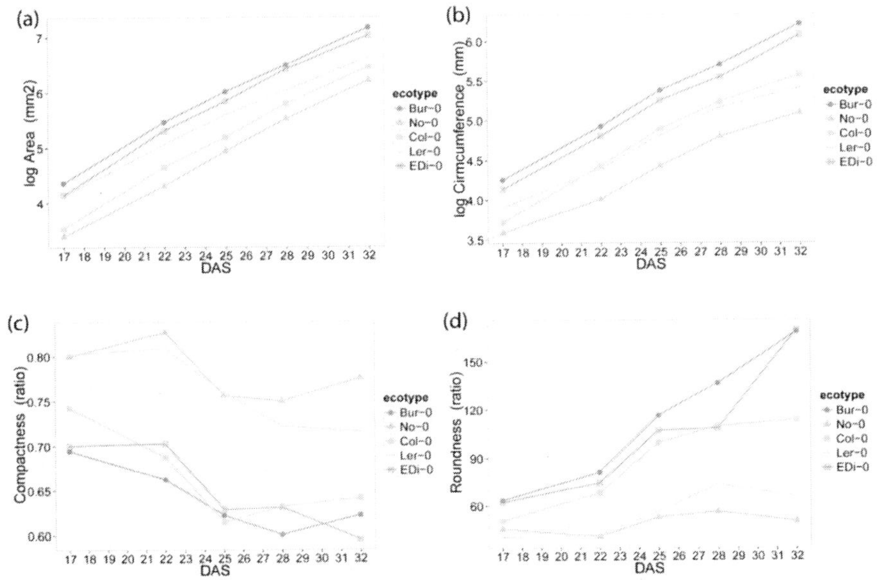


**Figure 3.** Time course for selected genotypes from statistical model for (A) $\log_e$Area (B) $\log_e$ Circumference (C) Compactness and (D) Roundness.

As the experiment was a split-plot design replicated in time (to asses changes over time), a linear mixed effect model that took in consideration the effects of the repeated measurements design and the variance and covariance of each shape descriptor was used. The model included a random intercept for each plant, an ecotype effect, a time effect, and an ecotype-time interaction effect. In addition for the Area group DAS squared was added to the model to allow for the quadratic trend with time. Eq. 3 is the model of Compactness for observation *j* in the group *i* at *t* time point. Eq. 4 is the model of Area for observation *j* in the group *i* at *t* time point.

$$Compactness_{ijt} = \beta_0(1) + \beta_1 \text{ecotype}_{ij} \beta_2 DAS_{tj} + \varepsilon_{ijt} \tag{3}$$

$$Area_{ijt} = \beta_0(1) + \beta_1 \text{ecotype}_{ij} \beta_2 DAS_{tj} + \beta_1 \text{ecotype}_{ij} \beta_2 DAS_{tj}^2 + \varepsilon_{ijt} \tag{4}$$

Results of the lme models for each shape descriptor confirmed that (a) there was a significant time effect ($P<0.05$), suggesting time dependency, (b) there was a significant ecotype effect ($P<0.05$), suggesting ecotype dependency and (c) there was a significant interaction effect ($P<0.05$) between time and ecotype. Plots of residuals showed normally distributed errors with homogenous variances providing an indication of the goodness of fit of the model describing each shape descriptor.

Figure **3** shows time courses from fitted models for 'Area', 'Circumference', 'Compactness' and 'Roundness' for selected ecotypes.

To determine over which time steps the differences in the shape parameters were significant across all ecotypes, a pairwise Tukey test over the lme model was applied between DAS. 'Normsmallpax', 'Normlargepax' and 'Normrotmo' showed significant differences only between $t_1$ and $t_2$. 'Mindistcenbdy' showed significant differences only between $t_2$ and $t_3$. 'Excentricity' showed significant differences only between $t_3$ and $t_4$. 'Compactness' is relatively constant with time and generally becomes stable after $t_2$ suggesting that 'Compactness' is defined early in development. Images of rosettes (Figure 4A) contrast the low 'Compactness' in Ct-1 due to long petioles with the greater 'Compactness' of No-0 with its much more closely spaced leaves. Other descriptors such as 'RRAGR' show most significant ($P<0.01$) differences between the pairs 'Tsu-0/Wil-2, 'Tsu-0/No-0' and 'Tsu-0/Ler-0' (Figure S7). Differences between all-time points were significant (P<0.05). 'Area' was significantly different between all time steps (P<0.05), as would be expected for a size parameter of growing plants (Figure 4). Between ecotypes 'Area', showed the most significant differences (P<0.01) between the pairs 'No-0/Bur-0', 'Bur-0/Wu-0' and 'EDi-0/No-0'. Images of Bur-0 and Wu-0 have been added to Figure 4C to illustrate the greater size of the rosette in Bur-0 than Wu-0. Figures 4B and 4D use box plots to illustrate the changes in 'Compactness' and 'RRAGR, and the variation between replicates, for each ecotype across time.

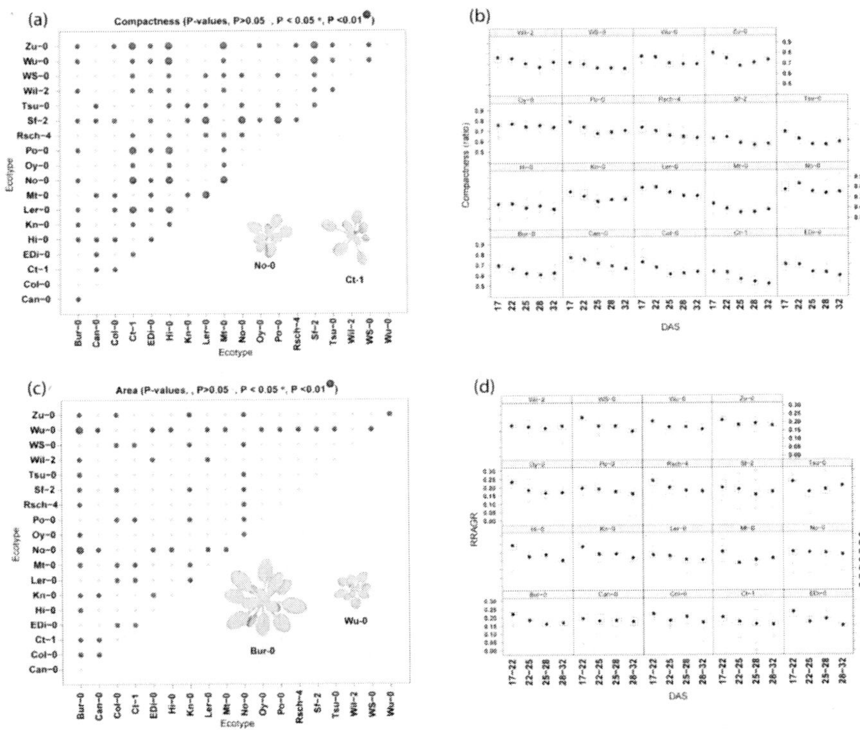


**Figure 4. Multiple comparisons of Compactness and Area between ecotypes.** Scatter plots showing significant (P>0.05•, P<0.05 •, P<0.01•, Post-hoc Tukey test between ecotypes) differences between ecotypes for (A) 'Compactness' and (C) 'Area' and boxplots for (B) 'Compactness' and (D) Area over time. Images have been added to (A) and (B) to show range of 'Compactness' and 'Area'.

Having established that shape descriptors changed at different rates through time and that this pattern of change differed between ecotypes, we asked whether ecotypes could be grouped on the basis of their shape parameters. Visual inspection of radar plots for each ecotype (Figure 5) indicate that Bur-0 and EDi-0, No-0 and Wu-0, Po-0 and Can-0 share a similar overall pattern of parameters, while Po-0 and Can-0 are very similar in terms of 'Compactness' and 'Area'. The plots also show that No-0 and Ler-0 are both quite compact but Ler-0 has a greater rosette 'Area'. The radar plot is an excellent way to rapidly identify groups that are common at a given descriptor.

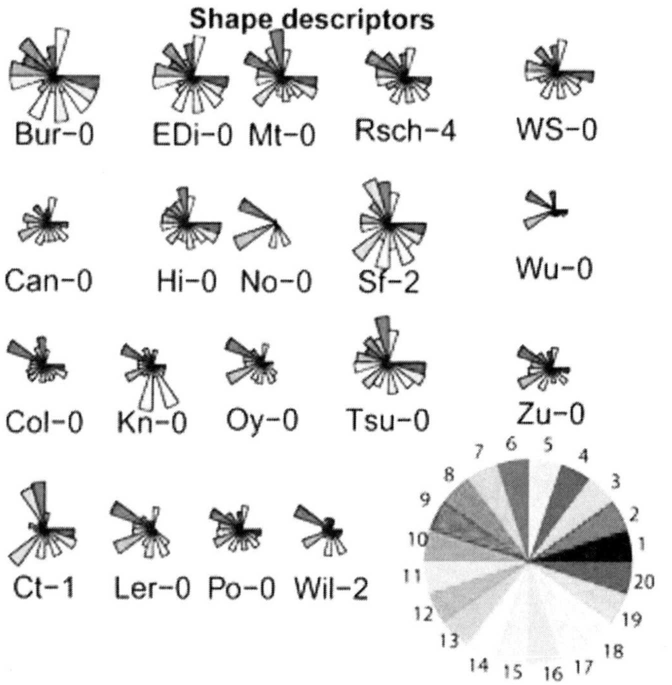


**Figure 5. Shape descriptor plots of ecotype's feature profile.** Radar plot of 20 shape features for each ecotype. Plots are average of 12 replicates over five time points. Variable assignment key for star plot is located at the bottom right corner. Each star plot or segment diagram represents one row of the input data. Variables (columns) start on the right and wind counter clockwise around the circle. The size of the (scaled) column is shown by the distance from the centre to the point on the star or the radius of the segment representing the variable. The columns of the data matrix are scaled independently so that the maximum value in each column is 1 and the minimum is 0. Segment numbers corresponding to descriptors are defined in Table 1.

## Feature selection

PCA was performed per time point to identify meaningful underlying variables and whether they show the same pattern across time. At 17 DAS 54.26% of the variation was captured by the first principal component and 19.53% by the second, (Figure 6A). PCA plots for 22, 25, 28 and 32 DAS are shown in Figure S3. In summary, the major contributors to PC1 were 'Maxdiam', 'Conhullcirc', 'Circumference', 'Mincirclediam', 'Bdrycount', 'Minrectarea' and 'Conhullarea'. The major contributors of PC2 were 'Bdrytoarearatio', 'Normlargepax', 'normrotmo' and 'Compactness'. PC3 captured 14.3% of the variation and the major contributors were: 'Normsmallpax', 'Paxratio' and 'Excentricity'. Variation captured in further components was: PC4: 5.14%, PC5: 2.68%, PC6: 2.04% and PC7 to PC20's summed was 2.04%. Interestingly, the major contributor of PC4 was 'Mindistcenbdy' (contributing 84%) suggesting a more detailed look to this descriptor in future analysis. Figures S4A–D show standard contributions for each descriptor.

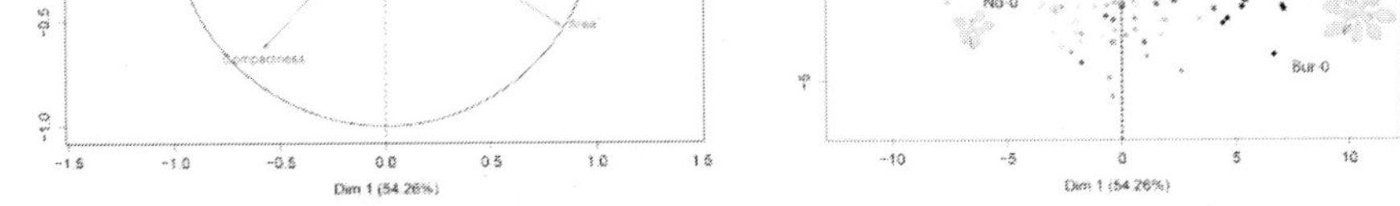


**Figure 6. Principal Component Analysis.** (A) Variable loadings for first and second principal components, 17 DAS and (B) Analysis by ecotype over first and second principal components, 17 DAS. Significance level is given by the size of the squares, the smaller the square the more significantly different (P<0.05). (C) Contrast in 'Area' between 'Bur-0' and 'Wu-0' and Contrast in 'Compactness' between 'Ct-1' and 'No-0') and where both ecotypes have similar Area as demonstrated in plot (A).

PCA of all observations labelled by time showed that there was more variability later than earlier in growth (Figure S5).

Further, we applied the ReliefF method for attribute estimation in the regression to reduce the dimensionality of the data. This method assesses a set of features in a dataset and ranks them according to their power to accurately differentiate classes (i.e. ecotypes) in the dataset. The test ranked 'Compactness', 'Normrotmo' and 'Normlargepax' in first, second and third place and 'Conhullcirc' in last, confirming that 'Compactness' is an important discriminatory descriptor of rosette shape. This analysis also shows that 'Area' and 'Area-related' descriptors are not good discriminators of ecotypes. The Area plots in Figure S5shows a similar trend for each ecotype.

## Growth patterns of ecotypes

To evaluate the extent to which the patterns of growth were influenced by the time, data points classified by time were added as supplementary information to the PCA analysis. Results in Figure S5 show data points are located at the centre of the plot at an early stage and become scattered around at a later stages which suggest that plants showed more variability as the get bigger. In addition to time, ecotype variation was also analysed, Figure 6 shows results. Some points to highlight from this analysis are: there were significant differences ($P<0.05$) between the ecotype's shapes (given by the size of the square, the smaller the square the more significant). Bur-0, EDi-0 and WS-0 are on the same PCA dimensions suggesting similarities between them in relation to shape. This result is consistent to what is shown in the radar plots of Figure 5 where Bur-0 and EDi-0 show similar patterns. Ct-1 shows similarities with the other ecotypes at 17 DAS but soon its data points are scatter along dimension 2 (Figure S6A–D). Data points of Oy-0, Ler-0, and Zu-0 are on the same coordinates of 'Compactness' (Figure S6A–D) which suggests that these three ecotypes are correlated in 'Compactness'. To help in the analysis, rosette images of some ecotypes were superimposed on the plot. For example, data points corresponding to No-0 are on the coordinates of 'Compactness' and data points corresponding to Ct-1 are at the opposite site. This data organization suggest low correlation in 'Compactness' which is confirmed by the rosettes images of Ct-1 and No-0. Similarly, Bur-0's data points are on the coordinates of 'Area' and Wu-0 are at the opposite site, suggesting low correlation in 'Area' which is confirmed by the rosettes images of Bur-0 Wu-0.

## Analysis of descriptors over time

Phenotypic traits can be classified as static or dynamic. Static traits are often complex characteristics that tend to be measured at a single point in time (for example, yield), whereas dynamic traits (growth and other spatiotemporal changes) change with and can reveal different trajectories to similar end points [28], [29]. We analysed the trajectory of each descriptor over time and found two main patterns. The first pattern, the 'Area' group, defined above (Table 1) contained descriptors with a continually increasing plant size component as seen for 'Area' (Figure 3 and S2). The trajectories appeared to be parallel between ecotypes with a time displacement, Bur-0 having the greatest and No-0 the smallest 'Area' at the last measurement. Comparisons indicate that the increases in 'Area' are attributable to growth rather than changes in plant shape as would be the case, for example, if petiole elongation played a major role. Areas were already different when seedlings were first imaged and these differences were largely maintained during the period of the experiment. Increased 'Area' at first measurement may be the result of increased seed size at sowing as seeds of Bur-0 have been reported as larger than those of Col-0 and Ler-0 [5], However, seed areas (a measure of seed size) were not correlated with rosette area from multiple replicates of each ecotype and from two batches of seeds from the same source as used here.

The second group, the NonArea group, (Table 1) show variable patterns of change (Figures 7B and S2). This group includes descriptors of shape that relate to how the area is distributed to form the resultant rosette shape. Rsch-4 had the greatest 'Mindistcenbdy' and Can-0 the lowest (Figure S2). Within the overall pattern of compactness described above, there were noticeable differences between ecotypes with No-0 decreasing less than Ct-1 (Figure 7B). 'Paxratio' generally decreases over time with Sf-0 having the lowest and Bur-0 the highest. However, Ct-1 shows a different pattern, increasing moderately until $t_4$ and thereafter decreasing moderately. 'Roundness' increases over time with Bur-0 being the highest and No-0 the lowest. Bur-0 becomes rounder at every time step, which contrasts with all the other ecotypes. 'Bdryround' increases over time with Bur-0 increasing fastest and Ler-0 increasing more slowly. 'Excentricity' decreases over time with Bur-0 being the most rapid and Sf-2 the slowest. 'Bdrytoarearatio' is defined as the length of the outline divided by the area, and this relationship would be expected decrease as the plant grows on purely mathematical grounds. The rate of decline in the 'Bdrytoarearatio' was greater in Ler-0 than in Ct-1, the two ecotypes display extreme values for this parameter. See distribution of shape descriptors over time in Figure S2.

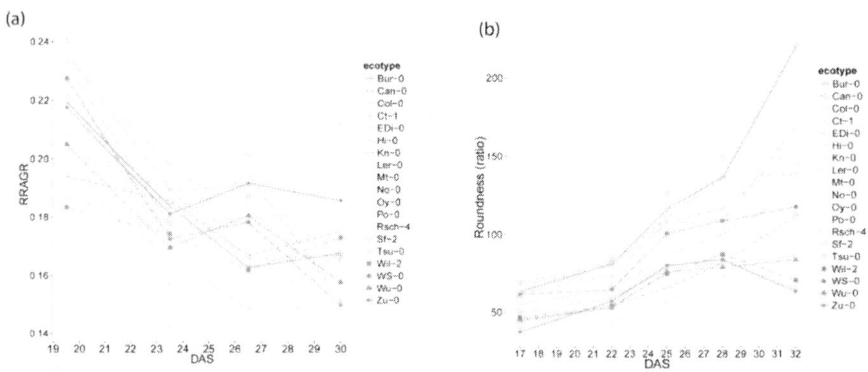


**Figure 7. Shape descriptors over time.** (A) Relative Rosette Area Growth Rate Over Time (RRAGR), (B) Compactness.

## Comparisons with a previous study

One of the principal problems in using a new approach such as the morphological descriptors used here is determining if the descriptors are universal To investigate this we have compared our results with a similar approach used previously [13]. Whilst both approaches were used on similar material, i.e. the rosettes of young *Arabidopsis* plants, there were important differences in the range of material used and cultivation (summarised in Table S3) and the previous data was collected at only one time point. Some comparable descriptors were present in both studies although in detail some were calculated slightly differently (see Table S4). PCA of the previous descriptors on our dataset (Figure S8A) produced a very similar distribution of principal components 1 and 2 to that in [13]. Although PC1 and PC2 accounted for more of the variation (82 and 13% for PCs 1 and 2 in our data compared with 78 and 11% respectively in [13]), probably an effect of the smaller number of variables used in our PCA. As in [13] most of the Correlations between area related parameters: Rosette area (RA), Rosette Perimeter (RP), Ellipse Area (EA), Ellipse Perimeter (EP) and Max Feret's diameter (RXF), were positive (Table S5, Figure S8B). Because of the wider range of the parameters due to the greater time for growth, these parameters appear to be more closely related than in [13]. Also the smaller number of ecotypes in our data set compared with the much larger number of lines in [13] may have resulted in the closer relationships in our data. As before the relations of the area based parameters with Rosette compactness (RC) were less well defined. Thus our results are largely in agreement with[13] but extend the approach to multiple time points, Also, our study took into account the repeated measurements and used statistical models to determine significant differences between ecotypes, time and their interaction, for each descriptor. We also reported more descriptors and define how each of was calculated to allow for other readers to repeat the analysis.

## DISCUSSION

Rosette shape and size are attractive traits on which to develop and evaluate automated approaches for objective machine-assisted plant phenotyping. The change in shape and size can describe how the plant (or crop) covers the ground surface, affecting traits such as photosynthetic potential and canopy closure. The latter affects a crop's ability to suppress competition [30] and, in dry climates, may affect soil water conservation. In *Arabidopsis*, rosettes lie approximately flat across the ground so simple 2D photography can acquire most of the relevant information.

Despite being intrinsically amenable to automated acquisition and analysis, there are few detailed studies of rosette shape surveying natural variation amongst a range of accessions as in the MAGIC plants here. In this study, aimed at developing non-destructive objective methods to monitor plant growth, we have used simple computational methods to process, analyse and compare the rosettes of 19 ecotypes of *Arabidopsis*. Images were taken at successive times to capture the patterns of growth, segmented to separate rosettes from background and features describing rosette shapes were extracted and analysed. Shape descriptors were compared to establish whether differences between ecotypes were significant. An advantage of this approach is that the descriptors used are either independent of plant orientation, or are calculated taking into account the principal axis of the rosette. The continuous and complex variation in rosette shape has been reduced to numerical descriptors, which was here examined for differences using established statistical techniques. Significant differences for the descriptors have been established between ecotypes (Figure 6) and two independent presentations revealed a similar pattern of relationships between the ecotypes (Figure 5). These two analyses suggested that shape descriptors were time and ecotype dependent because the time effect was significant ($P<0.05$), the ecotype effect was significant ($P<0.05$) and the interaction between time and ecotype was also significant ($P<0.05$). To confirm which of those ecotypes with apparently different time courses on initial visual inspection (Figure S2) were significantly different, post-hoc tests between pairs of ecotypes were used. Furthermore, the RRAGR interaction plots (Figure 7A) and the post-hoc tests suggested that descriptors such as 'Area' do not change with the same direction and amount in all ecotypes (Figure S7). Those changes could not be attributed to seed size as seed size was not correlated with rosette area.

In addition to the statistical results, PCA and machine learning analyses (such as the ReliefF method used here) concluded that 'Area' and

Compactness were among a set of candidates that could be used for rosette classification. Other studies have also demonstrated that 'Area' accounted for the highest variability [13]. As most of the shape descriptors used 'Area' as parameter, perhaps other descriptors associated with 'Area' could be used for classification, for example RRAGR (Figure S3E). Note that PCA plots (Figure 6 and Figure S3A-D) show Area as clustered with a number of other shape descriptors and not completely isolated from the rest.

While this paper describes the application of an initial set of unbiased quantitative characters to describe variation in rosette shape of *Arabidopsis*, other shape descriptors are available. Some of these may be more robust to differences in viewpoint and scale and some assess other aspects of shape that are not included here [31]. We restricted our study to two dimensions, an obvious over-simplification. Rosettes are significantly variable in 3-D; capturing the 3$^{rd}$ dimension requires more sophisticated image vision tools. Subsequent floral development is highly dynamic in all three spatial dimensions and requires additional descriptors. Furthermore, physiological processes contribute to colour variation that is super-imposed on morphological variation. Some techniques (such as LemnaTec 2.5D) provide a very rough proxy, but most other currently used methods are in effect multiple 2-D analyses, and the same pipeline for plant management, image processing and data analysis could be used. It remains a very significant challenge to screen populations in 3-D but 3D models have been produced from rotary imaging [32] or laser scanning [33] of single plants. Thus, the development of an optimal set of descriptors suitable for capturing general traits remains to be completed and is partly dependent on the imaging technology available.

A widespread and probably under-reported problem in plant biology is that, in spite of very careful control of growth conditions, it seems remarkably difficult to grow plants in a reproducible manner between laboratories [34]. As the measurements used in this report are non-destructive and rapid they provide a completely unbiased means of measuring growth responses for given genotypes across different locales, times and environments. Essentially this would use genetically defined plants as an environmental monitor with objectively acquired plant morphological descriptors as the readout, allowing results to be normalised. This could replace manual, often subjective, observations and allow improved comparisons between experiments across workers and laboratories. Also the information contained in the shape descriptors, together with the existing descriptions of leaf shape [17],[35], should allow reconstruction of a representation of the average plant with its statistically described range under given conditions. These reconstructions could then be developed for plants grown under a range of conditions and will allow a thorough cataloguing of environmental responses that can be used to diagnose those features of the environment that the plant is responding to. In that regard, we compared our results against the Perez-Perez study and found important similarities.

Both commercial (e.g Matlab, LemnaTec) and freeware (i.e. ImageJ [36], Octave [37] or Scilab [38]) packages are capable of extracting and analysing appropriate descriptors are readily available. However, in some commercial packages, the precise mathematical identity of the descriptor is obscure and can change without notification. This reduces their value to the general research community. We include a list of equations (Table S1) defining the majority of descriptors as used in version 2.1.0.8645 of LemnaTec. These equations were written in the Matlab environment to provide another way to calculate the shape descriptors. The definition of variables are in the files (Methods S1 and S2); variable names used to store final results of calculations in the Matlab program on a binary image are given in Table S6 to facilitate comparison of results using other software. It is also important to convert pixel-based values to appropriate dimensions to facilitate comparisons of images takes on different cameras with different optics and different distances. We suggest that all such descriptors should be clearly described by software purveyors, so that they can be used in the creation of technology-standard ontologies.

In general terms, the same principles should be applicable to more complex plant architectures, including later developmental stages of *Arabidopsis* as well as to crops and grasses of economic importance. The challenge will be to process and characterise large amounts of 2- and 3-D image and physiological data taken from automated capture systems handling large numbers of plants. Therefore, phenotype-genotype relationships for plant improvement can benefit hugely, and descriptions of shape phenotypes will become as accessible to analyses as currently available for genotypes. Here we have provided equivalent analysis in open source software and have provided the equations the calculation image descriptors which are closer to the ideal for reproducible computational research [39].

## ACKNOWLEDGMENTS

We are grateful to Paula Kover for supplying the accessions and to the European Commission (Erasmus program) for supporting PD and ZS. We are also grateful to Drs John Lane and Ruth Sanderson for their advice on the statistical analysis of the data.

## AUTHOR CONTRIBUTIONS

Conceived and designed the experiments: AC JHD APG. Performed the experiments: DP ZS. Analyzed the data: AC APG. Contributed reagents/materials/analysis tools: AC APG. Wrote the paper: AC KV JHD APG. Image recording: DP ZS.

## REFERENCES

1. Kover PX, Valdar W, Trakalo J, Scarcelli N, Ehrenreich IM, et al. (2009) A Multiparent Advanced Generation Inter-Cross to Fine-Map Quantitative Traits in*Arabidopsis thaliana*. PLoS Genet 5: e1000551.

2. Furbank RT, Tester M (2011) Phenomics – technologies to relieve the phenotyping bottleneck. Trends in Plant Science 16: 635–644.

3. Passardi F, Dobias J, Valério L, Guimil S, Penel C, et al. (2007) Morphological and physiological traits of three major *Arabidopsis thaliana* accessions. Journal of Plant Physiology 164: 980–992.

4. Juenger T, Pérez-Pérez JM, Bernal S, Micol JL (2005) Quantitative trait loci mapping of floral and leaf morphology traits in *Arabidopsis thaliana*: evidence for modular genetic architecture. Evolution & Development 7: 259–271.

5. Herridge R, Day R, Baldwin S, Macknight R (2011) Rapid analysis of seed size in*Arabidopsis* for mutant and QTL discovery. Plant Methods 7: 3.

6. Jansen M, Gilmer F, Biskup B, Nagel KA, Rascher U, et al. (2009) Simultaneous phenotyping of leaf growth and chlorophyll fluorescence via GROWSCREEN FLUORO allows detection of stress tolerance in *Arabidopsis thaliana* and other rosette plants. Functional Plant Biology 36: 902–914.

7. Ikram S, Bedu M, Daniel-Vedele F, Chaillou S, Chardon F (2012) Natural variation of*Arabidopsis* response to nitrogen availability. Journal of Experimental Botany 63: 91–105.

8. Ferrier T, Matus JT, Jin J, Riechmann JL (2011) *Arabidopsis* paves the way: genomic and network analyses in crops. Current Opinion in Biotechnology 22: 260–270.

9. Koornneef M, Meinke D (2010) The development of *Arabidopsis* as a model plant. The Plant Journal 61: 909–921.

10. Somerville C, Koornneef M (2002) A fortunate choice: the history of *Arabidopsis* as a model plant. Nat Rev Genet 3: 883–889.

11. Hoffmann MH (2002) Biogeography of *Arabidopsis* thaliana (L.) Heynh. (Brassicaceae). Journal of Biogeography 29: 125–134.

12. Kover PX, Valdar W, Trakalo J, Scarcelli N, Ehrenreich IM, et al. (2009) A Multiparent Advanced Generation Inter-Cross to Fine-Map Quantitative Traits in*Arabidopsis thaliana*. PLoS Genet 5: e1000551.

13. Pérez-Pérez JM, Rubio-Díaz S, Dhondt S, Hernández-Romero D, Sánchez-Soriano J, et al. (2011) Whole organ, venation and epidermal cell morphological variations are correlated in the leaves of *Arabidopsis* mutants. Plant, Cell & Environment 34: 2200–2211.

14. Arvidsson S, Pérez-Rodríguez P, Mueller-Roeber B (2011) A growth phenotyping pipeline for *Arabidopsis thaliana* integrating image analysis and rosette area modeling for robust quantification of genotype effects. New Phytologist 191: 895–907.

15. Granier C, Aguirrezabal L, Chenu K, Cookson SJ, Dauzat M, et al. (2006) PHENOPSIS, an automated platform for reproducible phenotyping of plant responses to soil water deficit in *Arabidopsis thaliana* permitted the identification of an accession with low sensitivity to soil water deficit. New Phytologist 169: 623–635.

16. Walter A, Scharr H, Gilmer F, Zierer R, Nagel KA, et al. (2007) Dynamics of seedling growth acclimation towards altered light conditions can be quantified via GROWSCREEN: a setup and procedure designed for rapid optical phenotyping of different plant species. New Phytologist 174: 447–455.

17. Bensmihen S, Hanna AI, Langlade NB, Micol JL, Bangham A, et al. (2008) Mutational spaces for leaf shape and size. HFSP Journal 2: 110–120.

18. Weight C, Parnham D, Waites R (2008) LeafAnalyser: a computational method for rapid and large-scale analyses of leaf shape variation. The Plant Journal 53: 578–586.

19. Gonzalez RC, Woods RE (2002) Digital Image Processing. Upper Saddle River, NJ, USA: Prentice Hall.

20. Devlin PF, Halliday KJ, Harberd NP, Whitelam GC (1996) The rosette habit of*Arabidopsis thaliana* is dependent upon phytochrome action: novel phytochromes control internode elongation and flowering time. The Plant Journal 10: 1127–1134.

21. Preuss D (2002) How to grow *Arabidopsis*. In: Weigel D, Glazebrook J, editors. In Arabidopsis, A Laboratory Manual: Cold Spring Harbour Laboratory Press, New York.

22. Lemnatec (2010) LemnaLauncher Image analysis. LemnaLauncher and LemnaMiner Manual. Würselen, Germany: Lemnatec. \pp. 112–186.

23. The MathWorks I (2012b) MATLAB and Statistics Toolbox Release. Natick, Massachusetts, United States.

24. Pinheiro J, Bates D (2000) Mixed-Effects Models in S and S-PLUS: Springer: New York.

25. R Development Core Team (2011) R: A Language and Environment for Statistical Computing. R Foundation for Statistical Computing.

26. Hall M, Eibe F, Holmes G, Pfahringer B, Reutemann P, et al.. (2009) The WEKA Data Mining Software: An Update. SIGKDD Explorations 11.

27. Robnik-Šikonja M, Kononenko I (1997) An adaptation of Relief for attribute estimation in regression. Proceedings of the Fourteenth International Conference on Machine Learning 296–304.

28. Clark RT, MacCurdy RB, Jung JK, Shaff JE, McCouch SR, et al. (2011) Three-Dimensional Root Phenotyping with a Novel Imaging and Software Platform. Plant Physiology 156: 455–465.

29. de Dorlodot S, Forster B, Pagès L, Price A, Tuberosa R, et al. (2007) Root system architecture: opportunities and constraints for genetic improvement of crops. Trends in Plant Science 12: 474–481.

30. Casler MD, Undersander DJ (2006) Selection for Establishment Capacity in Reed Canarygrass. Crop Science 46: 1277–1285.

31. Yang Y, Costa A, Leonhardt N, Siegel R, Schroeder J (2008) Isolation of a strong*Arabidopsis* guard cell promoter and its potential as a research tool. Plant Methods 4: 6.

32. Paproki A, Sirault X, Berry S, Furbank R, Fripp J (2012) A novel mesh processing based technique for 3D plant analysis. BMC Plant Biology 12: 63.

33. Côté J-F, Fournier RA, Frazer GW, Niemann KO (2012) A fine-scale architectural model of trees to enhance LiDAR-derived measurements of forest canopy structure. Agricultural and Forest Meteorology 166–167: 72–85.

34. Massonnet C, Vile D, Fabre J, Hannah MA, Caldana C, et al. (2010) Probing the Reproducibility of Leaf Growth and Molecular Phenotypes: A Comparison of Three*Arabidopsis* Accessions Cultivated in Ten Laboratories. Plant Physiology 152: 2142–2157.

35. Weight C, Parnham D, Waites R (2008) Techincal Advance: LeafAnalyser: a computational method for rapid and large-scale analyses of leaf shape variation. The Plant Journal 53: 578–586.

36. Schneider CA, Rasband WS, Eliceiri KW (2012) NIH Image to ImageJ: 25 years of image analysis. Nature Methods 9: 671–675.

37. Octave community (2014) GNU Octave 3.8.

38. Scilab Enterprises (2012) Scilab: Free and Open Source software for numerical computation.

39. Sandve GK, Nekrutenko A, Taylor J, Hovig E (2013) Ten Simple Rules for Reproducible Computational Research. PLoS Comput Biol 9: e1003285.

# Chapter 11

# Robust Pedestrian Tracking and Recognition from FLIR Video: A Unified Approach via Sparse Coding

**Xin Li [1,*], Rui Guo [2] and Chao Chen [3]**

[1]*Lane Department of CSEE, Morgantown, WV 26506-6109, USA*

[2]*Department of EECS, University of Tennessee, Knoxville, TN 37996, USA*

[3]*Department of Electrical and Computer Engineering, University of Missouri, Columbia, MO 65211, USA*

## ABSTRACT

Sparse coding is an emerging method that has been successfully applied to both robust object tracking and recognition in the vision literature. In this paper, we propose to explore a sparse coding-based approach toward joint object tracking-and-recognition and explore its potential in the analysis of forward-looking infrared (FLIR) video to support nighttime machine vision systems. A key technical contribution of this work is to unify existing sparse coding-based approaches toward tracking and recognition under the same framework, so that they can benefit from each other in a closed-loop. On the one hand, tracking the same object through temporal frames allows us to achieve improved recognition performance through dynamical updating of template/dictionary and combining multiple recognition results; on the other hand, the recognition of individual objects facilitates the tracking of multiple objects (*i.e.*, walking pedestrians), especially in the presence of occlusion within a crowded environment. We report experimental results on both the CASIAPedestrian Database and our own collected FLIR video database to demonstrate the effectiveness of the proposed joint tracking-and-recognition approach.

**Keywords:** Robust tracking; Pedestrian recognition; Sparse coding; Template updating; FLIR video

## 1. INTRODUCTION

The capability of recognizing a person at a distance in nighttime environments, which we call remote and night biometrics, has gained increasingly more attention in recent years. Fast advances in sensor technology (e.g., infrared cameras) and biometric systems (e.g., video-based recognition) have facilitated the task of remote and night biometrics. Object tracking and recognition are two basic building blocks in almost all video-based biometrics systems, including forward-looking infrared (FLIR)-based ones. The literature of object detection/tracking, face recognition and visual surveillance is huge; for recent advances, please refer to [1–3] and their references; pedestrian detection and tracking from FLIR video has also been studied in [4–7]. However, the relationship between detection/tracking and recognition has not been well studied in the literature. To the best of our knowledge, joint tracking and recognition has been considered under the context of particle filtering [8] only and specifically in the scenario of face biometrics [9].

In this paper, we propose to tackle joint object tracking and recognition under a unified sparse coding-based framework. Sparse coding originated from the research on compressed sensing theory [10] and has been recently leveraged into the problems of robust object tracking [11–13] and robust face recognition [14, 15]. For both tracking and recognition problems, the target patch/template of interest is sparsely represented in the space spanned by the dictionary (a collection of matching templates); and the final result is given by the candidate with the smallest projection error. Such a similarity motivates us to cast the two problems under the same framework and solve them simultaneously, *i.e.*, unlike previous works assuming a dictionary of templates (e.g., face portions) already cropped from the original image/video, ours obtains this dictionary by dynamically tracking the target of interest (e.g., a walking pedestrian).

We argue that tracking and recognition can benefit from each other for the following reasons. On the one hand, robust tracking of an object under a particle filter framework [16] often involves the updating of the matching templates on-the-fly. Such a dynamical strategy of template updating helps overcome the difficulties with occlusion and the cluttered background, which are also common adversary factors to the task of robust recognition. Moreover, persistently tracking allows the system to temporally combine the recognition results across multiple frames for improved accuracy (since we know it is the same object that has been tracked) [17, 18]. On the other hand, high-level vision tasks, such as recognition, often facilitates those at lower levels, including tracking, especially in the situation of multiple targets being involved [19]. More specifically, we suggest that the recognition result can be exploited by the template updating strategy to better fight against occlusion and a cluttered background. Such tracking-by-recognition offers some new insight to the challenging problem of multi-target tracking, which was often tackled by an energy optimization approach [20].

When applied to remote and night biometrics systems, the proposed approach has several advantages over other competing ones (e.g., gait-based [21] or silhouette-based [22]). First, previous approaches mostly count on image/video segmentation to extract relevant gait or silhouette information before recognition; consequently, segmentation errors have a significant impact on the accuracy of recognition [23]. By contrast, the proposed one directly works with image patches and does not involve any cropping or segmentation at all (note that in many previous works, such as [14], it is assumed that cropped image patches are already available). Second, it is widely known that occlusions and background clutters are often primary obstacles to various vision tasks, including tracking and recognition. Sparse coding has shown great potential in fighting against those adversary factors, thanks to the power of collaborative representation [15] (please refer to the Experimental Results section). Third, the unification of tracking and recognition allows us to jointly optimize these intrinsically connected components, which is highly desirable in the scenario of handling complicated cases, such as multi-target tracking in a crowd [24]. In other words, tracking and recognition can be viewed as two sides of the same coin: One helps the other and *vice versa*.

## 2. BACKGROUND ON SPARSE CODING

In this section, we review the current state-of-the-art in sparse coding and its applications into object tracking/recognition [25]. The basic idea behind sparse coding is to approximate a signal of interest $\mathbf{x} \in R^n$ by linear combination of a small number of atoms (elements in a dictionary $\mathbf{A}_{m\times n}$); namely, $\mathbf{x}_{m\times 1} = \mathbf{D}_{m\times n}\mathbf{a}_{n\times 1}$, where $\mathbf{a}$is the vector of sparse coefficients. Ideally, the sparsity constraint is enforced about the total number of nonzero coefficients in $\mathbf{a}$, which gives rise to the following constrained optimization problem:

$$\min_{\mathbf{a}} ||\mathbf{a}||_0 \ subject\ to\ ||\mathbf{x} - \mathbf{A}\mathbf{a}|| \leq \epsilon \tag{1}$$

However, the above problem is known to be NP-hard [26], and it is often suggested that the original $l_0$-norm be replaced by its $l_1$ counterpart. That is, one considers the following computationally tractable formulation:

$$\min_{\mathbf{a}} ||\mathbf{a}||_1 + \lambda||\mathbf{x} - \mathbf{A}\mathbf{a}|| \tag{2}$$

where λ is the Lagrangian multiplier converting the constrained optimization into an unconstrained one [27]. Various algorithms have been developed in recent years to solve this class of $l_1$-minimization problems (for a recent review, please refer to [28] and its references). Meanwhile, it is amazing to witness that many engineering problems across different disciplines can be reformulated into a variant of $l_1$-minimization problem. Within the scope of this paper, we opt to review two of them; namely, object tracking and object recognition.

## 2.1. Sparse Coding for Object Tracking

The fundamental assumption for appearance-based object tracking is that the global appearance of an object, despite varying illumination and viewpoint conditions, is still characterized by a low-dimensional space. Under the context of appearance-based object tracking, dictionary **A** is decomposed of target templates (image patches in $R^m$), as well as a collection of trivial templates (to model occlusion and noise in the real-world observation data), as shown in Figure 1. If one writes **A** as:

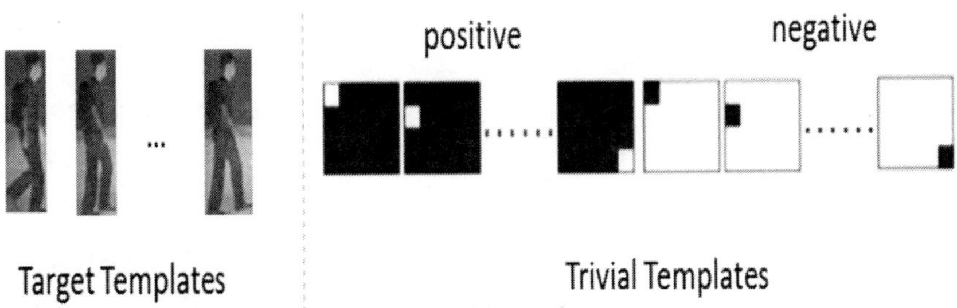


**Figure 1.** Decomposition of a dictionary into target and trivial templates in sparse coding-based object tracking.

$$\mathbf{x}_{m\times 1} = [\mathbf{T}\ \mathbf{I}\ -\mathbf{I}][\mathbf{b}\ \mathbf{e}^+\ \mathbf{e}^-]^t = \mathbf{A}_{m\times(n+2m)}\mathbf{a}_{(n+2m)\times 1} \quad (3)$$

where $\mathbf{T} = [\mathbf{t}_1, \ldots, \mathbf{t}_n]$ denotes $n$ target templates (note that $m >> n$) and $\mathbf{e}^+, \mathbf{e}^- \in R^m$ correspond to positive/negative trivial coefficient vectors, respectively.

For a good target candidate, there are only a small number of nonzero coefficients in positive and negative trivial coefficients accounting for the noise and partial occlusion. Such an observation has led to the formulation of object tracking into a $l_1$-minimization problem, as proposed in [11, 29-31]. The final tracking result is obtained by finding the smallest residual after projecting onto the subspace spanned by target templates, *i.e.*, $||\mathbf{x} - \mathbf{Tb}||_2$. Under a particle filtering framework [16], such minimum-error tracking admits a maximum *a posteriori*probability interpretation. Further improvement on robustness tracking can be brought by the idea of template updating. More specifically, the $l_2$-norm of template $\mathbf{t}_i$ intuitively indicates its significance to tracking; therefore, it is a plausible to eliminate the template of the least weight and replace it by the newly-obtained successful tracking result.

## 2.2. Sparse Coding for Object Recognition

Based on a similar observation to tracking, one can assume that the appearance of each individual subject lies in a unique low-dimensional subspace, and the structure of this subspace can be exploited to distinguish the subject of interest from others [14]. Therefore, if we consider a collection of $k$ subjects, each containing $n$ templates$\mathbf{t}_{i,j} \in R^m$ (again, $m$ is the size of the template of the image patch), the dictionary $\mathbf{A}_{m \times N}$ will consist of $N = nk$elements. For any given inquiry template $\mathbf{x}$, one can formulate the following sparse coding problem:

$$\min_{\mathbf{a}} ||\mathbf{a}||_1 + \lambda ||\mathbf{x}_{m\times 1} - \mathbf{A}_{m\times N}\mathbf{a}_{N\times 1}|| \quad (4)$$

where sparse coefficients a will be exploited to tell which subspace the inquiry is associated with. Ideally, the sparsest solution will associate the inquiry with the group of templates from a single subject class. However, due to noise and modeling errors, inference from other competing classes might arise; in other words, one might observe small nonzero entries associated with several subject classes. Therefore, it is often desirable to identify the subject by a twist of the above minimum-error strategy; namely, one can calculate the residual errors after projecting onto the subspace spanned by each class of target templates [14]:

$$E(i) = ||\mathbf{x}_{m\times 1} - \mathbf{A}_{m\times N}\delta_{(i)}(\mathbf{a}_{N\times 1})|| \quad (5)$$

where $\delta_{(i)}$ (**a**) is the characteristic function that assigns ones to the entries associated with subject $i$ in **a**. Then, the identity of inquiry **x** is obtained by $Id = \text{argmin}_i\, E(i)$, $1 \leq i \leq k$.

As articulated in [15], it is the idea of collaborative representation—namely, the formulation of joint dictionary A—that contributes to the good performance of Equation (5) in robust face recognition. It has been shown that replacing $l_1$-norm by its $l_2$-counterpart achieves comparable recognition performance, even though the computational complexity of the solution algorithm can be dramatically reduced (since the regularized least-square problem admits the analytical solution). When compared against previous $l_2$-based approaches (e.g., eigen-face [32]), we note that it is collaborative representation that enforces the global constraint on the collection of appearance subspaces spanned by individual subjects. In other words, the competition among sparse coefficients $a_i$ contributes to the effectiveness of the winner-take-all strategy, and therefore, it is possible to obtain robust recognition by searching for the smallest projection errors.

Despite the use of sparse coding in both object tracking and recognition, it should be emphasized that the relationship between them has not been studied in the open literature. To the best of our knowledge, joint tracking-and-recognition has only been addressed in two isolated scenarios: one is to embed them into a single particle filtering framework [8], and the other is to integrate tracking with recognition specially for the class of face biometrics [9]. The apparent similarity between Equations (3) and (5) inspires us to explore a unified sparse coding-based approach toward joint tracking-and-recognition. The primary objective of this paper is to demonstrate that such a joint approach can offer several new insights into the design of robust vision systems and find niche applications in challenging environments, such as remote and night biometrics using FLIR data.

## 3. JOINT TRACKING-AND-RECOGNITION: A UNIFIED APPROACH VIA SPARSE CODING

In this paper, we formally define a joint tracking-and-recognition problem as follows. Given an inquiry FLIR video $X$ containing walking pedestrians and a database of $k$ subjects each associated with $n$ video segments (training samples), establish the identity of the inquiry video. Note that unlike previous studies, [8] and [9], in which only one subject is considered, tracking and recognition are more tightly twisted in our multi-subject formulation (*i.e.*, one has to simultaneously track and recognize multiple subjects). At first sight, the interference among multiple subjects (e.g., one person could become occluded due to another person's presence) makes the joint tracking-and-recognition problem a lot more challenging than the single-subject scenario. To overcome this difficulty, we propose to gain a deeper understanding between tracking and recognition in this section.

### 3.1. Tracking-for-Recognition: Exploiting Temporal Redundancy

We first consider a simplified scenario where only one walking pedestrian is present in the inquiry video. When no interference is present, tracking a single pedestrian is a solved problem, and the recognition subproblem can be solved by sparse coding in a similar fashion to face recognition [14]. A more interesting question is: how can tracking help recognition? Here, we present a Bayesian interpretation of sparse coding-based recognition [14], which facilitates the exploitation of temporal redundancy arising from tracking a target template in the inquiry video. The key observation behind tracking-for-recognition lies in the fact that if it is known as *a priori* that multiple templates are associated with the same identity, such information can be exploited by the recognition system to improve the accuracy Each template can be viewed as an independent classifier, and accordingly, the idea of combining classifiers [33] can be easily implemented under the sparse coding framework.

Following the same notation used above, we consider a dictionary $\mathbf{A}_{m\times N}$ consisting of $k$ subjects each containing $n$ templates $\mathbf{t}_{i,j} \in R^m$ ($N = nk$). The subspace constraint of the appearance model for subject $i$ ($1 \leq i \leq k$) implies that a target template $\mathbf{x}$ associated with subject $i$ can be best approximated by the following sparse coding strategy:

$$\mathbf{x} \approx \mathbf{A}\delta_{(i)}(\mathbf{a}), \tag{6}$$

where $\delta_{(i)}$ ($\mathbf{a}$) is a binary vector in $R^N$, whose only nonzero elements are located at $j = (i - 1) * n + 1, \ldots, i * n$ (*i.e.*, those associated with subject $i$). If the approximation error is given by $E(i) = \mathbf{x} - \mathbf{A}_{m\times N}\, \delta_{(i)}\, (\mathbf{a}_{N\times 1})$ and assumed to observe an i.i.d. Gaussian model N(0,σ2w), then the likelihood function of observing a template $\mathbf{x}_i$ given subject $i$(denoted by $w_i$) can be written as:

$$p(\mathbf{x}|w_i) \approx exp(-\frac{||E(i)||_2^2}{2\sigma_w^2}) \tag{7}$$

Now, it follows from the Bayesian formula that the maximum *a posteriori* (MAP) classification of a given template $\mathbf{x}$ can be obtained from:

$$\max_i p(w_i|\mathbf{x}) = \max_i \frac{p(\mathbf{x}|w_i)p(w_i)}{p(\mathbf{x})} \tag{8}$$

which implies the equivalence between the MAP strategy in the Bayesian classifier and the minimum-distance classifier of Equation (5) used in SCR. Such a connection allows us to conveniently exploit the temporal redundancy of an inquiry video under the framework of combining classifiers, as we will elaborate next.

Similar to the setup in [33], we use $\{w_1, ..., w_k\}$ to denote $k$ different classes of subjects/identities and $\{\mathbf{x}_1, ..., \mathbf{x}_l\}$ the collection of measurement vectors. Given an inquiry FLIR video $X$, those measurement vectors are obtained by tracking a single target template $\mathbf{x}$ across multiple frames. Therefore, a Bayesian classifier works by assigning the label $Id = \max_i p(w_i|\mathbf{x}_1, ..., \mathbf{x}_l)$, which, in turn, can be written as:

$$\max_i p(w_i|\mathbf{x}_1, ..., \mathbf{x}_l) = \max_i \frac{p(\mathbf{x}_1, ..., \mathbf{x}_l|w_i)p(w_i)}{p(\mathbf{x}_1, ..., \mathbf{x}_l)} \tag{9}$$

Under the assumption that all measurement vectors are conditionally statistically independent, we have:

$$p(\mathbf{x}_1, ..., \mathbf{x}_l|w_i) = \prod_{j=1}^{l} p(\mathbf{x}_j|w_i) \tag{10}$$

Substituting Equations (7) and (8) into Equation (10), we can obtain the so-called feature-level fusion strategy:

$$p(\mathbf{x}_1, ..., \mathbf{x}_l|w_i) \approx exp(-\frac{\sum_{j=1}^{l} \|E_j(i)\|_2^2}{2\sigma_j^2}) \tag{11}$$

Therefore, the MAP decision boils down to a generalized minimum-distance classifier defined with respect to the group of measurement vectors. Alternatively, as suggested in [33], one can combine the decision outcomes instead of posterior probabilities, e.g., the final decision can be made by either sum rule $Id = \mathrm{argmin}_i \sum_{j=1}^{l} \|E_j(i)\|_2^2, 1 \leq i \leq k$ label returned by applying the minimum-distance classifier of Equation (8) to measurement vector $\mathbf{x}_j$. Even though the benefit of combining classifiers has been well-established in the literature (e.g., refer to [34]), the relationship between the number of classifiers *l* and performance gain is not. As we will show in the Experimental Results, even a small number of *l* (<10 frames) measurement vectors can dramatically boost the recognition accuracy.

## 3.2. Tracking-by-Recognition: Nonlocal Template Updating

Now, let us consider the more general situation: a multi-subject extension of the above joint tracking-and-recognition problem. In the literature, the problem of multi-object tracking is often addressed under the framework of energy minimization (e.g., refer to [35, 36] and their references). Two common technical challenges with tracking multiple objects is that the space of all possible trajectories is large and the appearance of a target might vary dramatically, due to the presence of occlusion or illumination variations. Consequently, it often requires special attention to design an appropriate cost function and a fast search strategy to solve the multi-object tracking problem. By contrast, we propose to cast multi-object tracking under the framework of sparse coding and explore the question of how the recognition result could help a multi-object tracking algorithm fight against adversary factors, such as occlusion and illumination variations. The basic assumption behind our tracking-by-recognition approach is that as long as the problem of multi-object tracking can be solved in a robust fashion, the recognition of multiple objects becomes straightforward (e.g., based on what we have discussed in the previous subsection on tracking-for-recognition).

The key observation behind our tracking-by-recognition is that one person's appearance along the moving trajectory behaves like the noise to the tracking of another person. For this reason, only the person of interest (that has been recognized) contributes to the formation of dictionary A in sparse coding-based tracking; all others can be handled the same way as background clutter. In other words, recognition facilitates the multi-object tracking problem by recognizing that for each appearance subspace of an individual subject, all other subjects, as well as the background can be modeled by the outliers. Such an observation leads us to rethink the template updating strategy proposed in [11], where the least-important template is eliminated from the dictionary and $\omega_i = ||\mathbf{t}_i||_2$ is adopted to quantify the importance of a template $\mathbf{t}_i$. Empirical studies have shown that such strategy is highly sensitive to occlusion, due to the reasons listed above. Instead, we propose a nonlocal alternative strategy of template updating; based on the recognition result, one can switch to a default set of templates upon the suspicion of occlusion. One way of implementing such a strategy is to save a copy of templates that have been recognized to be the same person (but likely in the distant history or even in the training set).

It is enlightening to appreciate the advantage of the above tracking-by-recognition formulation for multi-object tracking over existing energy minimization approaches. In energy minimization approaches, occlusion handling is often a thorny issue to address when coming up with an appropriate energy term for multi-object tracking. For example, a sophisticated global occlusion reasoning strategy is studied in [36], where a principled modeling of occlusion remains elusive, due to the complex dependency between a target's visibility and other targets' trajectories. By contrast, we argue that if the ultimate objective of the surveillance system is to recognize walking pedestrians, one can get around the tricky occlusion issue by stopping the tracker. In other words, the continuity of motion trajectory is unnecessary for the task of recognition; what matters is only the accumulated group size of measurement vectors (occlusion will reduce this size, but there is no need for accurate occlusion detection). In other words, tracking and recognition are essentially two sides of the same coin: tracking where a target template goes in the next frame is conceptually equivalent to recognizing whether a new hypothesized template in the next frame still belongs to the same class as the target one. With the recognition result available, tracking can always rely on a more trustworthy source (e.g., nonlocal rather than local) for template updating.

# 4. EXPERIMENTAL RESULTS

## 4.1. Experimental Setup

In this section, we report our experimental results with two FLIR pedestrian databases: one is collected by CASIA (Dataset C in the CASIA Gait Database, Publicly available athttp:// www. cbsr.ia.ac.cn/ english/Databases.asp), and the other is collected at the WVU Erickson Alumni Center (not publicly available, but it can be requested from http:// www.citer.wvu.edu/biometric _dataset_ collections). The CASIA Dataset C contains 153 subjects, each of which contains 11 video clips acquired by an FLIR camera. Each subject passes through the scene with and without carrying a bag, as well as at varying walking speeds; although silhouettes of those 153 subjects are supplied, we have found that they are error-prone, and therefore, we do not utilized them in our approach. The WVU dataset contains 30 subjects (18 males and 12 females) walking at three planned camera distances: 20, 25 and 30 m. In addition to the bag carrying option, the protocol includes both single-person and double-person scenarios. In the latter, two person walk toward each other, one carrying a bag and the other empty-handed; when they meet halfway, the bag will be handed to the other; then, they walk away from each other. Both occlusion and carrying a bag are adversary factors to pedestrian tracking and recognition in this setup.

To promote reproducible research, the source codes and saved experimental results accompanying this research can be accessed at http:// www.csee.wvu.edu/ xinl/code/FLIR.zip. In our MATLAB-based implementation, we have built upon two previous releases of sparse coding for tracking and recognition. The source codes of sparse coding for $l_1$-based tracking and recognition have been obtained fromhttp:// www.dabi.temple.edu/ hbling /code_data. htm#L1_Tracker and http://www.eecs.berkeley.edu/yang/software /l1benchmark/. More specifically, the dictionary needed for sparse coding-based recognition is obtained from the tracking result; we simply normalize the cropped templates to a common size. For the CASIA Dataset C, the following parameter setting is adopted: $k$ = 153, $n$ = 40.

## 4.2. Single-Object and Multi-Object Tracking

We first demonstrate the tracking result for single-object tracking. Figure 2 shows a collection of sample frames obtained from one typical FLIR video of CASIA Dataset C by $l_1$-based tracking. Since the background is relatively simple and only one pedestrian is present, the tracking is not a challenging issue for this data set. The new insight supplied by this experiment lies in that $l_1$-based tracking offers an automatic and robust cropping tool to obtain matching templates; *i.e.*, the elements of dictionary **A**. Note that the length of even a short video segment is a few seconds, which implies that at least dozens (or even hundreds) of matching templates can be cropped from the video clip. We note that this fact suggests that there is a significant amount of temporal redundancy that can be exploited by the recognition component.

A more interesting comparison result is in the scenario of multi-object tracking. For example, the WVU dataset contains test sequences in which two person walk toward each other. When the two pedestrians meet, one hands the bag to the other, and then, they continue walking away from each other. Such a protocol dictates that occlusion is present for a relatively long period of time. As shown in Figure 3, the straightforward application of the $l_1$-based tracking algorithm in [11] expectedly fails at the occlusion. The algorithm will be confused by the overlap of target templates associated with two pedestrians. By contrast, a recognition-based, nonlocal, template-updating

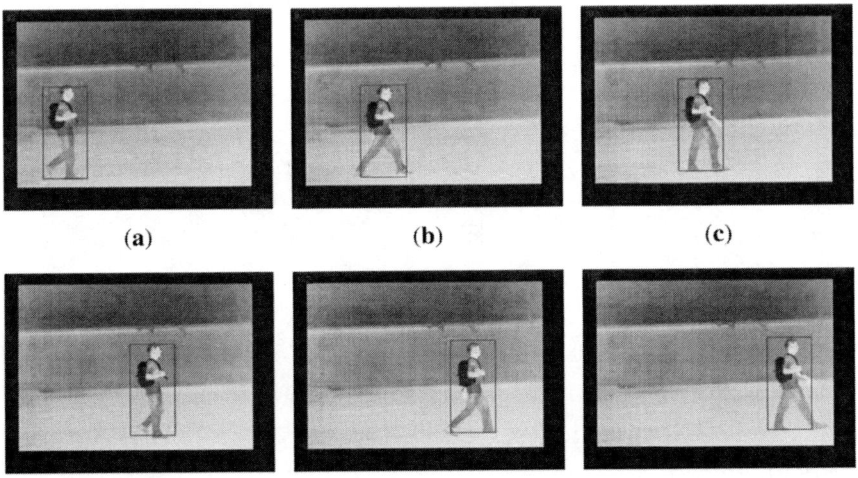

(a) (b) (c)

(d) (e) (f)

**Figure 2.** Sample tracking results for the forward-looking infrared (FLIR) video (red boxes highlight the locations of the walking pedestrian).

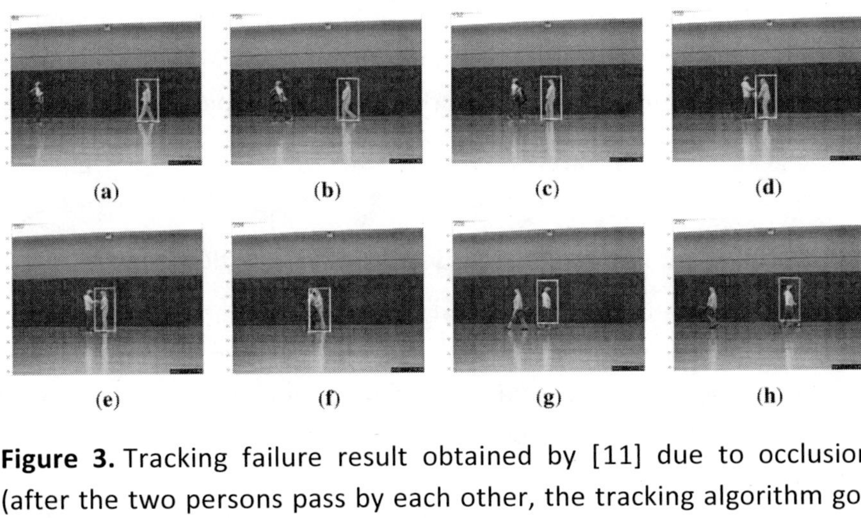

(a) (b) (c) (d)

(e) (f) (g) (h)

**Figure 3.** Tracking failure result obtained by [11] due to occlusion (after the two persons pass by each other, the tracking algorithm got confused; both red and green boxes get attached to the pedestrian walking to the right).

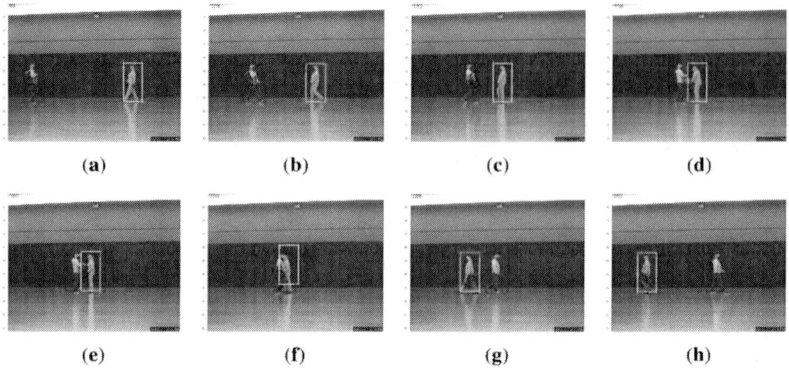


**Figure 4.** Joint tracking-and-recognition is capable of persistently tracking both pedestrians regardless of the occlusion and bad exchange (both red and green boxes are correctly associated with the correct identity).

strategy proposed in the previous section can produce robust and accurate tracking, even after one person hands the bag to the other (note that there are significant variations in terms of appearance), as shown in Figure 4. This is because when occlusion occurs, the recognition-based strategy will update the template stored from a distance past (in other words, nonlocal becomes more trustworthy than the local temporal neighborhood). Such experimental results justify the effectiveness of our tracking-by-recognition approach.

### 4.3. Robust Pedestrian Recognition from FLIR Video

Next, we report our experimental results with sparse coding-based recognition. In particular, we want to explore the gain brought by exploiting temporal redundancy (through combining classifiers) and the impact of occlusion on recognition performance. In the first experiment, we change the parameter *l*—the size of measurement vectors or the total number of frames for which we have successfully tracked for the inquiry video*X*. Two rules of combining the classification results have been implemented: sum *vs.* majority vote. Figure 5ashows how the accuracy of recognition evolves as l varies: it can be observed that the gain improves rapidly as l increases and quickly saturates. Therefore, even when a small number of measurement vectors (e.g., $l$ = 9 or <13second for 30 fps of video) is available, highly accurate recognition (close to 100%) is possible thanks to the power of temporal fusion. By contrast, we note that the best recognition performance reported for this data set is 96% in the open literature (e.g., gait energy image based [21]). Such a finding seems to suggest that video-based biometrics has a lot more potential than image-based, thanks to the blessing of redundancy.

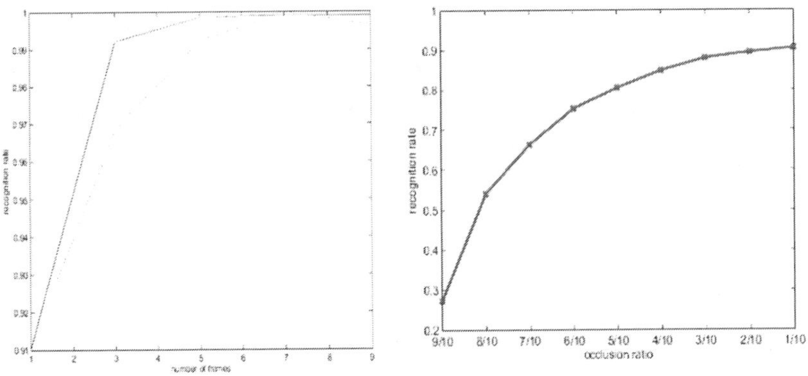


(a) (b)

**Figure 5.** The recognition performance of sparse coding-based recognition: (**a**) exploiting temporal redundancy improves the recognition accuracy (solid: sum rule; dashed: majority voting); (**b**) the recognition performance gracefully degrades as the occlusion ratio increases (no temporal fusion involved $l$ = 1).

In the second experiment, we artificially mask a certain percentage of the inquiry template (e.g., to simulate how the lower part of human body is occluded by bushes or deep grass in a real-world scenario) and test the performance of sparse coding-based recognition (no fusion is involved, *i.e.*, $l$ = 1). Figure 5b includes the result for the masking percentage varying from 10 to 90. It can be observed that sparse coding-based recognition is indeed insensitive to occlusion to some degree: about 30% occlusion degrades the recognition performance by about 5%. This is not surprising, because the lower part of the human body is not as discriminating as the upper part (more theoretical justifications can be found in the paper [14]). Combined with the result in Figure 5a, we conclude that when spatial clue becomes less reliable (e.g., due to occlusion), it is plausible to exploit temporal ones by a strategy, such as tracking-for-recognition.

Finally, we use experimental results to clarify the importance of obtaining a good dictionary for sparse coding-based recognition. One basic assumption behind sparse coding-based recognition is that the dictionary contains a densely sampled representation of appearance subspace; such an assumption is not always valid in practical situations. For instance, if the training set and testing set are significantly different (e.g., without and with a bag), the accuracy of recognition will be affected. Table 1 includes the experimental results of sparse coding-based recognition on CASIA Dataset C for a variety of different training/testing set situations. It shows that the walking speed of the pedestrian has a minor impact on the recognition performance; while the effect of carrying a bag or not is substantial. This is in contrast to what we have observed for the tracking experiments, where handing a bag over does not affect the result much. Nevertheless, the recognition accuracy achieved by SCR (even in the situation of no fusion being involved) is at least comparable to the template-matching-based approach, as reported in [37]. One can expect that much better recognition performance can be obtained by temporal fusion, as we have shown above.

**Table 1.** The recognition performance of the baseline algorithm for the training/testing data of different conditions.

| Training | Testing | This Work | [37] |
|---|---|---|---|
| Normal | Normal | 91.05% | 94% |
| Normal | Slow | 84.05% | 85% |
| Normal | Fast | 88.35% | 88% |
| Slow | Normal | 81.24% | - |
| Fast | Normal | 83.70% | - |
| with bag | with bag | 93.56% | - |
| w/obag | w/o bag | 92.94% | - |
| w/o bag | with bag | 57.61% | 51% |
| with bag | w/o bag | 49.75% | - |

## 5. CONCLUSIONS

In this paper, we studied a unified approach toward robust pedestrian tracking and recognition from FLIR video via sparse coding. Under the joint tracking-and-recognition framework, tracking helps recognition by generating matching templates needed for the dictionary and by facilitating the exploitation of temporal redundancy; recognition helps multi-object recognition by supplying a nonlocal template updating strategy instead of a local one. The main contributions of this work include: (1) an automatic night biometrics system capable of tracking and recognizing pedestrians from infrared video; and (2) an extension of sparse coding-based tracking from a single target to multiple targets, enabled by the proposed recognition-based template updating strategy. We have reported our experimental results on two FLIR video data sets: the CASIA gait database and the WVU Infrared Pedestrian database. On the former, we show how joint tracking-and-recognition can improve the accuracy and robustness of sparse coding-based recognition; on the latter, we demonstrate that the nonlocal template updating strategy based on the recognition result is capable of boosting the performance of sparse coding-based tracking in the presence of occlusion.

## ACKNOWLEDGMENTS

We want to acknowledge the authors of [11] and [28] for making their MATLAB codes available.

## REFERENCES

1. Yilmaz, A.; Javed, O.; Shah, M. Object tracking: A survey. *ACM Comput. Surv.* **2006**, *38*, 13.
2. Zhao, W.; Chellappa, R.; Rosenfeld, A.; Phillips, P. Face recognition: A literature survey. *ACM Comput. Surv.* **2003**, *35*, 399–458.
3. Hu, W.; Tan, T.; Wang, L.; Maybank, S. A survey on visual surveillance of object motion and behaviors.*IEEE Trans. Syst. Man Cybern. Part C: Appl. Rev.* **2004**, *34*, 334–352.
4. Nanda, H.; Davis, L. Probabilistic template based pedestrian detection in infrared videos. *IEEE Intell. Veh. Symp.* **2002**, *1*, 45–52.
5. Xu, F.; Liu, X.; Fujimura, K. Pedestrian detection and tracking with night vision. *IEEE Trans. Intell. Transp. Syst.* **2005**, *6*, 63–71.
6. Suard, F.; Rakotomamonjy, A.; Bensrhair, A.; Broggi, A. Pedestrian detection using infrared images and histograms of oriented gradients. Proceedings of the IEEE Intelligent Vehicles Symposium, Tokyo, Japan; 2006; pp. 206–212.

7. Dai, C.; Zheng, Y.; Li, X. Pedestrian detection and tracking in infrared imagery using shape and appearance. *Comput. Vis. Image Underst.* **2007**, *106*, 288–299.

8. Zhou, S.K.; Chellappa, R.; Moghaddam, B. Visual tracking and recognition using appearance-adaptive models in particle filters. *IEEE Trans. Image Process* **2004**, *13*, 1491–1506.

9. Lee, K.-C.; Ho, J.; Yang, M.-H.; Kriegman, D. Visual tracking and recognition using probabilistic appearance manifolds. *Comput. Vis. Image Underst.* **2005**, *99*, 303–331.

10. Candès, E.J.; Romberg, J.K.; Tao, T. Robust uncertainty principles: Exact signal reconstruction from highly incomplete frequency information. *IEEE Trans. Inf. Theory* **2006**, *52*, 489–509.

11. Mei, X.; Ling, H. Robust visual tracking using l1 minimization. Proceedings of the IEEE 12th International Conference on Computer Vision, Kyoto, Japan, 27 September– 4 October 2009; pp. 1436–1443.

12. Li, H.; Shen, C.; Shi, Q. Real-time visual tracking using compressive sensing. Proceedings of the IEEE Computer Vision and Pattern Recognition (CVPR), Providence, RI, USA, 20–25 June 2011; pp. 1305–1312.

13. Zhang, S.; Yao, H.; Sun, X.; Lu, X. Sparse coding based visual tracking: Review and experimental comparison. *Pattern Recognit.* **2013**, *46*, 1772–1788.

14. Wright, J.; Yang, A.; Ganesh, A.; Sastry, S.; Ma, Y. Robust face recognition via sparse representation. *IEEE Trans. Pattern Anal. Mach. Intell.* **2009**, *31*, 210–227.

15. Zhang, L.; Yang, M.; Feng, X. Sparse representation or collaborative representation: Which helps face recognition? *IEEE Int. Conf. Comput. Vis.* **2011**, 471–478.

16. Van Der Merwe, R.; Doucet, A.; De Freitas, N.; Wan, E. The unscented particle filter. *NIPS* **2000**, 584–590.

17. Lee, K.-C.; Ho, J.; Yang, M.-H.; Kriegman, D. Video-based face recognition using probabilistic appearance manifolds. Proceedings of the 2003 IEEE Computer Society Conference on Computer Vision and Pattern Recognition (CVPR 2003), Madison, WI, USA, 16–22 June 2003; pp. 313–320.

18. Lee, K.-C.; Kriegman, D. Online learning of probabilistic appearance manifolds for video-based recognition and tracking. *IEEE Conf. Comput. Vis. Pattern Recognit.* **2005**, *1*, 852–859.

19. Zhang, L.; Li, Y.; Nevatia, R. Global data association for multi-object tracking using network flows. Proceedings of IEEE Conference on Computer Vision and Pattern Recognition, Anchorage, AK, USA, 24–26 June 2008; pp. 1–8.

20. Milgram, S. The small world problem. *Psychol. Today* **1967**, *2*, 60–67.

21. Han, J.; Bhanu, B. Individual recognition using gait energy image. *IEEE Trans. Pattern Anal. Mach. Intell.* **2006**, *28*, 316–322.

22. Wang, L.; Tan, T.; Ning, H.; Hu, W. Silhouette analysis-based gait recognition for human identification. *IEEE Trans. Pattern Anal. Mach. Intell.* **2003**, *25*, 1505–1518.

23. Zhang, H.; Fritts, J.E.; Goldman, S.A. Image segmentation evaluation: A survey of unsupervised methods. *Comput. Vis. Imag. Underst.* **2008**, *110*, 260–280.

24. Zhan, B.; Monekosso, D.N.; Remagnino, P.; Velastin, S.A.; Xu, L.-Q. Crowd analysis: A survey. *Mach. Vis. Appl.* **2008**, *19*, 345–357.

25. Wright, J.; Ma, Y.; Mairal, J.; Sapiro, G.; Huang, T.S.; Yan, S. Sparse representation for computer vision and pattern recognition. *Proc. IEEE* **2010**, *98*, 1031–1044.

26. Zibulevsky, M.; Elad, M. L1-l2 optimization in signal and image processing. *IEEE Signal Process. Mag.* **2010**, *27*, 76–88.

27. Shoham, Y.; Gersho, A. Efficient bit allocation for an arbitrary set of quantizers. *IEEE Trans. Acoust. Speech Signal Proc.* **1988**, *36*, 1445–1453.

28. Yang, A.; Sastry, S.; Ganesh, A.; Ma, Y. *Fast l1-minimization Algorithms and an Application in Robust Face Recognition: A Review*; Technical Report No. UCB/EECS-2010-13; EECS Department University of California: Berkeley, CA, USA; 5; February; 2010.

29. Mei, X.; Ling, H. Robust visual tracking and vehicle classification via sparse representation. *IEEE Trans. Pattern Anal. Mach. Intell.* **2011**, *33*, 2259–2272.

30. Zhang, S.; Yao, H.; Sun, X.; Liu, S. Robust visual tracking using an effective appearance model based on sparse coding. *ACM Trans. Intell. Syst. Technol.* **2012**, *3*, 43.

31. Zhang, S.; Yao, H.; Zhou, H.; Sun, X.; Liu, S. Robust visual tracking based on online learning sparse representation. *Neurocomput* **2013**, *100*, 31–40.

32. Pentland, A. Fractal-based description of natural scenes. *IEEE Trans. Pattern Anal. Mach. Intell.* **1984**, *6*, 661–674.

33. Kittler, J.; Hatef, M.; Duin, R.; Matas, J. On combining classifiers. *IEEE Trans. PAMI* **1998**, *20*, 226–239.

34. Kuncheva, L. *Combining Pattern Classifiers: Methods and Algorithms*; Wiley-Interscience: New York, NY, USA, 2004.

35. Berclaz, J.; Fleuret, F.; Turetken, E.; Fua, P. Multiple object tracking using k-shortest paths optimization.*IEEE Trans. Pattern Anal. Mach. Intell.* **2011**, *33*, 1806–1819.

36. Schindler, K. Continuous energy minimization for multi-target tracking. *IEEE Trans. Pattern Anal. Mach. Intell.* **2014**, *36*.

37. Tan, D.; Huang, K.; Yu, S.; Tan, T. Efficient night gait recognition based on template matching. the Proceedings of the 18th International Conference on Pattern Recognition, Hong Kong, China, 20- 24 August 2006; pp. 1000–1003.

# Chapter 12

# Classification of Fruits Using Computer Vision and a Multiclass Support Vector Machine

**Yudong Zhang and Lenan Wu***

*School of Information Science and Engineering, Southeast University, Nanjing 210096, China*

## ABSTRACT

Automatic classification of fruits via computer vision is still a complicated task due to the various properties of numerous types of fruits. We propose a novel classification method based on a multi-class kernel support vector machine (kSVM) with the desirable goal of accurate and fast classification of fruits. First, fruit images were acquired by a digital camera, and then the background of each image was removed by a split-and-merge algorithm; Second, the color histogram, texture and shape features of each fruit image were extracted to compose a feature space; Third, principal component analysis (PCA) was used to reduce the dimensions of feature space; Finally, three kinds of multi-class SVMs were constructed, *i.e.*, Winner-Takes-All SVM, Max-Wins-Voting SVM, and Directed Acyclic Graph SVM. Meanwhile, three kinds of kernels were chosen, *i.e.*, linear kernel, Homogeneous Polynomial kernel, and Gaussian Radial Basis kernel; finally, the SVMs were trained using 5-fold stratified cross validation with the reduced feature vectors as input. The experimental results demonstrated that the Max-Wins-Voting SVM with Gaussian Radial Basis kernel achieves the best classification accuracy of 88.2%. For computation time, the Directed Acyclic Graph SVMs performs swiftest.

**Keywords:** Fruit classification; Principal component analysis; Color histogram; Unser's texture analysis; Mathematical morphology; Shape feature; Multi-class SVM; Kernel SVM; Stratified cross validation

## 1. INTRODUCTION

Recognizing different kinds of vegetables and fruits is a difficult task in supermarkets, since the cashier must point out the categories of a particular fruit to determine its price. The use of barcodes has mostly ended this problem for packaged products but given that most consumers want to pick their products, they cannot be prepackaged, and thus must be weighed. A solution is issuing codes for every fruit, but the memorization is problematic leading to pricing errors. Another solution is to issue the cashier an inventory with pictures and codes, however, flipping over the booklet is time consuming [1].

Some alternatives were proposed to address the problem. VeggieVision was the first supermarket produce recognition system consisting of an integrated scale and image system with a user-friendly interface [2]. Hong *et al.* [3] employed morphological examination to separate walnuts and hazelnuts into three groups. Baltazar *et al.* [4] first applied data fusion to nondestructive image of fresh intact tomatoes, followed by a three-class Bayesian classifier. Pennington *et al.* [5] used a clustering algorithm for classification of fruits and vegetables. Pholpho *et al.* [6] used visible spectroscopy for classification of non-bruised and bruised longan fruits, and combined this with principal component analysis (PCA), Partial Least Square Discriminant Analysis (PLS-DA) and Soft Independent Modeling of Class Analogy (SIMCA) to develop classification models.

The aforementioned techniques may have one or several of the following shortcomings: (1) they need extra sensors such as a gas sensor, invisible light sensor, and weight sensor. (2) The classifier is not suitable to all fruits, *viz.*, it can only recognize the varieties of the same category. (3) The recognition systems are not robust because different fruit images may have similar or identical color and shape features [7].

Support Vector Machines (SVMs) are state-of-the-art classification methods based on machine learning theory [8]. Compared with other methods such as artificial neural networks, decision trees, and Bayesian networks, SVMs have significant advantages because of their high accuracy, elegant mathematical tractability, and direct geometric interpretation. Besides, they do not need a large number of training samples to avoid overfitting [9].

In this paper, we chose an image recognition method which only needs a digital camera. To improve the recognition performance, we proposed a hybrid feature extraction technique which combines the color features, Unser's texture, and shape features, followed by the principal component analysis (PCA) to reduce the number of features. Three different multi-class SVMs were used for multi-class classification. We expect this method will solve the fruit classification problem.

The rest of the paper is organized as follows: Section 2 discusses the methods used in this paper. Section 2.1 shows the split-and-merge algorithm for fruits extraction; Section 2.2 gives the descriptors of fruits with respect to the color component, shape component, and texture component. In addition, PCA was introduced as a methodology to reduce the number of features used by the classifiers; Section 2.3 introduced in the kernel SVM, and then gives three schemes for multi-class SVMs, including Winner-Take-All SVM (WTA-SVM), Max-Wins-Voting (MWV-SVM), and Directed Acyclic Graph SVM (DAG-SVM); Section 3 shows the use of 1,653 images of 18 different types of fruits to test our method; and lastly Section 4 is devoted to conclusions.

# 2. METHODS

## 2.1. Image Segmentation with the Split-and-Merge Algorithm

First, we use image segmentation techniques to remove the background area since our research only focuses on the fruits. We choose a split-and-merge algorithm, which is based on a quadtree partition of an image. This method starts at the root of the tree that represents the whole image. If it is found inhomogeneous, then it is split into four son-squares (the splitting process), and so on so forth. Conversely, if four son-squares are homogeneous, they can be merged as several connected components (the merging process). The node in the tree is a segmented node. This process continues recursively until no further splits or merges are possible.

Figure 1 gives an example. Here the non-uniform light source causes color fluctuations on the surface of thes pear and background, therefore the gray value distributions of both pears and background mix together. Figure 1(b) shows the optimal threshold found by Otsu's method [10]. Figure 1(c) shows the fruits extracted from the Otsu threshold. Apparently the Otsu segmentation only extracts half of the fruits area.

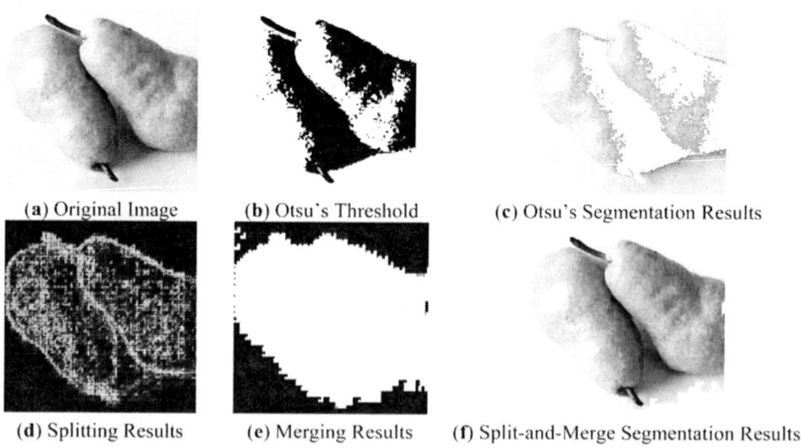


**Figure 1.** Comparison of Otsu's Method with split-and-merge segmentation.

Figure 1(d–f) show our method. The splitting process splits the image to homogeneous small squares (Figure 1(d)) according to the splitting rules, and then combines the connected squares according to the merging rules (Figure 1(e)). The final extraction (Figure 1(f)) shows this split-and-merge process neatly extracts the whole area of fruits.

## 2.2. Feature Extraction and Reduction

We propose a hybrid classification system based on color, texture, and appearance features of fruits. Here, we suppose the fruit images have been extracted by split-and-merge segmentation algorithm [11,12].

### 2.2.1. Color Histogram

At present, the color histogram is employed to represent the distribution of colors in an image [13]. The color histogram represents the number of pixels that have colors in a fixed list of color range that span the image's color space [14].

For monochromatic images, the set of possible color values is sufficiently small that each of those colors may be placed on a single range; then the histogram is merely the count of pixels that have each possible color. For color images using RGB space, the space is divided into an appropriate number of ranges, often arranged as a regular grid, each containing many similar color values.

Figure 2(a) is an original rainbow image with RGB channels from 0 to 255, so there are totally $256 \times 256 \times 256 = 2^{24}$colors. Figure 2(b) uses four bins to represent each color component, Bins 0, 1, 2, 3 denote intensities 0-63, 64-127, 128-191, 192-255, respectively, so there are in total $4 \times 4 \times 4 = 64$ colors. Figure 2(c) is the histogram of Figure 2(b), where the*x*-axis denotes the index of the 64 colors, and the *y*-axis denotes the number of pixels.

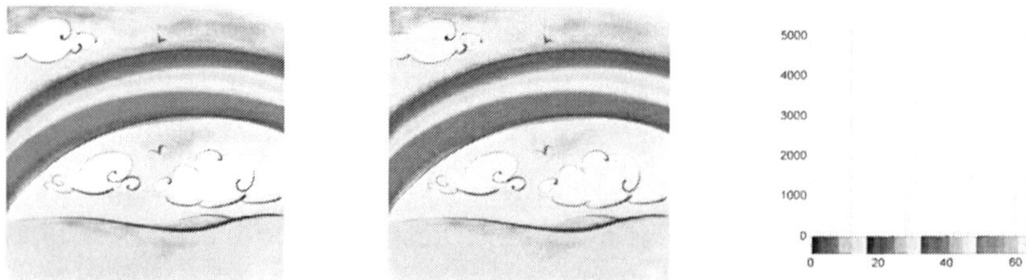


(a) Original Image (b) Reduced to 4 × 4 × 4 = 64 colors (c) Image Histogram

**Figure 2.** Rainbow image.

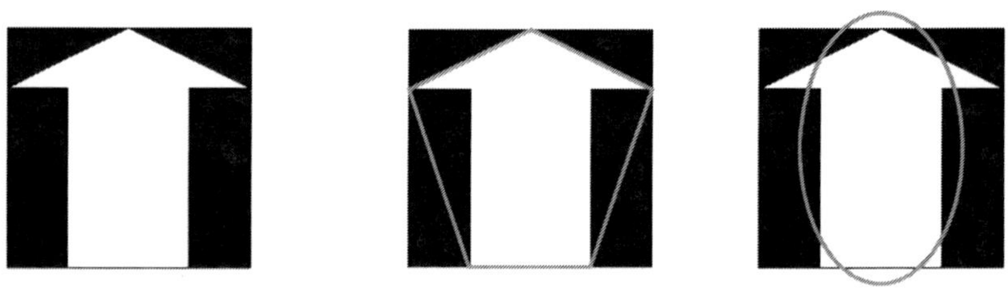

(a) Original Image (b) Convex Hull (c) Ellipse

**Figure 3.** Illustration of the morphology measures.

The histogram provides a compact summarization of the distribution of data in an image. The color histogram of an image is relatively invariant with translation and rotation about the viewing axis. By comparing histograms signatures of two images and matching the color content of one image with the other, the color histogram is well suited for the problem of recognizing an object of unknown position and rotation within a scene.

### 2.2.2. Unser's Texture Features

Gray level co-occurrence matrix and local binary pattern are good texture descriptors, however, they are excessively time consuming. In this paper, we chose the Unser feature vector. Unser proved that the sum and difference of two random variables with same variances are de-correlated and the principal axes of their associated joint probability function are defined. Therefore, we use the sum *s* and difference *d* histograms for texture description [15].

The non-normalized sum and difference associated with a relative displacement ($\delta_1$, $\delta_2$) for an image *I* are defined as:

$$s(k,l;\delta_1,\delta_2) = I(k,l) + I(k+\delta_1, l+\delta_2) \quad (1)$$

$$d(k,l;\delta_1,\delta_2) = I(k,l) - I(k+\delta_1, l+\delta_2) \quad (2)$$

The sum and difference histograms over the domain *D* are defined as:

$$h_s(i;\delta_1,\delta_2) = \text{card}\left((k,l) \in D, s(k,l;\delta_1,\delta_2) = i\right) \quad (3)$$

$$h_d(j;\delta_1,\delta_2) = \text{card}\left((k,l) \in D, d(k,l;\delta_1,\delta_2) = j\right) \quad (4)$$

Next, seven indexes can be defined on the basis of the sum and difference histogram. Those indexes and their corresponding formulas are listed in Table 1. In our method, we firstly abandoned the color information, followed by calculating the 64-bin histogram, and finally obtain the seven indexes.

**Table 1.** Sum and difference histogram based measures.

| Measure | Formula |
|---|---|
| Mean ($\mu$) | $\mu = (1/2) \times \sum_i i h_s(i;\delta_1,\delta_2)$ |
| Contrast ($C_n$) | $C_n = \sum_j j^2 h_d(j;\delta_1,\delta_2)$ |
| Homogeneity ($H_g$) | $H_g = \sum_j (1/(1+j^2)) h_d(j;\delta_1,\delta_2)$ |
| Energy ($E_n$) | $E_n = \sum_i h_s(i;\delta_1,\delta_2)^2 \sum_j h_d(j;\delta_1,\delta_2)^2$ |
| Variance ($\sigma^2$) | $\sigma^2 = (1/2) \times \left(\sum_i (i-2\mu)^2 h_s(i;\delta_1,\delta_2) + \sum_j j^2 h_d(j;\delta_1,\delta_2)\right)$ |
| Correlation ($C_r$) | $C_r = (1/2) \times \left(\sum_i (i-2\mu)^2 h_s(i;\delta_1,\delta_2) - \sum_j j^2 h_d(j;\delta_1,\delta_2)\right)$ |
| Entropy ($H_n$) | $H_n = -\sum_i h_s(i;\delta_1,\delta_2) \log(h_s(i;\delta_1,\delta_2)) - \sum_j h_d(j;\delta_1,\delta_2) \log(h_d(j;\delta_1,\delta_2))$ |

### 2.2.3. Shape Features

In this paper we propose eight measures based on mathematical morphology, which are listed in Table 2. The measures can be classified into four groups: (1) The "area", "perimeter", and the "Euler number" can be extracted directly from the object; (2) Create a convex hull using Graham Scan method [16] which is the smallest convex polygon that covers the object, then extract the "convex area" and "solidity" features; (3) Create an ellipse that has the same second-moments as the object, then extract the "minor length", "major length", and "eccentricity" features. Table 2 illustrates an example of generating the convex hull and the ellipse from original images.

**Table 2.** The Morphology based Measures.

| Measure | Meaning |
|---|---|
| Area ($A_r$) | The actual number of pixels inside the object |
| Perimeter ($P_r$) | The distance around the boundary of the object |
| Euler ($E_l$) | The Euler number of the object |
| Convex ($C_n$) | The number of pixels of the convex hull |
| Solidity ($S_l$) | The proportion of area to convex hull |
| MinorLength ($M_n$) | The length of the minor axis of the ellipse |
| MajorLength ($M_j$) | The length of the major axis of the ellipse |
| Eccentricity ($E_c$) | The eccentricity of the ellipse |

### 2.2.4. Principal Component Analysis

In total, there are 79 features (64 color features + seven texture features + eight shape features) extracted from a given image. Excessive features increase computation time and storage memory, which sometimes causes the classification process to become more complicated and even decrease the performance of the classifier. A strategy is necessary to reduce the number of features used in classification.

Principal component analysis (PCA) is an efficient tool to reduce the dimensionality of a data set consisting of a large number of interrelated variables while retaining the most significant variations [17]. It is achieved by transforming the data set to a new set of ordered variables according to their degree of variance or importance. This technique has three effects: (1) it orthogonalizes the components of the input vectors so that they are uncorrelated with each other, (2) it orders the resulting orthogonal components so that those with the largest variation come first, and (3) it eliminates the components in the data set that contributes the least variation [18].

It should be noted that the input vectors should be normalized to have zero mean and unity variance before performing PCA, which is shown in Figure 4. The normalization is a standard procedure. Details about PCA are given in [19].

**Figure 4.** Using normalization before PCA.

## 2.3. Multiclass Kernel SVMs

### 2.3.1. Kernel SVM

Traditional linear SVMs cannot separate complicated distributed practical data. In order to generalize it to nonlinear hyperplane, the kernel trick is applied to SVMs [20]. The resulting algorithm is formally similar, except that every dot product is replaced by a nonlinear kernel function. From another point of view, the kernel SVMs allow to fit the maximum-margin hyperplane in a transformed feature space. The transformation may be nonlinear and the transformed space is a higher dimensional space. Though the classifier is a hyperplane in the higher-dimensional feature space, it may be nonlinear in the original input space. Four common kernels [21] are listed in Table 3. For each kernel, there should be at least one adjusting parameter so as to make the kernel flexible and tailor itself to practical data.

**Table 3.** Four Common Kernels.

| Measure | Meaning |
|---|---|
| Area ($A_r$) | The actual number of pixels inside the object |
| Perimeter ($P_r$) | The distance around the boundary of the object |
| Euler ($E_l$) | The Euler number of the object |
| Convex ($C_n$) | The number of pixels of the convex hull |
| Solidity ($S_l$) | The proportion of area to convex hull |
| MinorLength ($M_n$) | The length of the minor axis of the ellipse |
| MajorLength ($M_j$) | The length of the major axis of the ellipse |
| Eccentricity ($E_c$) | The eccentricity of the ellipse |

SVMs were originally designed for binary classification. Several methods have been proposed for multi-class SVMs, and the dominant approach is to reduce the single multiclass problem into multiple binary classification problems [22]. Three popular types of methods are depicted as follow.

### 2.3.2. Winner-Takes-All SVM

Assume there are totally $C$ ($C > 2$) classes. For the one-versus-all approach, classification of new instances is done by a winner-takes-all (WTA) strategy [23]. We first train $c$ different binary SVMs, each one trained to distinguish the data in a single class from the data of all the remaining classes. When applied to a new test data, all the $C$ classifiers are run, and the classifier which outputs the largest value is chosen. If there are two identical output values, WTA selects the class with the smallest index.

The mathematical model is described as follow. Given a $p$-dimensional $N$-size training dataset of the form:

$$\left\{(x_n, y_n) \mid x_n \in R^p, y_n \in \{1,2,...,C\}\right\}, n = 1,2,...,N \quad (5)$$

where $x_n$ is a $p$-dimensional vector, and $y_n \in \{1,2,...,C\}$ is the class label of each $x_n$. The classification decision function for*i*th individual binary SVM can be defined as:

$$f_i(x) = \sum_{n=1}^{N} y_n^i \alpha_n^i k(x_n, x) - b_i, \quad i = 1,2,...,C \quad (6)$$

$$y_n^i = \begin{cases} +1 & \text{if } x_n \in i\text{th class} \\ -1 & \text{otherwise} \end{cases} \quad (7)$$

where $N$ is the number of training data; $C$ is the number of total classes; yin∈{+1,−1} depends on the class label of $x_n$, if$x_n$ belongs to the *i*th class, yin=+1, otherwise yin=−1; $k()$ is the predefined kernel function; αin is the Lagrange coefficient; and $b_i$ is the bias term. αin and $b^i$ are obtained by training the *i*th individual SVM. The output of *i*th SVM is the sign function of its decision function, namely:

$$O_i(x) = \text{sgn}\left(f_i(x)\right) \quad (8)$$

If $f_i(x) > 0$, then the output $O_i(x)$ is +1, denoting $x$ belongs to *i*th class; otherwise output is −1, denoting $x$ belongs to other classes.

### 2.3.3. Max-Wins-Voting SVM

For the one-versus-one approach, classification is done by a max-wins voting (MWV) strategy [23]. First we construct a binary SVM for each pair of classes, so in total we will get $C(C-1)/2$ binary SVMs. When applied to a new test data, each SVM gives one vote to the winning class, and the test data is labeled with the class having most labels. If there are two identical votes, MWV selects the class with the smallest index.

The mathematical model is described as follow. The *ij*th ($i$ = 1,2, ..., $C$-1, $j$ = $i$ + 1, ..., $C$) individual binary SVM is trained with all data in the *i*th class with +1 label and all data of the *j*th class with −1 label, so as to distinguish *i*th class from *j*th class. The decision function of *ij*th SVM is:

$$f_{ij}(x) = \sum_{n=1}^{N_i+N_j} y_n^{ij} \alpha_n^{ij} k(x_n^{ij}, x) - b_{ij} \tag{9}$$

$$i = 1, 2, \ldots, C-1,\ j = i+1, i+2, \ldots, C$$

$$y_n^{ij} = \begin{cases} +1 & x_n^{ij} \in i\text{th class} \\ -1 & x_n^{ij} \in j\text{th class} \end{cases} \tag{10}$$

where $N_i$ and $N_j$ denotes the total number of *i*th class and *j*th class, respectively. yijn∈{+1,−1} depends on the class label of xijn. If xijn belongs to *i*th class, yijn=+1; otherwise xijn belongs to *j*th class, yijn=−1. αijn is the Lagrange coefficient; and $b_{ij}$ is the bias term. αijn and $b_{ij}$ are obtained by training the *ij*th individual SVM. The output of *ij*th SVM is the sign function of its decision function, namely:

$$O_{ij}(x) = \operatorname{sgn}\left(f_{ij}(x)\right) \tag{11}$$

If $f_{ij}(x)>0$, then the output $O_{ij}(x)$ is +1, denoting $x$ belongs to *i*th class; otherwise output is −1, denoting $x$ belongs to *j*th class.

#### 2.3.4. Directed Acyclic Graph SVM

A Directed Acyclic Graph (DAG) is a graph whose edges have an orientation and no cycles. The DAG-SVM constructs the individual SVM as the MWV-SVM, however, the output of each individual SVM is explained differently. When $O_{ij}(x)$ is +1, it denotes that $x$ does not belong to *j*th class; when $O_{ij}(x)$ is −1, it denotes that $x$ does not belong to *i*th class. Therefore, the final decision cannot be reached until the leaf node is reached [24].

Figure 5 below shows the DAG for finding the best class out of six given classes. Here, the root node and intermediate nodes represents the individual binary SVM, whereas the leaf nodes represent the output label. Given a test sample *x*starting at the root node, the individual binary SVMs are evaluated. The node is then exited via the evaluation result to either left edge or right edge. The next SVM's function is evaluated again until the leaf node is reached. Therefore, DAG-SVM costs less computation time compared to MWV-SVM. In this case, the MWV-SVM needs to cover all nodes of 15 individual SVMs, yet the DAG-SVM only needs to evaluate only five individual SVMs.

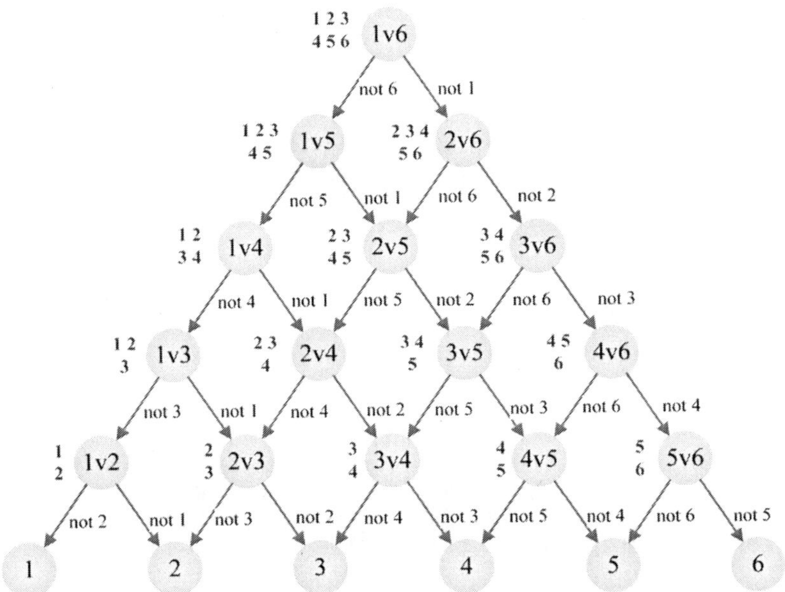


**Figure 5.** The DAG for finding best class out of six classes.

## 3. EXPERIMENTS & DISCUSSIONS

The experiments were carried out on a P4 IBM platform with 3 GHz main frequency and 2 GB memory running under the Microsoft

Windows XP operating system. The algorithm was developed in-house on the Matlab 2011b (The Mathworks©) platform. The programs can be run or tested on any computer platforms where Matlab is available.

### 3.1. Fruit Recognition System

Below are the steps explaining the flowchart of the proposed fruit recognition system shown in Figure 6.

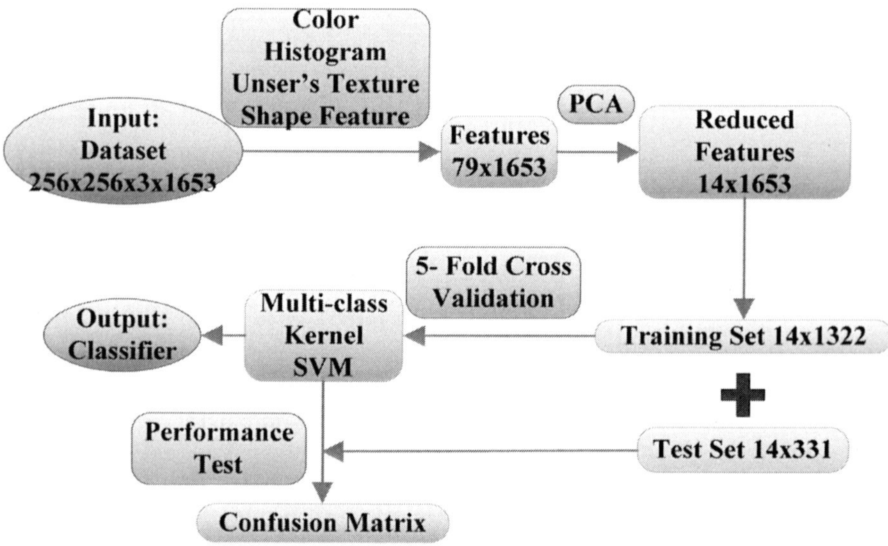


**Figure 6.** The flowchart of the proposed fruit recognition system.

Numbers in the figure are achieved by experiments below:

- **Step 1.** The input is a database of 1,653 images consisting of 18 categories of fruits, and each image size is 256 × 256.
- **Step 2.** The 79 features are extracted from each 256 × 256 image. These 79 features contain 64 color features, seven texture features, and eight shape features.

- **Step 3.** The 79 features are reduced to only 14 features via PCA, and the selection standard is to preserve 95% energy.
- **Step 4.** The 1,653 images are divided into training set (1,322) and test set (331) in the proportion of 4:1. Meanwhile, the training set is treated by 5-fold cross validation.
- **Step 5.** The training set is used to train the multi-class SVM. The weights of the SVM are adjusted to make minimal the average error of 5-fold cross validation.
- **Step 6.** The test dataset is constructed by randomly sampling in each group, and is used to analyze the performance of the classifier and to calculate the Confusion Matrix. If acceptable, then output the classifier, otherwise return to step 5 to re-train the weights of SVM.

### 3.2. Dataset

The fruit dataset was obtained after six months of on-site data collecting via digital camera and online collecting using images.google.com as the main search engine. The split-and-merge algorithm was used to remove the background areas; later images were cropped to leave the fruit in the center of the image, and finally downsampled to 256 × 256 in size.

The data set comprises 18 different categories: Granny Smith Apples (64), Rome Apples (83), Yellow Bananas (132), Green Plantains (61), Tangerines (112), Hass Avocados (105), Watermelons (72), Cantaloupes (129), Gold Pineapples (89), Passion Fruits (72), Bosc Pears (88), Anjou Pears (140), Green Grapes (74), Red Grapes (45), Black Grapes (122), Blackberries (97), Blueberries (95), and Strawberries (73). In total, there are 1s653 images. Table 4 depicts the samples of different types of fruits in the data set.

### 3.3. Stratified Cross Validation

Typically, a statistical model that deals with the inherent data variability is inferred from the database (*i.e.*, the training set) and employed by statistical learning machines for the automatic construction of classifiers. The model has a set of adjustable parameters that are estimated in the learning phase using a set of examples. Nevertheless, the learning machine must ensure a reliable estimation of the parameters and consequently good generalization, *i.e.*, correct responses to unseen examples, including classifying new images correctly. Hence, the learning device must efficiently find a trade-off between its complexity, which is measured by several variables, such as the effective number of free parameters of the classifier and the feature input space dimension, and the information on the problem given by the training set (e.g., measured by the number of samples).

Cross validation methods are usually employed to assess the statistical relevance of the classifiers. It consists of four types: Random subsampling, *K*-fold cross validation, leave-one-out validation, and Monte Carlo Cross-Validation [25]. The *K*-fold cross validation is applied due to its simple and easy properties, while using all data for training and validation. The mechanism is to create a *K*-fold partition of the whole dataset, repeat *K* times to use *K*-1 folds for training and a left fold for validation, and finally average the error rates of *K* experiments. The schematic diagram of 5-fold cross validation is shown in Figure 7.

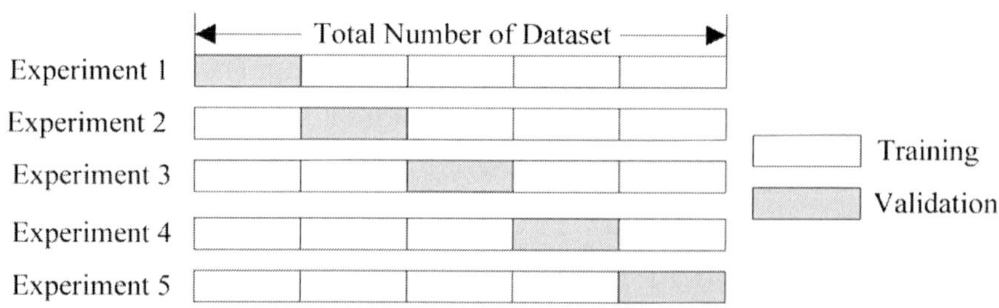


**Figure 7.** A 5-fold Cross Validation.

The *K* folds can be purely random partitioned; however, some folds may have quite different distributions from other folds. Therefore, the stratified *K*-fold cross validation was employed, in which every fold has nearly the same class distributions [26]. The folds are selected so that the mean response value is approximately equal in all the folds. In the case of a dichotomous classification, this means that each fold contains roughly the same proportions of the two types of class labels.

Another challenge was to determine the number of folds. If *K* is set too large, the bias of the true error rate estimator will be small, but the variance of the estimator will be large and the computation will be time consuming. Alternatively, if *K* is set too small, the computation time will decrease, the variance of the estimator will be small, but the bias of the estimator will be large [27]. In this study, we empirically determined *K* to be 5 through the trial-and-error method.

### 3.4. PCA Results

The curve of cumulative sum of variance versus number of reduced vectors via PCA is shown in Figure 8. The detailed data results are listed in Table 5. It shows that merely 14 features can preserve 95.08% energy. The reduced features only cost 17.7% (14/79) of the memory needed for the original 79 features. Consequently, the algorithm can be accelerated remarkably. Seventy nine features are not a burden to the latest computers. But after they are reduced to 14 features, we can accelerate the training and test speed, and meanwhile removing extra features will enhance the classification accuracy.

The loading plot on principal component 1&2 is shown in Figure 9, from which we can analyze the subsequent role of 79 features for classification. It will guide us to select features more effectively and to identify the relationship between samples and features.

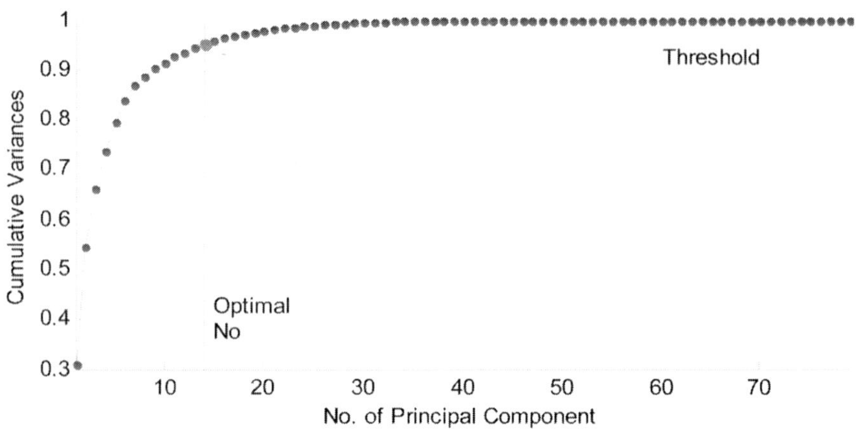


**Figure 8.** Feature selection via PCA (threshold is set as 95%).

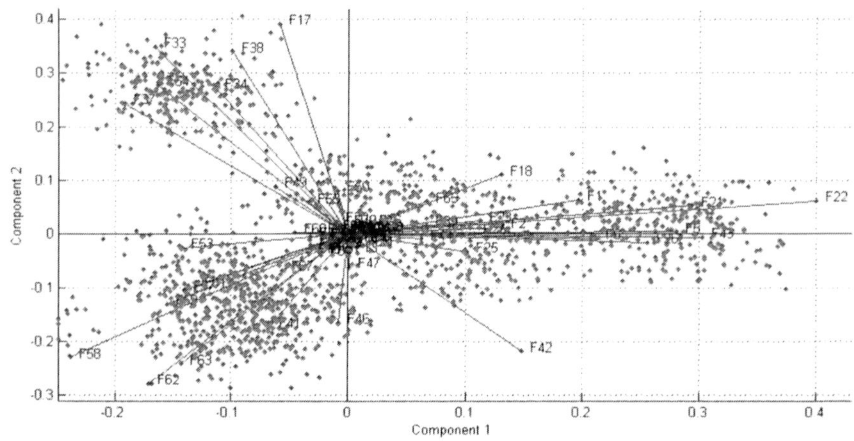


**Figure 9.** The biplot (red dots represent the samples, and blue lines represent the 79 original features, and x-axis & y-axis represent the two principal components).

### 3.5. SVM Results

We tested three multi-class SVMs (WTA-SVM, MWV-SVM, and DAG-SVM) using the reduced feature vectors and using 5-fold cross validation. Meanwhile, we chose the Linear (LIN) kernel, *d*th Homogeneous Polynomial (HPOL) kernel, and the Gaussian Radial

Basis (GRB) kernel as listed in Table 3. We computed hundreds of simulations in order to estimate the optimal parameters of the kernel functions, such as the order *d* in HPOL kernel and the scaling factor *γ* in GRB kernel.

Tables 6 and 7 show the classification accuracy and calculation time in five-fold cross-validation for those SVMs with optimized parameters, respectively. For LIN kernel, the classification accuracies of MWV-SVM and DAG-SVM are the same of 53.5%, higher than the WTA-SVM of 48.1%; for the HPOL kernel, the classification accuracy of MWV-SVM is 75.6%, higher than WTA-SVM of 61.7% and DAG-SVM of 70.1%; for the GRB kernel, the classification accuracy of MWV-SVM is 88.2%, still higher than WTA-SVM of 55.4% and DAG-SVM of 84.0%. Therefore, the best results are achieved using the GRB kernel MWV-SVM with a classification accuracy of 88.2%.

As for the classification speed, the WTA-SVM is the slowest, for it uses one-*versus*-all strategy so the dataset needed for training is relatively large. The MWV-SVM is faster than WTA-SVM for it uses one-versus-one strategy so every individual binary SVM only takes about 2/18 portion of the data. The DAG-SVM is yet four times faster than MWV-SVM. The reason leans upon that the MWV-SVM needs all 153 individual SVMs to make the final decision, nevertheless the DAG-SVM needs only 17 binary SVMs to complete the equivalent task.

### 3.6. Confusion Matrix

The confusion matrix of GRB kernel MWV-SVM is shown in Figure 10. Each column of the matrix represents the instances in target class (actual class), while each row represents the instances in the output class (predicted class). The number in *i*th row and *j*th column represents samples whose target is the *j*th class that was classified as *i*th class. All the misclassification cases are highlighted in yellow.

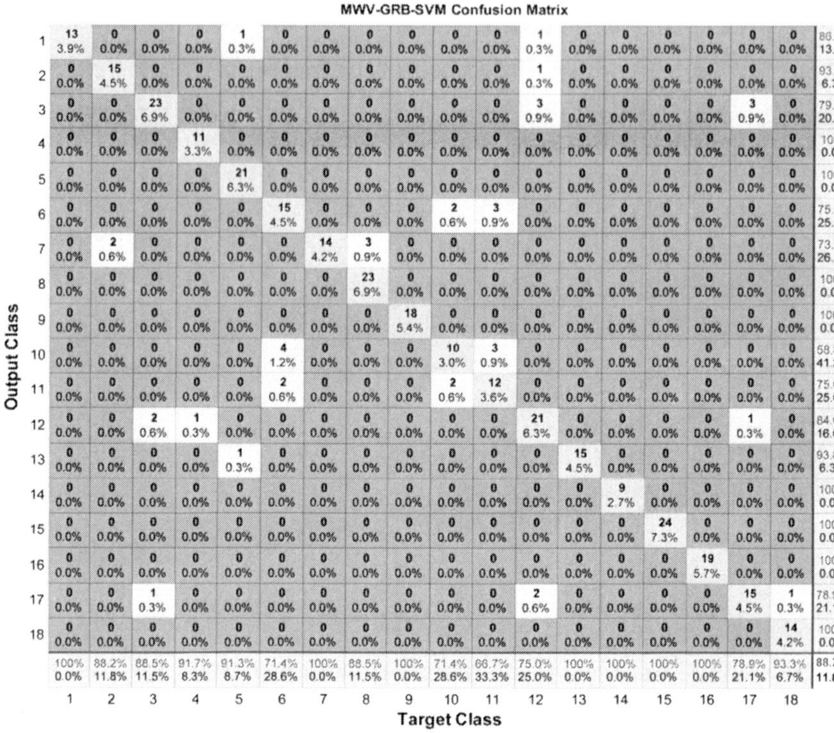


**Figure 10.** Confusion matrix of GRB kernel MWV-SVM with overall classification accuracy of 88.2%.

By looking at the bottom line of Figure 10, we found that 1st class (Granny Smith Apples), 7th class (Water melon), 9th class (Golden Pineapple), 13th class (Green Grape), 14th class (Red Grape), 15th class (Black Grape), 16th class (Black berry) are all recognized successfully.

Notwithstanding, a few types of fruits were not recognized so successfully. The SVM for the 11th class (Bosc Pears) performs the worst. In the test dataset, there are 18 different pictures of Bosc Pears, however, three of them are misclassified as 6th class (Avocado), and another three of them are misclassified as 10th class (Passion Fruits), so the rest are recognized correctly leading to a 66.7% (12/18) success rate. For the 6th class (Avocado), it has twenty-one samples in the test dataset, but four are misclassified as 10th class (Passion Fruits) and two are misclassified as 11th class (Bosc Pears), so with the rest fifteen samples recognized, this give us a 71.43% (15/21) success rate. For the 10th class (Passion Fruits), it has fourteen samples in the test dataset, two are misclassified as 6th class (Avocado), and another two are misclassified as 11th class (Bosc Pears), so with the rest recognized, it give us a 71.43% (10/14) success rate. In other words, the 6th, 10th, and 11th classes are not distinct in the view of SVM, which is a motivation for our future work in order to solve this misclassification.

## 4. CONCLUSIONS

This work proposed a novel classification method based on multi-class kSVM. The experimental results demonstrated that the MWV-SVM with GRB kernel achieves the best classification accuracy of 88.2%. The combination of color histogram, Unser's texture, and shape features are more effective than any single kind of feature in classification of fruits. Using PCA to reduce features, we tested three different multi-class SVMs (WTA-SVM, MWV-SVM, and DAG-SVM) with linear kernel, *d*th Homogeneous Polynomial kernel, and Gaussian Radial Basis kernel in the dataset of 1,653 fruit images. The best results were obtained for MWV-SVM with the GRB kernel with an overall classification accuracy of 88.2%. Future research will concentrate on: (1) extending our research to sliced, dried, canned, and tinned fruits; (2) include additional features to increase the classification accuracy; (3) accelerate the algorithm; and (4) find distinguishable features for Bosc Pears, Passion Fruits, and Avocado.

## ACKNOWLEDGMENTS

The authors give special thanks to Roberto Lam from The City College of New York-CUNY for the review of the whole paper.

## REFERENCES


1. Rocha, A.; Hauagge, D.C.; Wainer, J.; Goldenstein, S. Automatic fruit and vegetable classification from images.*Comput. Electron. Agric.* **2010**, *70*, 96–104.
2. Bolle, R.M.; Connell, J.H.; Haas, N.; Mohan, R.; Taubin, G. VeggieVision: A Produce Recognition System. Proceedings 3rd IEEE Workshop on Applications of Computer Vision, WACV'96, Sarasota, FL, USA, 2– 4 December 1996; pp. 244–251.
3. Hong, S.G.; Maccaroni, M.; Figuli, P.J.; Pryor, B.M.; Belisario, A. Polyphasic Classification of alternaria isolated from hazelnut and walnut fruit in Europe. *Mycol. Res.* **2006**, *110*, 1290–1300.
4. Baltazar, A.; Aranda, J.I.; González-Aguilar, G. Bayesian classification of ripening stages of tomato fruit using acoustic impact and colorimeter sensor data. *Comput. Electron. Agric.* **2008**, *60*, 113–121.
5. Pennington, J.A.T.; Fisher, R.A. Classification of fruits and vegetables. *J. Food Compos. Anal.* **2009**, *22*, S23–S31.
6. Pholpho, T.; Pathaveerat, S.; Sirisomboon, P. Classification of longan fruit bruising using visible spectroscopy. *J. Food Eng.* **2011**, *104*, 169–172.
7. Seng, W.C.; Mirisaee, S.H. A New Method for Fruits Recognition System. Proceedings of International Conference on Electrical Engineering and Informatics, ICEEI'09, Selangor, Malaysia, 5–7 August 2009; Volume 1. pp. 130–134.
8. Patil, N.S.; Shelokar, P.S.; Jayaraman, V.K.; Kulkarni, B.D. Regression models using pattern search assisted least square support vector machines. *Chem. Eng. Res. Des.* **2005**, *83*, 1030–1037.
9. Li, D.; Yang, W.; Wang, S. Classification of foreign fibers in cotton lint using machine vision and multi-class support vector machine. *Comput. Electron. Agric.* **2010**, *74*, 274–279.

10. Min, T.-H.; Park, R.-H. Eyelid and eyelash detection method in the normalized iris image using the parabolic Hough model and Otsu's thresholding method. *Pattern Recognit. Lett.* **2009**, *30*, 1138–1143.

11. Xiao, Y.; Zou, J.; Yan, H. An adaptive split-and-merge method for binary image contour data compression. *Pattern Recognit. Lett.* **2001**, *22*, 299–307.

12. Damiand, G.; Resch, P. Split-and-merge algorithms defined on topological maps for 3D image segmentation.*Graph. Models* **2003**, *65*, 149–167.

13. Siang Tan, K.; Mat Isa, N.A. Color image segmentation using histogram thresholding—Fuzzy C-means hybrid approach. *Pattern Recognit. Lett.* **2011**, *44*, 1–15.

14. Maitra, M.; Chatterjee, A. A hybrid cooperative-comprehensive learning based PSO algorithm for image segmentation using multilevel thresholding. *Expert Syst. Appl.* **2008**, *34*, 1341–1350.

15. Unser, M. Texture classification and segmentation using wavelet frames. *IEEE Trans. Image Process* **1995**, *4*, 1549–1560.

16. Lou, S.; Jiang, X.; Scott, P.J. Algorithms for morphological profile filters and their comparison. *Precis. Eng.* **2012**,*36*, 414–423.

17. Kwak, N. Principal Component Analysis Based on L1-Norm Maximization. *IEEE Trans. Patt. Anal. Mach. Int.***2008**, *30*, 1672–1680.

18. Lipovetsky, S. PCA and SVD with nonnegative loadings. *Pattern Recognit. Lett.* **2009**, *42*, 68–76.

19. Jackson, J.E. *A User's Guide to Principal Components*; John Wiley & Sons: Hoboken, NJ, USA, 1991.

20. Acevedo-Rodríguez, J.; Maldonado-Bascón, S.; Lafuente-Arroyo, S.; Siegmann, P.; López-Ferreras, F. Computational load reduction in decision functions using support vector machines. *Signal Process* **2009**, *89*, 2066–2071.

21. Deris, A.M.; Zain, A.M.; Sallehuddin, R. Overview of Support Vector Machine in Modeling Machining Performances. *Procedia Eng.* **2011**, *24*, 308–312.

22. Maddipati, S.; Nandigam, R.; Kim, S.; Venkatasubramanian, V. Learning patterns in combinatorial protein libraries by Support Vector Machines. *Comput. Chem. Eng.* **2011**, *35*, 1143–1151.

23. Lingras, P.; Butz, C. Rough set based 1-v-1 and 1-v-r approaches to support vector machine multi-classification.*Inform. Sci.* **2007**, *177*, 3782–3798.

24. Platt, J.C.; Cristianini, N.; Shawe-Taylor, J. Large margin DAGs for multiclass classification. *Adv. Neural. Inform. Process. Syst.* **2000**, *12*, 547–553.

25. Pereira, A.C.; Reis, M.S.; Saraiva, P.M.; Marques, J.C. Madeira wine ageing prediction based on different analytical techniques: UV–vis, GC-MS, HPLC-DAD. *Chemometr. Intel. Lab. Syst.* **2011**, *105*, 43–55.

26. May, R.J.; Maier, H.R.; Dandy, G.C. Data splitting for artificial neural networks using SOM-based stratified sampling. *Neural Netw.* **2010**, *23*, 283–294.

27. Armand, S.; Watelain, E.; Roux, E.; Mercier, M.; Lepoutre, F.-X. Linking clinical measurements and kinematic gait patterns of toe-walking using fuzzy decision trees. *Gait Posture* **2007**, *25*, 475–484.

# Chapter 13

## FAST AND FLEXIBLE MOVABLE VISION MEASUREMENT FOR THE SURFACE OF A LARGE-SIZED OBJECT

**Zhen Liu, Xiaojing Li, Fengjiao Li, Xinguo Wei * and Guanjun Zhang**

*Ministry of Education Key Laboratory of Precision Opto-Mechatronics Technology, Beihang University, No.37 Xueyuan Rd., Haidian District, Beijing 100191, China*

## ABSTRACT

The presented movable vision measurement for the three-dimensional (3D) surface of a large-sized object has the advantages of system simplicity, low cost, and high accuracy. Aiming at addressing the problems of existing movable vision measurement methods, a more suitable method for large-sized products on industrial sites is introduced in this paper. A raster binocular vision sensor and a wide-field camera are combined to form a 3D scanning sensor. During measurement, several planar targets are placed around the object to be measured. With the planar target as an intermediary, the local 3D data measured by the scanning sensor are integrated into the global coordinate system. The effectiveness of the proposed method is verified through physical experiments.

**Keywords:** Machine vision; Binocular vision sensor; Planar target

# 1. INTRODUCTION

In the process of manufacture and assembly of large-sized objects the use of sensor feedback to guide the processing and assembly by the rapid online measurement of large-sized surface morphologies can significantly improve the machine efficiency and quality of the resulting parts. With advances in computer technology, image processing, and pattern-recognition technologies, vision measurement technology has rapidly developed. Vision measurement systems have gradually become the most important means of three-dimensional (3D) surface topography measurement for large-sized objects [1,2,3,4,5]. Currently, the main characteristic of 3D surface topography measurements for large-sized objects is that the measuring position is essentially fixed because in the industrial field each batch of large-sized product does not change significantly in shape. However, the fast-paced production and the small measuring space require that the measurement system be highly accurate, its speed rapid, and the structures be simple and flexible. However, most existing vision measurement systems cannot meet the needs of fast-paced on-site production. Thus, research on fast and high-precision 3D shape measurement of large-sized objects is important in the industrial field.

At present, 3D shape measurement of objects basically uses three methods: structured light vision measurement, Fourier profilometry, and phase profilometry. Structured light vision measurement includes the multi-line structured light method and the encoding structured light method. Light strip matching is more difficult, so the multi-line structured light method [6,7] is usually applied in object geometric measurement. Meanwhile, the coded structured light method [8,9,10] is an effective means of obtaining dense 3D point clouds of object 3D surface morphology; the method operates on a simple principle and has a high degree of automation, so it is the most commonly used among the 3D shape measurement methods. The biggest advantage of Fourier transform profilometry [11,12,13] is that by using only one image, it can achieve 3D object surface topography measurement. Therefore, it is suitable for dynamic 3D measurements. Its disadvantages are its long operation time and low automated performance, so it is not suitable for industrial measurements. Phase measurement profilometry [14,15,16] has high accuracy and is currently the most frequently used 3D shape measurement method, however, the algorithm is more complex and the phase unwrapping problem exists.

Single-vision sensors cannot achieve overall large-sized object 3D surface topography measurement because of the occlusions. The usual method is to divide the area to be measured into a plurality of sub-regions, and all the sub-region 3D data are integrated into the global coordinate system to obtain a 3D morphology of the entire surface of the object. Depending on the different overall unified approaches, the surface 3D morphology vision measurement of large-sized objects can be divided into two categories: movable single-vision sensor measurement and fixed multiple vision sensor measurement.

Movable single-vision sensor measurement method measures the 3D morphology of the entire surface of a large-sized object using a movable single-vision sensor. It uses simple equipment and is low cost. This method affixes labels on the object or uses a planar target to integrate the subregion 3D data into the global coordinate system. A typical method using adhesive markers is the ATOS movable 3D optical measurement system developed by the GOM Company. However, many of the objects to be measured (e.g., soft objects, liquids, or high-precision mechanical components) cannot be labeled. Meanwhile, this method has a long adhesive marking time and the marker is easily deformed. By contrast, using the planar target method [17], errors caused in the single movable measurement can easily accumulate. In addition, the planar target needs to be placed before the measured object in this method, the measuring time is long, and the operation is complex.

Fixed multiple-vision sensor measurement [18,19,20] needs to employ more on-site vision sensors and complete the global calibration of multiple vision sensors. Based on the global calibration results, data obtained by each vision sensor are united into the global coordinate system. Currently, typical measurement systems using fixed multiple-vision sensors include those of the American company Perceptron, with its auto-body geometry detection system, and Italian company MERMEC, with its online trial of full profile measurement systems. The principle of the method is simple, but the systems are complex and on-site calibration is difficult. After the measurement system is moved or the measured objects are changed, the measurement system needs to be reconfigured and recalibrated. At present, the method is often used in the geometry size measurement of the mass-produced large-sized products in the industrial field, but it is not suitable for large-sized and complex 3D surface reconstruction.

Based on the above analysis, compared with the fixed multiple-vision sensors measurement, the movable single-vision sensor measurement method seems more suitable for 3D surface topography measurement of the large-sized object. To achieve rapid measurement of the 3D surface topography of large-sized object, particularly mass-produced large-sized objects in the industrial field, the method proposed herein combines a raster binocular vision sensor with a wide-field camera to form a 3D scanning sensor. Multiple plane targets arranged in the surroundings of the measured object are used as intermediaries and the local 3D data obtained from the 3D scanning sensor are integrated into the global coordinate system. The remainder of the paper is organized as follows: Section 2 describes the structure and the mathematical model of the 3D scanning sensor, Section 3 provides a detailed description of the basic principles of the algorithm, and Section 4 verifies the effectiveness of the proposed algorithm through experiments.

## 2. SYSTEM MEASUREMENT PRINCIPLE

The structural schematic of the measurement system is shown in Figure 1. The coordinate systems of planar targets 1 and 2 are Ot1xt1yt1zt1 and Ot2xt2yt2zt2, respectively. Ooxoyozois the 3D scanning sensor coordinate system. The coordinate system of planar target 1 Ot1xt1yt1zt1 is selected as the global coordinate system OGxGyGzG. The 3D scanning sensor is placed in front of the measured object to ensure that the wide-field camera can "see" the target plane. TC,t1 and TC,t2 are the transformation matrices from the 3D scanning sensor coordinate system Ooxoyozo to the coordinate systems of plane targets 1 and 2, respectively. Tt2,t1 is the transformation matrix from the plane target 2 to plane target 1.

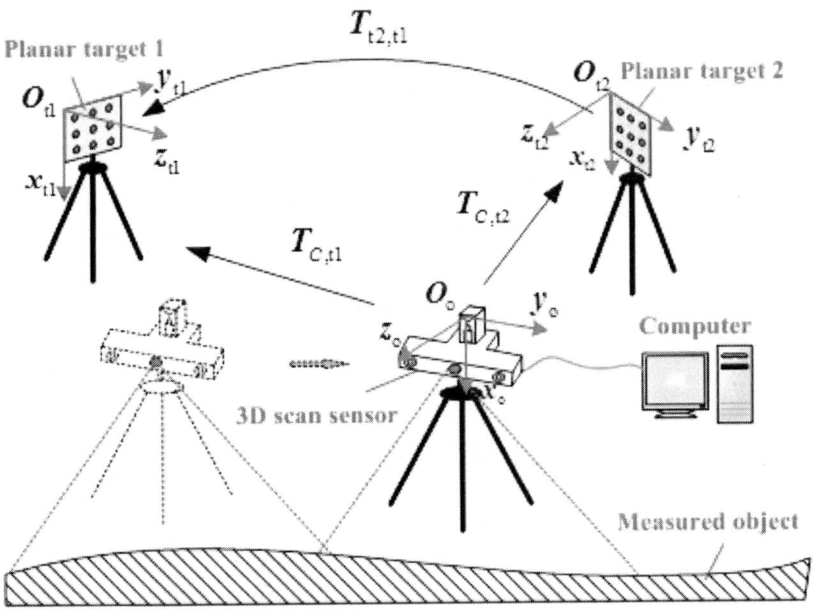


**Figure 1.** The structural schematic of the measurement system.

The proposed system includes a 3D scanning sensor, multiple planar targets, a high-speed image acquisition system, a computer, measurement software, and the corresponding mechanical structure. The basic principle of the measurement system is as follows: first, multiple planar targets are arranged around the measured object. Second, the raster binocular stereo vision sensor of the 3D scanning sensor measures the local 3D surface of the object, and the wide-field camera of the 3D scanning sensor measures the planar target. Finally, these planar targets function as the mediators to integrate all local 3D data measured by the 3D scanning sensor into the global coordinate system *OGxGyGzG.*

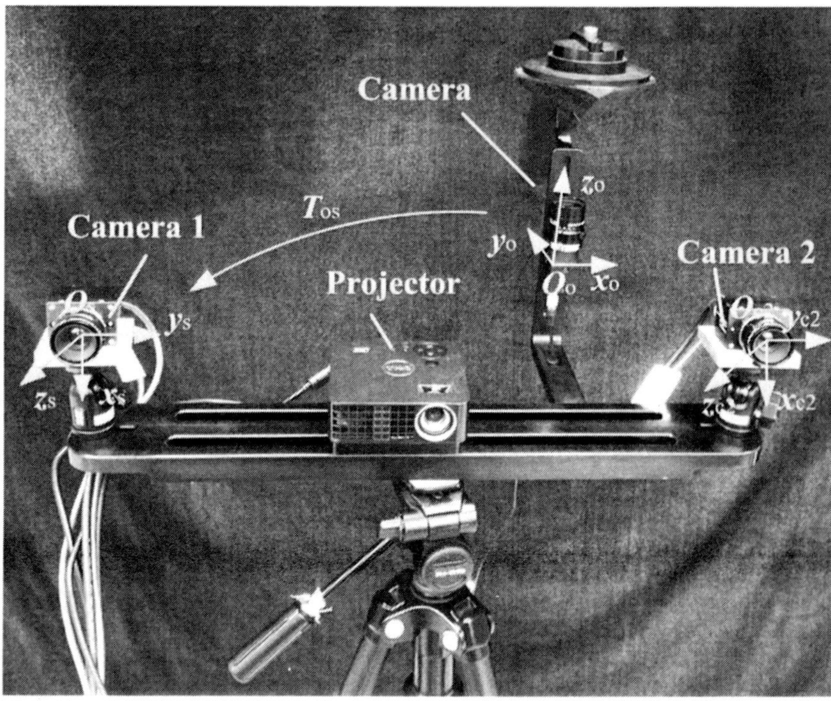


**Figure 2.** Structure of the 3D scanning sensor.

### 2.1. 3D Scanning Sensor

As shown in Figure 2, the 3D scanning sensor includes a raster binocular stereo vision sensor and a wide-field camera. The raster binocular stereo vision sensor consists of two cameras and a projector. The wide-field camera is a combination of a high-resolution camera and a four-sided mirror. The wide-field camera also can be considered as a four-mirror camera to achieve multi-angle measurement. The 3D scanning sensor coordinate system *Ooxoyozo* is established under the wide-field camera coordinate system *Olxlylzl.*

The raster binocular stereo vision sensor coordinate system *Osxsyszs* is established under the left camera coordinate system Oc1xc1yc1zc1 of the raster binocular vision sensor and Tos is the transformation matrix from *Ooxoyozo* to *Osxsyszs.* Schematic images of the wide-field camera and the image captured by the wide-field camera are shown in Figure 3a,b, respectively.

Compared with the curved mirror in current panoramic cameras, the model of the wide-field camera with a four-surface mirror is simpler and its measurement accuracy is higher. However, the field of views of the wide-field camera has a blind area. The size and measuring location of mass-produced large-sized products are basically fixed in industrial production sites, so each movement position of the 3D scanning sensor can be determined in advance, and the planar targets used in the proposed method can optimize those positions based on each moving point of the 3D scanning sensor. Therefore, compared with using a panoramic camera with curved mirrors, the wide-field camera with a four-surface mirror is suitable for industrial production. It is also the main reason why flat mirrors are used in the proposed method instead of curved mirrors.

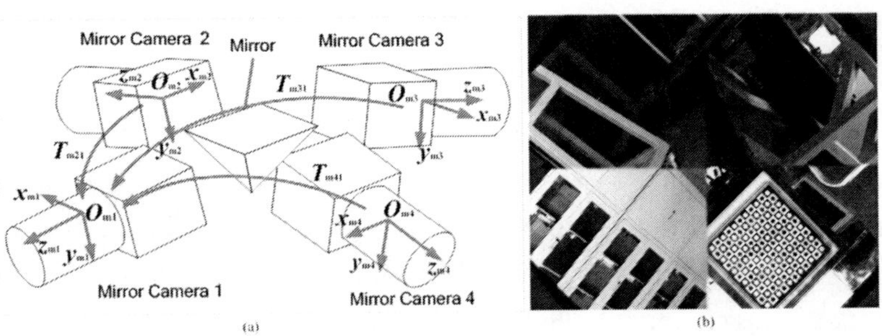


**Figure 3.** (**a**) Schematic image of the wide-field camera; (**b**) Image captured by the wide-field camera.

As shown in Figure 3a, *Omixmiymizmi*(i=1,2,3,4) is the coordinate system of the four mirror cameras of the wide-field camera, respectively. Tm21,Tm31,Tm41 are the transformation matrixes from the coordinate system of mirror cameras 2, 3, and 4 to that of mirror camera 1, respectively. The coordinate system Olxlylzl of the wide-field camera is established based on the coordinate system Om1xm1ym1zm1 of mirror camera 1. According to Equation (1), the 3D coordinates ***Po***=[xo,yo,zo,1] of *P* under the coordinate system *Ooxoyozo* can be obtained under the coordinate system of the 3D scanning sensor:

$$P_{O} = T_{OS}^{-1} P_{S} \tag{1}$$

where Ps is the 3D coordinates of P under the coordinate system *Osxsyszs.* Tos can be obtained by calibration before measuring [21].

## 2.2. Light Strip Image Center Extraction and Coding

### Light Strip Coding

The proposed method uses the existing binary-coded method [22] to achieve the match with the left and right cameras' light strips. The projector is first arranged according to Figure 4a–f to cast six black and white images. Supposing that the black is defined as 0 and the white is 1. The coding index of the first black light bar region in the left side of the 64 black and white light bar region is 000000 in Figure 4f. From left to right, the successive light bar coding is 000001, 000010, 000011, and so on.

As shown in Figure 4a–f, after the projection of six black and white images, 64 black and white light bar regions can be formed, and they have been encoded. Four light strip images are constructed, and each image has 64 vertical light strips, as shown in Figure 4g–j. In each graph of Figure 4g–j, 64 light strips are in 64 black and white coding light bar regions formed inFigure 4a–f. According to the four light strip images above, 64 × 4 = 256 light strips can be obtained. The distribution schematic diagram of all projected images is shown in Figure 5. At the same time, the number of light strip images can be increased or decreased based on need; 64 × 2 = 128 light strips can be obtained by projecting two images, 64 × 6 = 384 light strips can be obtained by projecting six images, and so on.

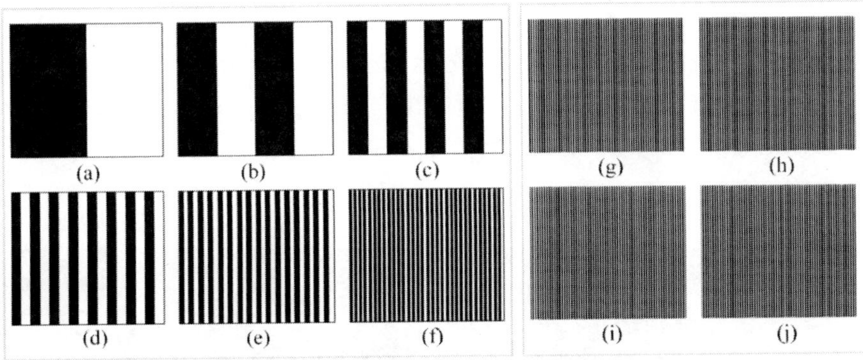


**Figure 4.** All projected images.

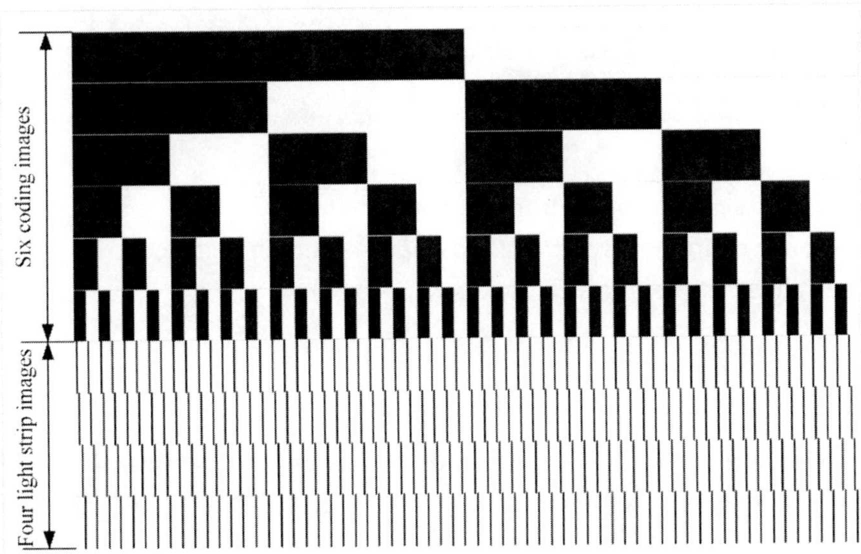


**Figure 5.** Line distribution diagram of all projected images.

In Figure 4a–f, the black and white light bar region is only used for constructing the coding region to identify 64 light strips of each light strip image in Figure 4g–j. In the four light strip images shown in Figure 4g–j, the Steger [23] algorithm is used to extract the light strip center point of the light strip image in this paper. First, the Hessian matrix is used to determine the pixel-level coordinate and the normal direction of the light strip center Then, the sub-pixel level coordinate of the light strip center is obtained by solving the extreme points in the normal direction, as shown in Figure 6a. Finally, a link constraint method is used to remove the wrong center of the light bar and to link the correct light strip centers together to form a plurality of segments, as shown in Figure 6b.

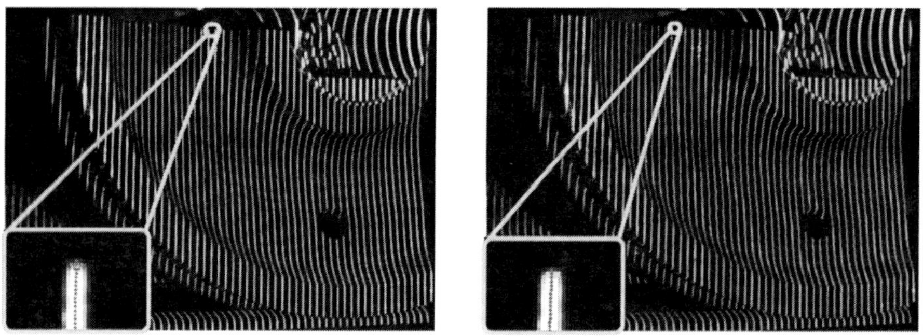

(a) (b)

**Figure 6.** Light stripe extraction results. (**a**) Extraction result of the sub-pixel coordinates of the light stripe center; (**b**) Extraction result of the light stripe center after linking.

## 2.3. Partial 3D Reconstruction

Section 2.2 shows that each light strip in the projected image corresponds to a unique code index. The light strips captured by the left and right cameras of the raster binocular stereo vision sensor can be matched according to the code index. The corresponding points of the light strip captured by two cameras can be obtained according to the epipolar constraints. Finally, the corresponding points are substituted into the raster binocular stereo vision model to calculate the 3D coordinates of the corresponding points.

The schematic of the grating binocular vision sensor model is shown in Figure 7. The left camera's coordinate system is Oc1xc1yc1zc1 and the right camera's coordinate system is Oc2xc2yc2zc2. The transformation matrix from $O_{c1}x_{c1}y_{c1}z_{c1}$ to $O_{c2}x_{c2}y_{c2}z_{c2}$ is $\boldsymbol{T}_{21}=\begin{bmatrix}\boldsymbol{R}_{21} & \boldsymbol{t}_{21}\\ 0 & 1\end{bmatrix}$ (where R21 and t21 are the rotation matrix and translation vectors, respectively).

Without loss of generality, the raster binocular stereo vision sensor coordinate system Osxsyszs is built under $O_{c1}x_{c1}y_{c1}z_{c1}$. $\boldsymbol{p}_1=[u_1,v_1,1]^{\mathrm{T}}$ and $\boldsymbol{p}_2=[u_2,v_2,1]^{\mathrm{T}}$ are undistorted homogeneous image coordinates of the light strip point P at the left and right camera coordinate system (obtained from the distorted image of homogeneous coordinates through lens distortion correction [24]). l1 is the pole line of p2 in the left camera and l2 is the pole line of p1 in the right camera. The 3D coordinates Ps=[xs,ys,zs,1]T of P under Osxsyszs can be solved by the binocular stereo vision model, as shown in Equation (2):

$$\begin{cases}\rho_1\boldsymbol{p}_1=\boldsymbol{K}_1\begin{bmatrix}\boldsymbol{I} & \boldsymbol{0}\end{bmatrix}\boldsymbol{P}_{\mathrm{s}}\\ \rho_2\boldsymbol{p}_2=\boldsymbol{K}_2\begin{bmatrix}\boldsymbol{R}_{21} & \boldsymbol{t}_{21}\end{bmatrix}\boldsymbol{P}_{\mathrm{s}}\end{cases} \tag{2}$$

where K1 and K2 are intrinsic parameters of the left and right cameras, respectively.

The light strip matching of the left and right cameras can be achieved by light strip coding. The epipolar constraints are added to achieve the corresponding light strip center points of the left and right cameras. The corresponding points are substituted into Equation (4) to calculate their 3D coordinates.

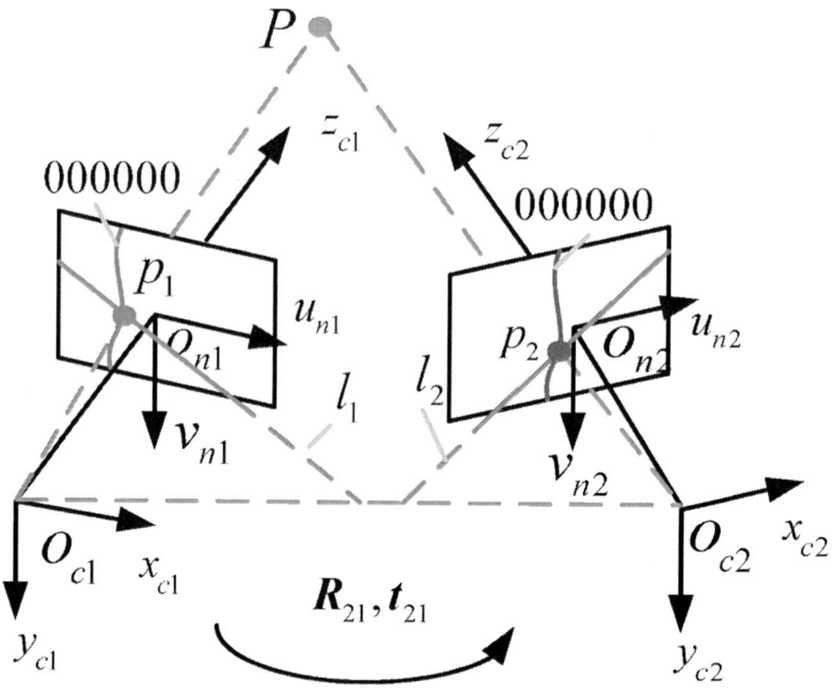


**Figure 7.** Schematic of the grating binocular vision sensor model.

### 2.4. Global Unity of Partial 3D Data

The partial 3D reconstruction process of the 3D scanning sensor is introduced in Section 2.3. However, limited by the vision sensor's field of view, the partial 3D reconstruction of the 3D scanning sensor can only measure the local 3D data of large-sized objects. To achieve the overall 3D reconstruction of large-sized objects, all local 3D data need to be integrated into the global coordinate system.

The planar target 1 coordinate Ot1xt1yt1zt1 is selected as the global coordinate system *OGxGyGzG*. PO is the 3D coordinate of the light strip center point *P* measured by the raster binocular vision sensor in the 3D scanning sensor coordinate system *OOxOyOzO* and PG is the 3D coordinate of *P* in the global coordinate system *OGxGyGzG.* As shown in Figure 1, the wide-field camera of the 3D scanning sensor can "see" two plane targets placed around the large-sized object to calculate TC,t1 and TC,t2, then calculate Tt2,t1. The local 3D coordinates measured by 3D scanning sensor can be integrated into the global coordinate system using Equation (3):

$$P_G = T_{C,t1} P_O \tag{3}$$

The wide-field camera may not "see" planar target 1, but it can "see" plane target 2. Then, the local 3D data can be integrated into the global coordinate system using Equation (4):

$$P_G = T_{t2,t1} T_{C,t2} P_O \tag{4}$$

To improve system efficiency and flexibility, multiple plane targets can be arranged around the large-sized object on the measurement site.

## 3. PHYSICAL EXPERIMENTS

The setup of the physical experiment is shown in Figure 8. The raster binocular stereo vision sensor of the 3D scanning sensor consists of two cameras (AVTGC1380H with 17 mm lenses and a resolution of 1360 × 1024 and a field of view of 500 mm × 380 mm × 400 mm, Allied Vision Technologies, Stadtroda, Germany) and one projector (Dell M110 with a resolution of 1360 × 768, Dell, Round Rock, TX, USA). The wide-field camera of the 3D scanning sensor consists of one camera (Pointgray with 12 mm lenses and a resolution of 2448 × 2048, Point Grey Research, Richmond, Canada) and one mirror with four surfaces. The characteristic point of the planar target is unified as 10 × 10, with a machining accuracy of 5 μm.

### 3.1. System Calibration Results

First, the raster binocular stereo vision and the intrinsic parameters of the wide-field camera are calibrated based on [24,25]. Then, the transformation matrix Tm21, Tm31, Tm31 and Tos are calibrated by [21]. The planar target used for calibration is the same as the planar target for the measurement system.

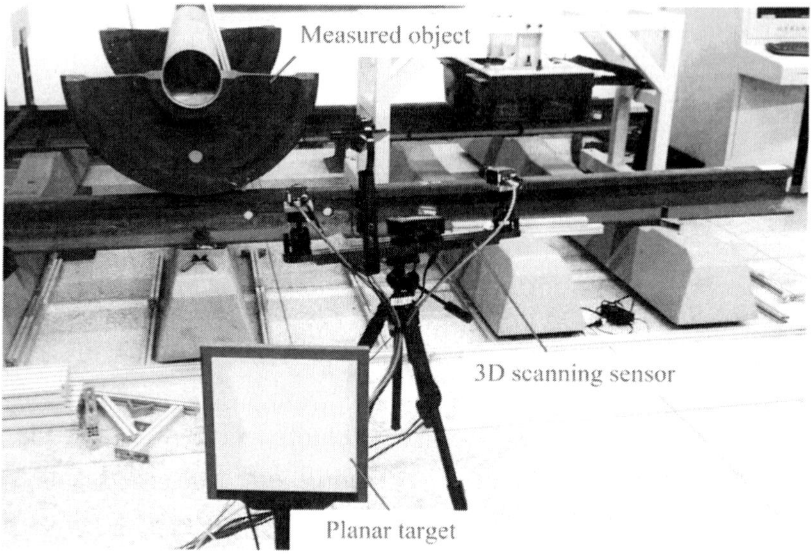


**Figure 8.** Layout of the physical experiments.

All calibration results of 3D scanning sensor are shown as follows:

(1) Binocular stereo vision sensor

Intrinsic parameters of left camera: $fx$ = 2744.3; $fy$ = 2745.9; $\gamma$ = 0; $u_0$ = 750.2; $v_0$ = 480.6; $k_1$ = −0.14; $k_2$ = −0.51.

Intrinsic parameters of right camera: $fx$ = 2754.6; $fy$ = 2753.5; $\gamma$ = 0; $u_0$ = 709.7; $v_0$ = 538.4; $k_1$ = −0.15; $k_2$ = 0.02.

$\boldsymbol{T}_{21}$: $\boldsymbol{r}_{21}$ = [0.0387, 0.416, 0.00024]; $\boldsymbol{t}_{21}$ = [−489.501, 13.515, 90.88667].

The uncertainty of intrinsic parameters of left camera: ufx=1.75; ufy=1.89; uu0=3.67; uv0=2.18; uk1=5.0×10−3; uk2=6. 29×10−2.

The uncertainty of intrinsic parameters of right camera: ufx=1.70; ufy=1.74; uu0=3.43; uv0=2.52; uk1=5.91×10−3; uk2= 7.51×10−2.

A planar target is placed before the binocular stereo vision sensor at two positions, which measures the distance of character points of the target. Compared the real distance and the measurement distance, the RMS error is 0.09 mm. The binocular stereo vision sensor measure the character points of planar target 100 times, the deviation error is 0.03 mm.

(2) Wide-field camera

Intrinsic parameters: $fx = 3705.8$; $fy = 3706.5$; $\gamma = 0$; $u_0 = 1222.5$; $v_0 = 997.4$; $k_1 = -0.14$; $k_2 = 0.26$.

$\boldsymbol{T}_{m21}$: $\boldsymbol{r}_{m21} = [-0.036, -1.528, -0.798]$; $\boldsymbol{t}_{m21} = [85.327, -55.294, 94.977]$.

$\boldsymbol{T}_{os}$: $\boldsymbol{r}_{os} = [1.413, 1.002, -1.257]$; $\boldsymbol{t}_{os} = [97.625, -103.644, 261.717]$.

To verify the effectiveness of the proposed method, the following experiments were conducted to evaluate the measurement accuracy. The following subsection is a detailed description of the procedures and results.

A self-designed method is used to evaluate the global measurement precision. The specific experimental procedure is as follows: a one-dimensional (1D) target with two characteristic points (the distance between the two points is 1234.15 mm, with a precision of 0.01 mm) is placed before the 3D scanning sensor, which measures the characteristic point of the 1D target, as shown in Figure 9. Firstly, the 3D scanning sensor measures the left characteristic point of the 1D target at the first position, then it measures the right characteristic point of the 1D target at the second position. Finally, all characteristic points of 1D target measured by the scanning sensor at two positions are integrated into the global coordinate system by the planar target. The above progress is repeated eight times. The distance between the two points is calculated as the measurement distance ($d$m). The real distance between the two points of 1D target is the ideal distance ($d$t = 1234.15 mm). The deviation ($\Delta d$) between $d_m$ and $d_t$ and the RMS error are calculated to evaluate the global accuracy of the proposed method.

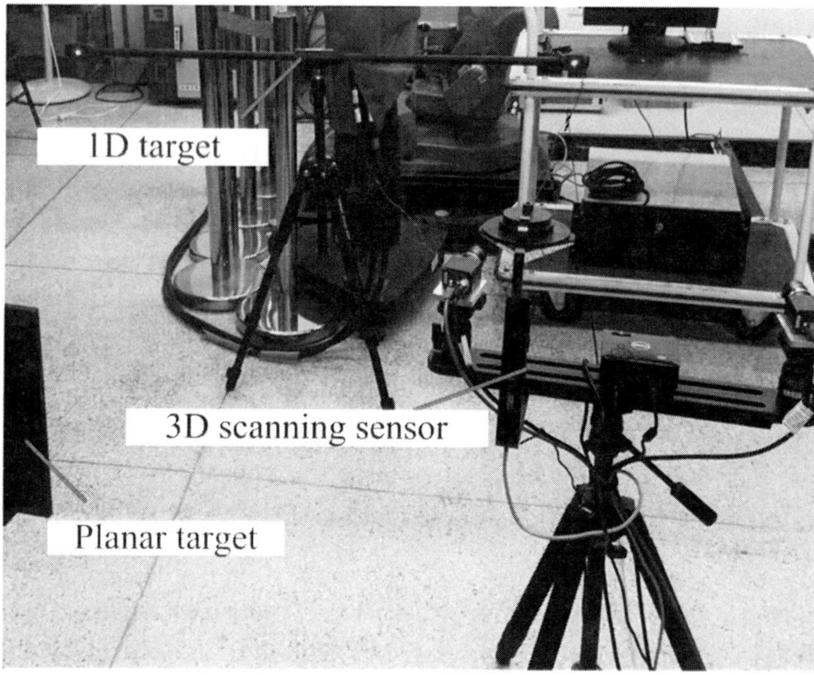


**Figure 9.** Schematic of global measurement precision evaluation.

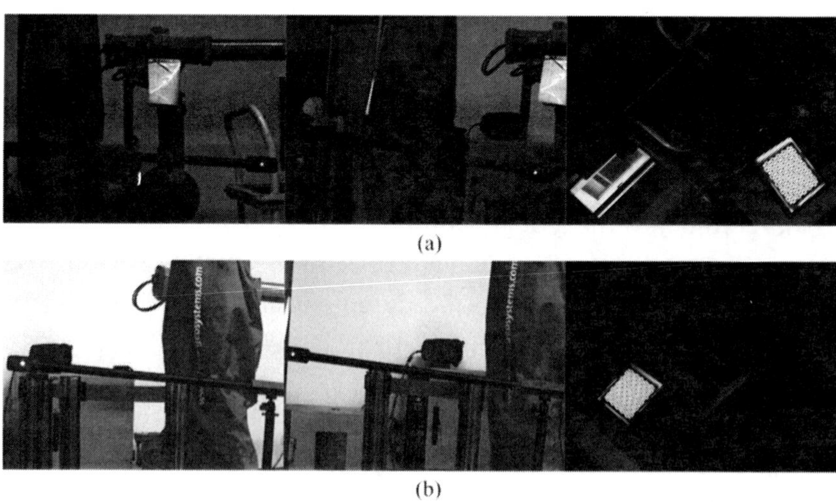


**Figure 10.** Images captured by two sensors for global precision calibration.

The images captured by the wide-field camera and the two cameras of the raster binocular stereo vision sensor at the first position are shown in Figure 10a. The images captured by the wide-field camera and the two cameras of the raster binocular stereo vision sensor at the second position are shown in Figure 10b. The distances between the two points of the 1D target by the 3D scanning sensor at eight positions and the RMS error are listed in Table 1. The result shows the global measurement accuracy of the proposed method can reach 0.14 mm.

**Table 1.** Evaluation of the global measurement accuracy (mm).

| | Left Point | | | Right Point | | | $dt$ (mm) | $dm$ (mm) | $\Delta d$ (mm) |
|---|---|---|---|---|---|---|---|---|---|
| | $x$ (mm) | $y$ (mm) | $z$ (mm) | $x$ (mm) | $y$ (mm) | $z$ (mm) | | | |
| 1 | −38.93 | 69.70 | 944.18 | 1136.60 | 10.56 | 1315.73 | 1234.15 | 1234.27 | −0.12 |
| 2 | −58.28 | −0.67 | 942.06 | 1145.09 | 34.81 | 1213.41 | 1234.15 | 1234.06 | 0.09 |
| 3 | −207.67 | 163.54 | 1177.13 | 1002.70 | 13.97 | 988.70 | 1234.15 | 1234.05 | 0.10 |
| 4 | −253.61 | 44.32 | 1147.33 | 915.61 | 294.11 | 1452.90 | 1234.15 | 1234.04 | 0.11 |
| 5 | 109.48 | 102.07 | 852.49 | 1265.76 | 31.61 | 1278.49 | 1234.15 | 1234.27 | −0.12 |
| 6 | −214.85 | 36.15 | 1012.34 | 1011.10 | 162.10 | 942.91 | 1234.15 | 1233.36 | −0.21 |
| 7 | 55.09 | 16.89 | 1160.02 | 1160.73 | 67.45 | 613.74 | 1234.15 | 1234.27 | −0.12 |
| 8 | 58.98 | 1.35 | 838.59 | 1191.43 | −109.66 | 1316.00 | 1234.15 | 1233.97 | 0.18 |
| | | | | | | | RMS error | | 0.14 |

### *3.2. Real Data Measurement Experiment*

To verify the effectiveness of the proposed method, the following real data measurement experiment was designed. In the experiment, the 3D scanning sensor is moved twice to measure the 3D morphology of the two parts of the train wheels.

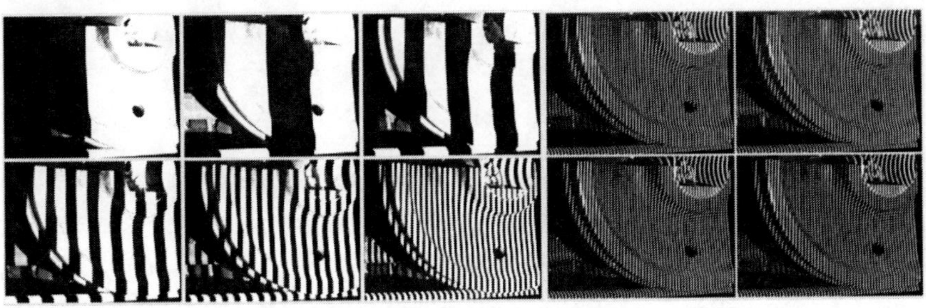

**Figure 11.** Coded image and light strip image captured by 3D scanning sensor at the first position.

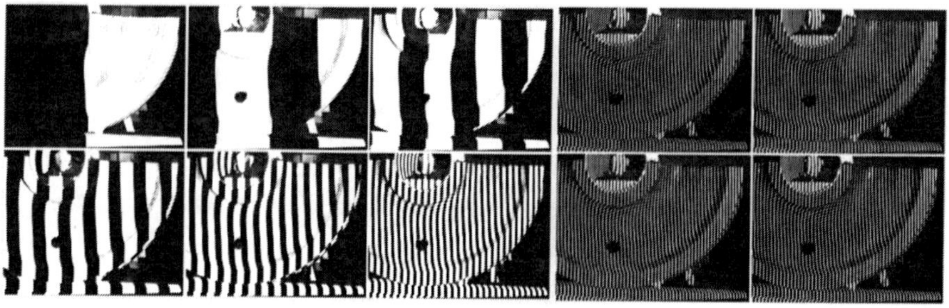

**Figure 12.** Coded image and light strip image captured by 3D scanning sensor at the second position.

The wide-field camera of the 3D scanning sensor is used to measure the arranged planar target. With the plane target as an intermediary, the local 3D data from two measurements is united to the global coordinate system. The coded images and the light strip images are shown in Figure 11 and Figure 12, respectively.

The 3D morphology of the object measured by the 3D scanning sensor at the first position is shown in Figure 13a. The 3D morphology of the object measured by the 3D scanning sensor at the second position is shown in Figure 13b. The united 3D morphology of the object measured by the 3D scanning sensor at two positions is shown in Figure 13c.

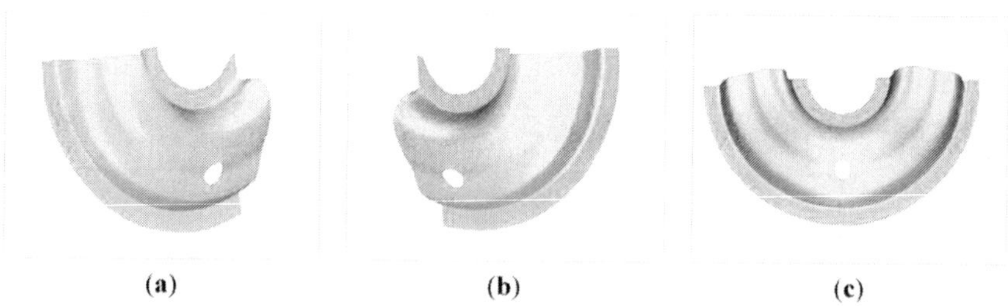


**Figure 13.** (**a**) 3D morphology of the object measured by the 3D scanning sensor at the first position; (**b**) 3D morphology of the object measured by the 3D scanning sensor at the second position; (**c**) united 3D morphology of the object measured by the 3D scanning sensor at two positions.

In order to further validate the effectiveness of the proposed algorithm, we measured the missile model, and their 3D morphology are shown in Figure 14.

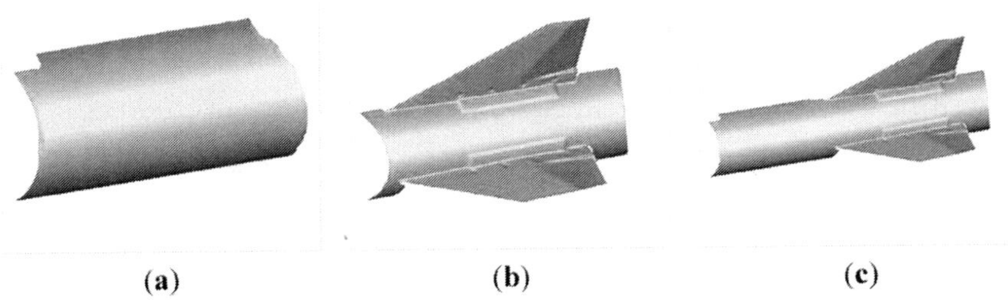

**Figure 14.** (**a**) 3D morphology of the missile model measured by the 3D scanning sensor at the first position; (**b**) 3D morphology of the missile model measured by the 3D scanning sensor at the second position; (**c**) united 3D morphology of the missile model measured by the 3D scanning sensor at two positions.

## 4. CONCLUSIONS

Given that existing movable vision measurement methods for the 3D surface of large-sized objects have some problems, such as long operation times, low efficiency, and unsuitability for soft surfaces, a fast and high-precision movable vision measurement method for 3D surface of large-sized objects is introduced in this paper.

Compared with the existing measurement methods, the proposed method combines a raster binocular vision sensor with a wide-field camera to form a scanning sensor, and it is not necessary to past marks on the object's surface in front of the object. Meanwhile, the proposed method realizes the synchronous measurement of partial 3D measurement and local 3D data integrating, which is not needed to move target repeatedly in front of the object and the 3D scanning sensor, so it greatly improving the measurement efficiency. Physical experiment confirms that when the size of 1D target is about 1.2 m, the accuracy of the proposed method could reach 0.14 mm. Meanwhile, the proposed method is s of high flexibility and efficiency.

Since the size and measuring location of mass-produced large-sized products are basically fixed, so each moved position of the 3D scanning sensor can be determined in advance, and those positions of the planar targets used in the proposed method can be optimized based on each moving point of the 3D scanning sensor. Thus, the proposed method is especially suitable for the measurement for the mass-produced large-sized products in the industrial site.

## ACKNOWLEDGMENTS

This work is supported by the National Natural Science Foundation of P. R. China under Grant no. 51175027, 61127009 and the Beijing Natural Science Foundation under Grant no. 3132029.

## AUTHOR CONTRIBUTIONS

Zhen Liu and Xinguo Wei conceived and designed the experiments; Zhen Liu, Xiaojing Li and Fenjiao Li performed the experiments and analyzed the data; Guangjun Zhang contributed analysis tools; Zhen Liu wrote the paper.

## REFERENCES

1. Chen, F.; Brown, G.M.; Song, M. Overview of three-dimensional shape measurement using optical methods. *Opt. Eng.* **2000**, *39*, 10–22.

2. Malamas, E.N.; Petrakis, E.G.M.; Zervakis, M.; Petit, L.; Legat, J.D. A survey on industrial vision systems, applications and tools. *Image Vis. Comput.* **2003**, *21*, 171–188.

3. Kovac, I. Flexible inspection system in the body-in white manufacturing. In Proceedings of the International Workshop on Robot Sensing, 2004 (ROSE 2004), Graz, Austria, 24–25 May 2004; pp. 41–48.

4. Okamoto, A.; Wasa, Y.; Kagawa, Y. Development of shape measurement system for hot large forgings. *Kobe Steel Eng. Rep.* **2007**, *57*, 29–33.

5. Furferi, R.; Governi, L.; Volpe, Y.; Carfagni, M. Design and assessment of a machine vision system for automatic vehicle wheel alignment. *Int. J. Adv. Robot. Syst.* **2013**, *10*.

6. Zeng, L.; Hao, Q.; Kawachi, K. A scanning projected line method for measuring a beating bumblebee Wing. *Opt. Commun.* **2000**, *183*, 37–43.

7. Jang, W.; Je, C.; Seo, Y.; Lee, S.W. Structured-light stereo: Comparative analysis and integration of structured-light and active stereo for measuring dynamic shape. *Opt. Lasers Eng.* **2013**, *51*, 1255–1264.

8. Morano, R.A.; Ozturk, C.; Conn, R.; Dubin, S.; Zietz, S.; Nissano, J. Structured light using pseudorandom codes. *IEEE Trans. Pattern Anal. Mach. Intell.* **1998**, *20*, 322–327.

9. Salvi, J.; Pagès, J.; Batlle, J. Pattern codification strategies in structured light systems.*Pattern Recognit.* **2004**, *37*, 827–849.

10. Koninckx, T.; Griesser, A.; van Gool, L. Real-time range scanning of deformable surfaces by adaptively coded structured light. In Proceedings of the International Conference on 3-D Digital Imaging and Modelling, Banff, AB, Canada, 6–10 October 2003; pp. 293–300.

11. Su, X.Y.; Chen, W.J.; Zhang, Q.C.; Chao, Y.P. Dynamic 3-D shape measurement method based on FTP. *Opt. Lasers Eng.* **2001**, *36*, 49–64.

12. Zappa, E.; Busca, G. Static and dynamic features of Fourier transform profilometry: A review. *Opt. Lasers Eng.* **2012**, *50*, 1140–1151.

13. Su, X.Y.; Zhou, W.S.; Bally, G.; Vukicevic, D. Automated phased-measuring profilometry using defocused projection of a Ronchi grating. *Opt. Commun.* **1992**, *94*, 561–573.

14. Quan, C.G.; Chen, W.; Tay, C.J. Phase-retrieval techniques in fringe-projection profilometry. *Opt. Lasers Eng.* **2010**, *48*, 235–243.

15. Huang, P.S.; Zhang, C.P.; Chiang, F.P. High-speed 3-D shape measurement based on digital fringe projection. *Opt. Eng.* **2003**, *42*, 163–168.

16. Zhang, S. Recent progresses on real-time 3D shape measurement using digital fringe projection techniques. *Opt. Lasers Eng.* **2010**, *48*, 149–158.

17. Sun, J.H.; Zhang, G.J.; Wei, Z.Z.; Zhou, F.Q. Large 3D free surface measurement using a movable coded light-based stereo vision system. *Sens. Actuators A Phys.* **2006**, *132*, 460–471.

18. Lu, R.S.; Li, Y.F.; Yu, Q. On-line measurement of straightness of seamless steel pipe using machine vision technique. *Sens. Actuators A Phys.* **2001**, *94*, 95–101.

19. Li, Q.; Ren, S. A Real-Time Visual Inspection System for Discrete Surface Defects of Rail Heads. *IEEE Trans. Instrum. Meas.* **2012**, *61*, 2189–2199.

20. Li, Y.; Li, Y.F.; Wang, Q.L.; Xu, D.; Tan, M. Measurement and defect detection of the weld bead based on online vision inspection. *IEEE Trans. Instrum. Meas.* **2010**, *59*, 1841–1849.

21. Liu, Z.; Zhang, G.J.; Wei, Z.Z.; Sun, J.H. A global calibration method for multiple vision sensors based on multiple targets. *Meas. Sci. Technol.* **2011**, *22*.

22. Posdamer, J.L.; Altschuler, M.D. Surface measurement by space-encoded projected beam systems Comput. *Graph. Image Process* **1982**, *18*, 1–17.

23. Steger, C. An unbiased detector of curvilinear structures. *IEEE Trans. Pattern Anal. Mach. Intell.* **1998**, *20*, 113–125.

24. Zhang, Z.Y. A flexible new technique for camera calibration. *IEEE Trans. Pattern Anal. Mach. Intell.* **2000**, *22*, 1330–1334.

25. Bouguet, J.Y. Camera Calibration Toolbox for Matlab. Available online: http:// www.vision. caltech.edu/bouguetj /calib_doc/ (accessed on 17 February 2015).

# Index

## M



## N



## P



## R



## S



## T